Practice Workbook

Contents

Chapter 1

Practice 1-1: Example Exercises 9
Practice 1-1: Mixed Exercises 10
Practice 1-2: Example Exercises 11
Practice 1-2: Mixed Exercises 12
Practice 1-3: Example Exercises 13
Practice 1-3: Mixed Exercises 14
Practice 1-4: Example Exercises 15
Practice 1-4: Mixed Exercises 16
Practice 1-5: Example Exercises 17
Practice 1-5: Mixed Exercises 18
Practice 1-6: Example Exercises 19
Practice 1-6: Mixed Exercises 20
Practice 1-7: Example Exercises 21
Practice 1-7: Mixed Exercises 22
Practice 1-8: Example Exercises 23
Practice 1-8: Mixed Exercises 24
Practice 1-9: Example Exercises 25
Practice 1-9: Mixed Exercises 26

Chapter 2

Practice 2-1: Example Exercises 27
Practice 2-1: Mixed Exercises 28
Practice 2-2: Example Exercises 29
Practice 2-2: Mixed Exercises 30
Practice 2-3: Example Exercises 31
Practice 2-3: Mixed Exercises 32
Practice 2-4: Example Exercises 33
Practice 2-4: Mixed Exercises 34
Practice 2-5: Example Exercises 35
Practice 2-5: Mixed Exercises 36
Practice 2-6: Example Exercises 37
Practice 2-6: Mixed Exercises 38
Practice 2-7: Example Exercises 39
Practice 2-7: Mixed Exercises 40
Practice 2-8: Example Exercises 41
Practice 2-8: Mixed Exercises 42

Practice Workbook

Contents (continued)

Chapter 3

Practice 3-1: Example Exercises 43
Practice 3-1: Mixed Exercises 44
Practice 3-2: Example Exercises 45
Practice 3-2: Mixed Exercises 46
Practice 3-3: Example Exercises 47
Practice 3-3: Mixed Exercises 48
Practice 3-4: Example Exercises 49
Practice 3-4: Mixed Exercises 50
Practice 3-5: Example Exercises 51
Practice 3-5: Mixed Exercises 52
Practice 3-6: Example Exercises 53
Practice 3-6: Mixed Exercises 54
Practice 3-7: Example Exercises 55
Practice 3-7: Mixed Exercises 56
Practice 3-8: Example Exercises 57
Practice 3-8: Mixed Exercises 58

Chapter 4

Practice 4-1: Example Exercises 59
Practice 4-1: Mixed Exercises 60
Practice 4-2: Example Exercises 61
Practice 4-2: Mixed Exercises 62
Practice 4-3: Example Exercises 63
Practice 4-3: Mixed Exercises 64
Practice 4-4: Example Exercises 65
Practice 4-4: Mixed Exercises 66
Practice 4-5: Example Exercises 67
Practice 4-5: Mixed Exercises 68
Practice 4-6: Example Exercises 69
Practice 4-6: Mixed Exercises 70
Practice 4-7: Example Exercises 71
Practice 4-7: Mixed Exercises 72
Practice 4-8: Example Exercises 73
Practice 4-8: Mixed Exercises 74
Practice 4-9: Example Exercises 75
Practice 4-9: Mixed Exercises 76

ALGEBRA
TOOLS FOR A CHANGING WORLD

Practice
Workbook

PRENTICE HALL
Upper Saddle River, New Jersey
Needham Heights, Massachusetts

ISBN: 0-13-433069-2

Printed in the United States of America
    6 7 8   02 01 00 99 98

Editorial, design, and production services:
Publishers Resource Group, Inc.

PRENTICE HALL
Simon & Schuster Education Group
A VIACOM COMPANY

Chapter 5

Practice 5-1: Example Exercises 77
Practice 5-1: Mixed Exercises 78
Practice 5-2: Example Exercises 79
Practice 5-2: Mixed Exercises 80
Practice 5-3: Example Exercises 81
Practice 5-3: Mixed Exercises 82
Practice 5-4: Example Exercises 83
Practice 5-4: Mixed Exercises 84
Practice 5-5: Example Exercises 85
Practice 5-5: Mixed Exercises 86
Practice 5-6: Example Exercises 87
Practice 5-6: Mixed Exercises 88
Practice 5-7: Example Exercises 89
Practice 5-7: Mixed Exercises 90
Practice 5-8: Example Exercises 91
Practice 5-8: Mixed Exercises 92
Practice 5-9: Example Exercises 93
Practice 5-9: Mixed Exercises 94

Chapter 6

Practice 6-1: Example Exercises 95
Practice 6-1: Mixed Exercises 96
Practice 6-2: Example Exercises 97
Practice 6-2: Mixed Exercises 98
Practice 6-3: Example Exercises 99
Practice 6-3: Mixed Exercises 100
Practice 6-4: Example Exercises 101
Practice 6-4: Mixed Exercises 102
Practice 6-5: Example Exercises 103
Practice 6-5: Mixed Exercises 104
Practice 6-6: Example Exercises 105
Practice 6-6: Mixed Exercises 106
Practice 6-7: Example Exercises 107
Practice 6-7: Mixed Exercises 108
Practice 6-8: Example Exercises 109
Practice 6-8: Mixed Exercises 110

Practice Workbook

Contents (continued)

Chapter 7

Practice 7-1: Example Exercises 111
Practice 7-1: Mixed Exercises 112
Practice 7-2: Example Exercises 113
Practice 7-2: Mixed Exercises 114
Practice 7-3: Example Exercises 115
Practice 7-3: Mixed Exercises 116
Practice 7-4: Example Exercises 117
Practice 7-4: Mixed Exercises 118
Practice 7-5: Example Exercises 119
Practice 7-5: Mixed Exercises 120
Practice 7-6: Example Exercises 121
Practice 7-6: Mixed Exercises 122
Practice 7-7: Example Exercises 123
Practice 7-7: Mixed Exercises 124

Chapter 8

Practice 8-1: Example Exercises 125
Practice 8-1: Mixed Exercises 126
Practice 8-2: Example Exercises 127
Practice 8-2: Mixed Exercises 128
Practice 8-3: Example Exercises 129
Practice 8-3: Mixed Exercises 130
Practice 8-4: Example Exercises 131
Practice 8-4: Mixed Exercises 132
Practice 8-5: Example Exercises 133
Practice 8-5: Mixed Exercises 134
Practice 8-6: Example Exercises 135
Practice 8-6: Mixed Exercises 136
Practice 8-7: Example Exercises 137
Practice 8-7: Mixed Exercises 138
Practice 8-8: Example Exercises 139
Practice 8-8: Mixed Exercises 140

Chapter 9

Practice 9-1: Example Exercises 141
Practice 9-1: Mixed Exercises 142
Practice 9-2: Example Exercises 143
Practice 9-2: Mixed Exercises 144
Practice 9-3: Example Exercises 145
Practice 9-3: Mixed Exercises 146
Practice 9-4: Example Exercises 147
Practice 9-4: Mixed Exercises 148
Practice 9-5: Example Exercises 149
Practice 9-5: Mixed Exercises 150
Practice 9-6: Example Exercises 151
Practice 9-6: Mixed Exercises 152
Practice 9-7: Example Exercises 153
Practice 9-7: Mixed Exercises 154
Practice 9-8: Example Exercises 155
Practice 9-8: Mixed Exercises 156

Chapter 10

Practice 10-1: Example Exercises 157
Practice 10-1: Mixed Exercises 158
Practice 10-2: Example Exercises 159
Practice 10-2: Mixed Exercises 160
Practice 10-3: Example Exercises 161
Practice 10-3: Mixed Exercises 162
Practice 10-4: Example Exercises 163
Practice 10-4: Mixed Exercises 164
Practice 10-5: Example Exercises 165
Practice 10-5: Mixed Exercises 166
Practice 10-6: Example Exercises 167
Practice 10-6: Mixed Exercises 168
Practice 10-7: Example Exercises 169
Practice 10-7: Mixed Exercises 170

Practice Workbook

Contents (continued)

Chapter 11

Practice 11-1: Example Exercises 171
Practice 11-1: Mixed Exercises 172
Practice 11-2: Example Exercises 173
Practice 11-2: Mixed Exercises 174
Practice 11-3: Example Exercises 175
Practice 11-3: Mixed Exercises 176
Practice 11-4: Example Exercises 177
Practice 11-4: Mixed Exercises 178
Practice 11-5: Example Exercises 179
Practice 11-5: Mixed Exercises 180
Practice 11-6: Example Exercises 181
Practice 11-6: Mixed Exercises 182
Practice 11-7: Example Exercises 183
Practice 11-7: Mixed Exercises 184

Practice 1-1

Example Exercises

Example 1

Find the mean for each set of data. Round to the nearest tenth.

1. 0, 5, 5, 10

2. 2, 9, 7, 3, 9, 4, 9, 8, 3, 2

3. 2.7, 5.6, 8.1, 10.9, 12.7, 9.5

4. 5.5, 5.8, 6.2, 6.4, 5.9, 6.1

5. 9, 10, 10, 11, 12

6. 10, 12, 13, 9, 4, 8, 7, 9, 15

Find the median for each set of data.

7. 1, 4, 6, 9, 12

8. 6.3, 12.2, 9.5, 3.1, 4.8

9. 2, 6, 8, 10

10. 11.8, 8.2, 3.8, 9.6, 8.9

11. 3, 9, 5, 7, 4, 7

12. 2, 12, 8, 7, 3, 8, 2, 5, 9

Find the mode for each set of data.

13. 6, 4, 8, 2, 4, 7

14. 2, 5, 8, 2, 3, 8, 4

15. 9, 7, 8, 9, 10, 9, 8, 10

16. 2.8, 7.4, 4.8, 2.8, 6.4, 7.1

17. 3, 8, 2, 9, 10, 4, 6, 12, 15

18. 6.4, 7.5, 9.8, 3.9, 7.5, 8.3

Example 2

Draw a multiple bar graph for the table.

19.   **Population of the Three Largest U.S. Cities (rounded to the nearest hundred thousand)**

City	1970	1980	1990
New York	7,900,000	7,100,000	7,300,000
Los Angeles	2,800,000	3,000,000	3,500,000
Chicago	3,400,000	3,000,000	2,800,000

Source: Bureau of the Census, U.S. Dept. of Commerce

20. Which cities showed a decrease in population between 1970 and 1980?

21. What city showed both an increase and a decrease?

Example 3

Draw a double line graph for the table.

22.   **Technology in Public Schools**

Year	Interactive Video	Modems
1992	6502	13,597
1993	11,729	18,471
1994	17,489	22,611

Source: Quality Education Data, Inc.

23. Which technology showed the smaller increase from 1992 to 1994?

24. What trend do you see in the number of schools with modems?

Name _____ Class _____ Date _____

Practice 1-1
• •
Mixed Exercises

Find the mean for the following data. Round to the nearest tenth.

1. 8, 1, 2, 9, 5

2. 2.1, 9.2, 6.4, 7.3, 10.3, 9.6

3. 3.3, 7.2, 6.3, 8.3, 9, 12, 4, 5.6

Draw a multiple bar graph for the table.

4.
Population of States
(rounded to the nearest hundred thousand)

State	1960	1970	1980	1990
Arkansas	1,800,000	1,900,000	2,300,000	2,400,000
Indiana	4,700,000	5,200,000	5,500,000	5,500,000
Michigan	7,800,000	8,900,000	9,300,000	9,300,000
New Jersey	6,100,000	7,200,000	7,400,000	7,700,000

Source: Bureau of the Census, U.S. Dept. of Commerce

5. What happened to Indiana's population during these years?

6. Which state had the greatest increase in population?

Find the median for the following data.

7. 3, 9, 2, 7, 5

8. 3, 8, 4, 0, 1, 6, 7

9. 89, 94, 96, 86, 93, 95, 89, 92

10. 9.25, 10.75, 8.25, 7.50, 6.25

11. 16.4, 19.7, 13.4, 9, 12

12. 8, 9, 12, 17, 12, 13, 9, 6, 4, 12

Draw a double line graph for the table.

13.
Life Expectancy at Birth

Year	Male	Female
1940	60.8	65.2
1950	65.6	71.1
1960	66.6	73.1
1970	67.1	74.7
1980	70.0	77.5
1990	71.8	78.8

Source: National Center for Health Statistics

14. What is the trend for the life expectancy of males and females?

15. Which group's life expectancy has increased more, males or females?

16. During which decade did life expectancy increase most?

Find the mode for the following data.

17. 97, 84, 85, 93, 85, 92

18. 11, 16, 13, 18, 19, 17, 12

19. 9.1, 9.5, 9.4, 9.8, 9.2, 9.5

Find the mean for the following data. Round to the nearest tenth.

20. 5.6, 8.3, 9.1, 2.4, 1.8

21. 0.5, 1.4, 6.2, 4.8

22. 19, 17, 12, 15, 16, 18, 18, 11

23. 5, 6, 7, 8, 8, 7, 6, 5

24. 92, 91, 84, 86, 87, 91, 75, 73, 91, 85, 87, 81

© Prentice-Hall, Inc.

Practice 1-2

••

Example Exercises

Example 1

In Excercises 1-5, use an equation to model each situation.

1. The total cost equals the number of bottles times $1.95.

2. The total amount of money earned is the number of hours worked times $6.50.

3. The amount of money in a bag of nickels is the number of nickels times $.05.

4. The cost of buying 10 gal of gas is 10 times the price per gallon.

5. What is the total cost of renting several videos at $2.50 each?

6. The equation for the total cost of buying tickets to a movie at $3.50 per ticket is $c = 3.50t$.

   a. What do the variables c and t represent?

   b. Write the equation that you would use when the price of tickets is raised to $4.00.

   c. Suppose the equation for the total cost of tickets is $c = 3.25t$. What does this mean?

7. Your teacher wants you to write the equation that could be used to find the total cost of bananas at 0.39 per pound. You write $c = 0.39n$ and Maria writes $b = 0.39p$. Explain why both equations are correct.

Example 2

Use an equation to model the relationship in each table.

8.

Tickets	Cost
2	$7
4	$14
6	$21
8	$28

9.

Hours	Distance
1	55 mi
3	165 mi
5	275 mi
7	385 mi

10.

Hours	Pay
8	$40
12	$60
16	$80
20	$100

11.

Cost	Change
$10.00	$0
$9.00	$1.00
$7.50	$2.50
$5.00	$5.00

12.

Days	Length
1	0.45 in.
4	1.80 in.
8	3.60 in.
10	4.50 in.

13.

Miles Traveled	Miles Remaining
0	500
125	375
350	150

© Prentice-Hall, Inc.

Practice 1-2

Mixed Exercises

Use an equation to model each situation.

1. How does the amount of money in five-dollar bills relate to the number of five-dollar bills?

2. What is the total cost of buying several shirts that are $24.95 each?

3.
Tapes	Cost
1	$7.50
2	$15.00
3	$22.50
4	$30.00

4.
Hours	Pay
4	$28
6	$42
8	$56
10	$70

5.
Miles Hiked	Miles To Go
1.5	3.5
2.5	2.5
5.0	0

6. The number of gallons of water used to water trees is 30 times the number of trees.

7. What is the amount of money in a bank containing only dimes?

8. What is the number of marbles left from a 48-piece bag after some have been given away?

9.
Gallons	Miles
3	75
5	125
7	175
9	225

10.
Cost	Change
$15.00	$0
$12.00	$3.00
$11.50	$3.50
$10.21	$4.79

11.
Books	Cost
1	$3.50
2	$7.00
3	$10.50
4	$14.00

12. The total cost equals the price of the tickets times eight people.

13. What is the cost of buying several pairs of pants at $32.95 a pair?

14.
Days	Hours
2	48
4	96
7	168
11	264

15.
Weeks	Length
1	1.25 cm
3	3.75 cm
5	6.25 cm
7	8.75 cm

16.
Tickets Sold	Empty Seats
100	150
230	20
250	0

17.
Sales	Profits
$10	$3
$20	$6
$30	$9
$40	$12

18.
Apples Eaten	Apples Remaining
3	21
7	17
12	12

19.
Years	Months
1	12
2	24
6	72
10	120

20. The equation for the total cost of buying gasoline at $1.20/gal is $c = 1.20g$.

    a. What do the variables c and g represent?

    b. Write the equation for the total cost of gasoline at $1.25/gal.

Modeling Relationships with Variables   Algebra Chapter 1

Practice 1-3
••
Example Exercises

Example 1

Use the expression $p + r \times p$ to calculate the total cost of the following.

1. A jacket costs $39.95 with a sales tax rate of 7%. What is the total cost of the jacket?

2. A CD player costs $129.95 with a sales tax rate of 8%. What is the total cost of the CD player?

Example 2

Simplify each expression.

3. $6 \times 2 - 4$ **4.** $8 + 12 \div 3$ **5.** $2 \times 5 + 3 \times 4$

Evaluate each expression for $a = 3$ and $b = 4$.

6. $7b - 6a$ **7.** $12a + 5b$ **8.** $6b \div 4a$

9. $a + 3b$ **10.** $4a - 6 + 3b$ **11.** $8 - b + 2a$

Evaluate each expression for $m = 8$ and $n = 2$.

12. $2m - 3n$ **13.** $5m + 7n - 12$ **14.** $6m - 4n \div 8$

15. $m + 2n$ **16.** $12 \div n + 12m$ **17.** $3m - 8n$

18. Thuy evaluated the expression $3m - 2n \div 3$ for $m = 6$ and $n = 6$. Her result was 2. Is this answer correct? If not, what error did she make?

Example 3

Evaluate each expression for $x = 11$ and $y = 8$.

19. $(x + y)^2$ **20.** $x^2 + y^2$ **21.** xy^2 **22.** $(xy)^2$

Example 4

Simplify each expression.

23. $\dfrac{8 + 4}{7 - 3}$ **24.** $\dfrac{2(4 + 1)}{4 - 2}$ **25.** $25\left(\dfrac{6 + 8}{2}\right)$

Evaluate the following for $x = 4$, $y = 8$, and $z = 12$.

26. $\dfrac{3x + y}{10}$ **27.** $\dfrac{y + z}{x}$ **28.** $\dfrac{4(x + y)}{2z}$

Practice 1-3
• •

Mixed Exercises

Simplify each expression.

1. $4 + 6(8)$

2. $\dfrac{4(8 - 2)}{3 + 9}$

3. $21 \times 3 + 2$

4. $40 \div 5(2)$

5. $2.7 + 3.6 \times 4.5$

6. $3[4(8 - 2) + 5]$

7. $4 + 3(5 - 2)$

8. $17 - [(3 + 2) \times 2]$

9. $6 \times (3 + 2) \div 15$

Evaluate each expression.

10. $\dfrac{a + 2b}{5}$ for $a = 1$ and $b = 2$

11. $\dfrac{5m + n}{5}$ for $m = 6$ and $n = 15$

12. $x + 3y$ for $x = 3.4$ and $y = 3$

13. $7a - 4(b + 2)$ for $a = 5$ and $b = 2$

Simplify each expression.

14. $\dfrac{100 - 15}{9 + 8}$

15. $\dfrac{2(3 + 4)}{7}$

16. $\dfrac{3(4 + 12)}{2(7 - 3)}$

17. $14 + 3 \times 4$

18. $8 + 3(4 + 3)$

19. $3 + 4[13 - 2(6 - 3)]$

20. $8(5 + 30 \div 5)$

21. $(3.4)(2.7) + 5$

22. $50 \div 2 + 15 \times 4$

23. $7(9 - 5)$

24. $5(3) - 2(4)$

25. $4 + 8 \div 2 + 6 \times 3$

26. $(7 + 8) \div (4 - 1)$

27. $5[2(8 + 5) - 15]$

28. $(6 + 8) \times (8 - 4)$

29. $12\left(\dfrac{6 + 30}{9 - 3}\right)$

30. $14 + 6 \times 2 - 8 \div 4$

31. $\dfrac{7(14) - 3(6)}{2}$

32. $14 \div [3(8 - 2) - 11]$

33. $3\left(\dfrac{9 + 13}{6}\right)$

34. $\dfrac{4(8 - 3)}{3 + 2}$

35. $3 + 4 \times 8 - 8 \div 4$

36. $13 + 4 \times 9$

37. $5(8 + 2) + 3(11 - 7)$

Evaluate each expression for $a = 2$ and $b = 6$.

38. $2(7a - b)$

39. $(a + b) \div a$

40. $3b \div (2a - 1) + b$

41. $\dfrac{5a + 2}{b}$

42. $\dfrac{3(b - 2)}{4(a + 1)}$

43. $9a + 4b \div 3$

Use the expression $r + 0.12m$ to calculate the cost of renting a car. The basic rate is r. The miles is driven is m. Determine the cost for the following.

44. The basic rate is \$15.95. The car is driven 150 miles.

45. The basic rate is \$32.50. The car is driven 257 miles.

Evaluate each expression for $s = 3$ and $t = 9$.

46. $8(4s - t)$

47. $(2t - 3s) \div 4$

48. $4t \div (6 + s)$

Use grouping symbols to make each equation true.

49. $6 + 8 \div 4 \times 2 = 7$

50. $4 \div 3 + 1 \times 2 = 2$

51. $5 + 4 \times 3 - 1 = 18$

Practice 1-4
• •
Example Exercises

Example 1

Find the value of each expression.

1. $|3.4|$ **2.** $|-6|$ **3.** $|-11.9|$

4. $|3|$ **5.** $\left|-\frac{2}{3}\right|$ **6.** $\left|-\frac{4}{9}\right|$

Find each sum.

7. $6 + (-4)$ **8.** $-2 + (-13)$ **9.** $-18 + 4$

10. $15 + (-32)$ **11.** $-27 + (-14)$ **12** $8 + (-3)$

13. $|-13 + 6|$ **14.** $|14 + 13|$ **15.** $|-23 + (-19)|$

16. $-12.2 + 31.9$ **17.** $-47 + 47$ **18.** $-2.3 + (-13.9)$

19. $|-12| + |-21|$ **20.** $-17 + (-3) + 26$ **21.** $|14| + |-7|$

22. $19.8 + (-27.4)$ **23.** $5 + (-12) + 2$ **24.** $-9.4 + 6.8$

Example 2

Find each difference.

25. $13 - 6$ **26.** $19 - 35$ **27.** $-4 - 8$

28. $-14 - (-6)$ **29.** $18 - (-25)$ **30.** $-32 - 17$

31. $-6.8 - 14.6$ **32.** $-9.3 - (-23.9)$ **33.** $-8.2 - 0.8$

34. $|18 - 26.8|$ **35.** $|3.7 - (-6.8)|$ **36.** $|9.8| - |-15.7|$

37. $|-8 - (-32)|$ **38.** $|6 - 23|$ **39.** $|-4| - |13|$

40. $18.3 - (-8.1)$ **41.** $-3 - (-15)$ **42.** $6.4 - 17$

Example 3

Evaluate each expression for $c = -4$ and $d = -7$.

43. $|-c - d|$ **44.** $c - d$ **45.** $-c + d$

46. $|c + d|$ **47.** $|8 - c - d|$ **48.** $4 + c + d$

49. $-c - d - (-13)$ **50.** $c + d + 7$ **51.** $|25 - d + c|$

52. $|-c - 19 + d|$ **53.** $|c| - |-d|$ **54.** $|c - d| + |-17|$

Practice 1-4

•••

Mixed Exercises

Simplify each expression.

1. $-12 + (-16)$ **2.** $5 + (-12)$ **3.** $5 + (-13)$

4. $\left| -32 - (-45) \right|$ **5.** $\left| -18 + 7 \right|$ **6.** $182 - (-240)$

7. $-6 - 9$ **8.** $-7 + (-26)$ **9.** $\left| 9 - 12 \right|$

10. $\left| -4 - 8 \right|$ **11.** $\left| -13 \right| + \left| 9 \right|$ **12.** $\left| -11 \right| - \left| -29 \right|$

Evaluate each expression.

13. $\left| b + 4 \right|$ for $b = -12$ **14.** $a - b$ for $a = 4$ and $b = 15$

15. $-x - y$ for $x = -2$ and $y = 5$ **16.** $\left| m - n \right|$ for $m = -6$ and $n = -13$

17. $-r - s$ for $r = -7$ and $s = -9$ **18.** $-u + v$ for $u = -2$ and $v = -12$

19. $\left| a - b \right|$ for $a = -7$ and $b = 14$ **20.** $\left| 13 - a + b \right|$ for $a = 7$ and $b = -15$

21. $6 - m + n$ for $m = 10$ and $n = -2$ **22.** $2 + x - y$ for $x = 5$ and $y = -3$

23. $\left| g \right| - \left| h \right|$ for $g = -11$ and $h = -29$ **24.** $-d + (-e) - 7$ for $d = 8$ and $e = -4$

Simplify each expression.

25. $-3 + (-6) + 14$ **26.** $-5 - 7$ **27.** $-4.2 - (-6.8)$

28. $\left| 14 \right| + \left| -19 \right|$ **29.** $-15 + (-29)$ **30.** $-6 + 2$

31. $2.83 - 3.82$ **32.** $4 + (-8) + 15$ **33.** $-6.3 + 8.2$

34. $\left| -4.8 - (-7.2) \right|$ **35.** $60 + (-125)$ **36.** $\left| -9 + 4 \right|$

37. $\left| 8 - 17 \right|$ **38.** $17 + (-13)$ **39.** $6 - 14 - (-20)$

40. $-2.62 + (-6.24)$ **41.** $\left| 4 + (-8) - 15 \right|$ **42.** $54 + (-72)$

43. $28 - (-16)$ **44.** $\left| -27 \right| - \left| 8 \right|$ **45.** $-13.9 - (-34.6)$

Evaluate each expression.

46. $3 - b + c$ for $b = -4$ and $c = -8$ **47.** $15 - m + n$ for $m = -2$ and $n = 40$

48. $\left| x + y \right|$ for $x = 12$ and $y = -7$ **49.** $a - b$ for $a = 15.8$ and $b = -27.4$

50. $r - s$ for $r = 120$ and $s = -150$ **51.** $\left| p - q + 5 \right|$ for $p = -2.5$ and $q = 3.8$

52. $-x + y$ for $x = 4$ and $y = -6$ **53.** $\left| s - t \right|$ for $s = 13$ and $t = 19$

54. $f - g$ for $f = -0.84$ and $g = -1.72$ **55.** $x + y$ for $x = 7$ and $y = -18$

56. $\left| k \right| - \left| -j \right|$ for $j = -2.76$ and $k = -9.28$ **57.** $\left| c + 5 \right| - \left| d \right|$ for $c = -9$ and $d = -11$

Practice 1-5
•••
Example Exercises

Example 1

Simplify each expression.

1. $-48 \div 6$ **2.** $(-23)(-3)$ **3.** $(-6)(32)$

4. $16 \div (-4)$ **5.** $(14)(-5)(-3)$ **6.** $(24)(-2) - 15$

7. $-13 + (-2)(17)$ **8.** $(-3)(4) + 8(-7)$ **9.** $(-7)(-3) - (-11)(-6)$

10. $\frac{-64}{8} + 3(-4)(2)$ **11.** $(-32) \div (-16) + 2(-6)$ **12.** $(-7)(-15) - \left(\frac{-18}{3}\right)$

Evaluate each expression for $x = -6$, $y = 3$, and $z = -5$.

13. $7x - z$ **14.** xyz **15.** $4y \div (-3z)$

16. $\frac{10x}{y-1}$ **17.** $\frac{xy}{z-1}$ **18.** $5z - 4xy$

19. $\frac{2(x-y)}{5}$ **20.** $xy + 8z$ **21.** $\frac{-5(x+y)}{3}$

Example 2

Find the mean rounded to the nearest tenth.

22. $2, -7, 9, -7, -2, 8, 7$ **23.** $23, -10, -8, 33, 28, -13$

24. $-4, -7, 12, 10, -1, -7, 1, -9, 1, 12, -15$ **25.** $-25, -28, -6, 8, 2, -1, 9, -11, 3, 7$

26. $-1, 5, 0, 1, -4, -1, -8, 1, -4, 1, 0, -7, -19$ **27.** $-3, 8, 2, -11, 5, 0, 1, -5, -8, 1, 12, 17, 30$

Example 3

Simplify each expression.

28. $(-5)^3$ **29.** $(-4)^4$ **30.** -2^4

31. $4^2 + (-7)^2$ **32.** $-(-3)^3$ **33.** $-8^2 - (-9)^2$

34. $\left(\frac{-18}{6}\right)^3$ **35.** $-(-6)^3 \div (-3)^2$ **36.** $\frac{12^2}{(-2)^3}$

Evaluate each expression for $x = -4$, $y = -3$, and $z = 2$.

37. x^3 **38.** x^2z **39.** y^5

40. $(x+z)^3$ **41.** $\frac{-6y^2}{z}$ **42.** $4x^2 - z$

43. $3x^2 \div y$ **44.** $3x - y^2$ **45.** x^2y^3

46. $\frac{6x}{-y} + z^3$ **47.** $x^3 \div z^2$ **48.** $(xyz)^2$

Practice 1-5
Mixed Exercises

Simplify each expression.

1. $(-2)(8)$

2. $(-6)(-9)$

3. $(-3)^4$

4. -2^5

5. $(6)(-8) + 30 \div (-6)$

6. $(-14)^2$

7. $2(-4)(-6)$

8. $(-4)(-5)$

9. $5(-6)$

10. $(-8)(5)(-3)$

11. -7^2

12. -3^5

13. $\frac{-68}{17}$

14. $\frac{(-4)(-13)}{-26}$

15. $\frac{225}{(-3)(-5)}$

Evaluate each expression.

16. x^3 for $x = -5$

17. $s^2t - 10$ for $s = -2$ and $t = 10$

18. $-2m + 4n^2$ for $m = -6$ and $n = -5$

19. $7v^2$ for $v = -7$

20. $-cd^2$ for $c = 2$ and $d = -4$

21. $(x + 4)^2$ for $x = -11$

22. $\left(\frac{a}{b}\right)^2 + b^3$ for $a = 24$ and $b = -6$

23. $4p^2 + 7q^3$ for $p = -3$ and $q = -2$

24. $(e + f)^4$ for $e = -3$ and $f = 7$

25. $5f^2 - z^2$ for $f = -1$ and $z = -4$

Simplify each expression.

26. $2^4 - 3^2 + 5^2$

27. $(-8)^2 - 4^3$

28. $32 \div (-7 + 5)^3$

29. $(-3)(14)$

30. $18 + 4^2 \div (-8)$

31. $26 \div (4 - (-9))$

32. $4^3 - (2 - 5)^3$

33. $-(-4)^3$

34. $(-8)(-5)(-3)$

35. $(-3)^2 - 4^2$

36. $3 \times (-15)$

37. $(-2)^6$

38. $(-6)(15)$

39. $\frac{-15}{(7 - 4)}$

40. $\frac{195}{-13}$

Evaluate each expression.

41. $(a + b)^2$ for $a = 6$ and $b = -8$

42. $d^3 \div e$ for $d = -6$ and $e = -3$

43. $(m + 5n)^3$ for $m = 2$ and $n = -1$

44. $j^5 - 5k$ for $j = -4$ and $k = -1$

45. $xy + z$ for $x = -4, y = 3,$ and $z = -3$

46. $4s \div (-3t)$ for $s = -6$ and $t = -2$

47. $\frac{r^3}{s}$ for $r = -6$ and $s = -2$

48. $\frac{-h^5}{-4}$ for $h = 4$

Find the mean rounded to the nearest integer.

49. $5, 8, 2, -4, 7, -5$

50. $-15, 18, -13, 14, -17, -9, 1, -8$

51. $-30, -5, -18, 12, 6, 3, -19, 0, -3, 2$

52. $35, 27, -13, -19, 1, -3, 8, 15, -39$

53. $24, 7, 1, -9, -12, -32, 8, -11, 29, -11, -9$

54. $15, 19, -2, -7, -13, -21, 16, -22, 8, -9$

© Prentice-Hall, Inc.

Practice 1-6

Example Exercises

Example 1

Use a number line to compare the following.

1. $-\frac{11}{15}$ and $-\frac{4}{5}$ **2.** $\frac{3}{4}$ and $\frac{13}{16}$ **3.** $-\frac{7}{8}$ and $-\frac{4}{5}$ **4.** $-2\frac{3}{4}$ and -2.76

Example 2

Write in order from least to greatest.

5. $-\frac{3}{4}, -\frac{7}{8}, -\frac{2}{3}$ **6.** $-\frac{1}{3}, -0.3, -\frac{4}{11}$ **7.** $-\frac{5}{6}, \frac{1}{3}, -\frac{1}{2}$ **8.** $-2\frac{3}{4}, -2\frac{5}{8}, -2.7$

Example 3

Evaluate each expression for $f = \frac{3}{4}$ and $g = -\frac{2}{3}$.

9. fg **10.** $-\frac{9}{10}g$ **11.** $-2f$

12. $\frac{2}{3}f + \frac{3}{4}g$ **13.** $f - g - \frac{1}{2}$ **14.** $5f + g$

Evaluate each expression.

15. $5x - 7y$ for $x = -\frac{3}{4}$ and $y = -\frac{2}{3}$

16. $3m + 2n$ for $m = \frac{5}{6}$ and $n = -\frac{3}{8}$

17. $\frac{1}{2}a - \frac{2}{5}b$ for $a = \frac{2}{3}$ and $b = -\frac{5}{7}$

18. $5(a - b)$ for $a = -\frac{1}{2}$ and $b = -\frac{2}{3}$

Example 4

Evaluate each expression for $a = 20, b = 8,$ and $c = -25$.

19. $-\frac{5}{9}(c - 29)$ **20.** $-\frac{1}{2}(b + c)$ **21.** $\frac{3}{4}(a - b)$ **22.** $\frac{2}{3}(b - a)$

Use the expression $\frac{5}{9}(F - 32)$ to change the following from Fahrenheit to Celsius.

23. $14°F$ **24.** $68°F$ **25.** $-40°F$ **26.** $-13°F$

Example 5

Evaluate each expression.

27. $\frac{2a}{b}$ for $a = -\frac{2}{3}$ and $b = -\frac{1}{2}$ **28.** $\frac{x}{y}$ for $x = 4$ and $y = -\frac{4}{7}$

Practice 1-6

• •

Mixed Exercises

Use $<$, $=$, or $>$ to compare.

1. -10.98 ■ -10.99

2. $-\frac{1}{3}$ ■ -0.3

3. $-\frac{1}{2}$ ■ $-\frac{5}{10}$

4. $-\frac{3}{8}$ ■ $-\frac{7}{16}$

Evaluate each expression.

5. xy for $x = \frac{3}{5}$ and $y = -\frac{3}{4}$

6. $\frac{m + n}{m}$ for $m = -\frac{3}{4}$ and $n = \frac{2}{3}$

7. $\frac{2a}{b}$ for $a = -\frac{3}{4}$ and $b = \frac{1}{2}$

8. $6xy$ for $x = -\frac{7}{3}$ and $y = -\frac{1}{6}$

9. $\frac{x}{y}$ for $x = -\frac{7}{8}$ and $y = 7$

10. xyz for $x = \frac{5}{6}$, $y = -\frac{3}{4}$, and $z = -\frac{1}{2}$

11. ab for $a = \frac{2}{3}$ and $b = -\frac{5}{6}$

12. $-12mn$ for $m = -\frac{7}{9}$ and $n = \frac{1}{8}$

Evaluate each expression for $a = 33$ and $b = -15$.

13. $\frac{3}{4}(b - 13)$

14. $-\frac{1}{4}(a - b)$

15. $\frac{2}{3}(a + b)$

16. $\frac{9}{4}(13 + b)$

17. $\frac{9}{5}(20 - b)$

18. $-\frac{5}{9}(-25 + a)$

Write in order from least to greatest.

19. $-\frac{8}{9}$, $-\frac{7}{8}$, $-\frac{22}{25}$

20. $-3\frac{4}{9}$, -3.45, $-3\frac{12}{25}$

21. $-\frac{1}{4}$, $-\frac{1}{5}$, $-\frac{1}{3}$

22. -1.7, $-1\frac{3}{4}$, $-1\frac{7}{9}$

Evaluate each expression for $x = -\frac{1}{2}$ and $y = -\frac{2}{3}$.

23. $x - y - \frac{1}{2}$

24. $\frac{2}{3}x + \frac{3}{4}y$

25. $4xy$

26. $\frac{1}{4}xy$

27. $\frac{x}{y}$

28. $-3x - 6y$

Evaluate each expression.

29. $\frac{4}{3}cd$ for $c = -\frac{1}{2}$ and $d = -\frac{2}{3}$

30. $-\frac{3}{7}(x - 52)$ for $x = 10$

31. $4x + 7y$ for $x = \frac{3}{4}$ and $y = -\frac{1}{3}$

32. $\frac{3a}{b}$ for $a = -\frac{5}{6}$ and $b = -\frac{3}{4}$

33. st for $s = -\frac{1}{4}$ and $t = -\frac{4}{5}$

34. mn for $m = -\frac{2}{5}$ and $n = -\frac{2}{3}$

Change the following from Fahrenheit to Celsius. Use $C = \frac{5}{9}(F - 32)$.

35. $-22°F$

36. $95°F$

37. $-31°F$

38. $50°F$

Practice 1-7
• •
Example Exercises

Example 1

In a shipment of radios, 200 are selected at random. Four are found to be defective.

1. Find P(radio is defective).

2. Find P(radio is not defective).

3. Find the sum: P(radio is defective) + P(radio is not defective).

4. There are 1500 radios in the shipment. Predict how many of the radios will not work.

5. A basketball player made 35 of 50 free throws. What is the probability that she will make the next one?

Some students conducted a taste test at lunch. The results are in the table below.

Type	Brand X	Brand Y	Brand Z
Number	18	15	17

6. What is the probability that the next student will prefer Brand X?

7. What is the probability that the next student will prefer Brand Z?

8. There are 400 students in that school. Predict the number that prefer Brand Y.

9. Will exactly 144 students prefer Brand X? Explain.

Example 2

Use the random number table to perform the following simulations.

10. A baseball player gets a hit 30% of the time.
    a. What is P(hits in each of the next two at bats)?
    b. What is P(no hits in the next two at bats)?
    c. What is P(at least one hit in the next two at bats)?
    d. What is P(exactly 1 hit in the next two at bats)?

Random Number Table			
23948	71477	12573	05954
65628	22310	09311	94684
41261	09943	34078	78481
34831	94510	21490	93312

11. There is a 60% chance of rain for each of the next three days.
    a. What is P(rain exactly one day)?
    b. What is P(rain exactly two days)?
    c. What is P(rain all three days)?
    d. What is P(it does not rain)?

© Prentice-Hall, Inc.

Name_____ Class_____ Date_____

Practice 1-7
Mixed Exercises

Use the random number table to perform the following simulations.

1. Suppose there are two stop lights on your way to school. Each one has a 20% chance of stopping you.

   a. Find P(stopped by both lights).

   b. Find P(stopped by no lights).

   c. Find P(stopped by exactly one light).

   d. Find P(stopped by at least one light).

Random Number Table			
23948	71477	12573	05954
65628	22310	09311	94684
41261	09943	34078	78481
34831	94510	21490	93312

2. Suppose there is a 50% chance of rain each of the next three days.

   a. Find P(will rain each of the next three days).

   b. Find P(will rain exactly one of the next three days).

   c. Find P(it will not rain the next three days).

A driver collected data on how long it takes her to drive to work.

Minutes	20	25	30
Times	4	8	2

3. Find P(the trip will take 25 minutes).

4. Find P(the trip will take 20 minutes).

5. Find P(the trip will take at least 25 minutes).

Use the data in the line plot to find each probability.

Student Birth Months

				X						X
X		X		X				X		X
X		X		X	X		X	X		X
X	X	X	X	X	X	X	X	X	X	X
JAN	FEB	MAR	APR	MAY	JUN	JUL	AUG	SEP	OCT	NOV	DEC

6. Find P(June).   7. Find P(October).   8. Find P(first six months of year).

9. Find P(May).   10. Find P(not December)   11. Find P(last three months of year).

A cereal manufacturer selects 100 boxes of cereal at random. Ninety-nine of the boxes are the correct weight.

12. Find P(the cereal box is the correct weight).

13. Find P(the cereal box is not the correct weight).

14. There are 24,000 boxes of cereal. Predict how many of the boxes are the correct weight.

© Prentice-Hall, Inc.

Practice 1-8
Example Exercises

Example 1

Find each sum.

1. $\begin{bmatrix} 3.9 \\ -5.2 \end{bmatrix} + \begin{bmatrix} -6.3 \\ -2.7 \end{bmatrix}$ **2.** $\begin{bmatrix} -0.5 & -5.3 \\ 8.1 & 1.5 \end{bmatrix} + \begin{bmatrix} -1.8 & 9.5 \\ -8.7 & 4.3 \end{bmatrix}$

3. $\begin{bmatrix} 0 & 0 \\ 0 & 0 \end{bmatrix} + \begin{bmatrix} -5 & 11 \\ 8 & -1 \end{bmatrix}$ **4.** $\begin{bmatrix} 1 & 0 & -5 \\ 2 & -3 & 0 \end{bmatrix} + \begin{bmatrix} -2 & 7 & 1 \\ -3 & 1 & 8 \end{bmatrix}$

5. $\begin{bmatrix} \frac{1}{2} & \frac{1}{4} \\ \frac{2}{3} & -\frac{1}{2} \end{bmatrix} + \begin{bmatrix} -\frac{1}{3} & \frac{1}{2} \\ -\frac{1}{6} & \frac{3}{4} \end{bmatrix}$ **6.** $\begin{bmatrix} -8 & 7 & 2 \end{bmatrix} + \begin{bmatrix} 4 & -8 & -4 \end{bmatrix}$

Find each difference.

7. $\begin{bmatrix} 0.7 & 1.8 \\ 2.1 & 0 \end{bmatrix} - \begin{bmatrix} -1.9 & 2.4 \\ -3 & 0.9 \end{bmatrix}$ **8.** $\begin{bmatrix} 1 & 3 \\ -4 & 8 \end{bmatrix} - \begin{bmatrix} 2 & -8 \\ -1 & 2 \end{bmatrix}$ **9.** $\begin{bmatrix} -\frac{4}{5} & \frac{3}{4} \end{bmatrix} - \begin{bmatrix} \frac{4}{5} & -\frac{1}{6} \end{bmatrix}$

10. $\begin{bmatrix} 1 & -5 & 7 \\ 2 & -3 & 6 \end{bmatrix} - \begin{bmatrix} 5 & 2 & -1 \\ 0 & 2 & -3 \end{bmatrix}$ **11.** $\begin{bmatrix} 3.9 \\ -7.1 \end{bmatrix} - \begin{bmatrix} -4.2 \\ 10.8 \end{bmatrix}$ **12.** $\begin{bmatrix} -\frac{1}{2} & -\frac{7}{4} \\ \frac{1}{3} & \frac{1}{2} \end{bmatrix} - \begin{bmatrix} -\frac{3}{4} & \frac{2}{3} \\ -\frac{5}{6} & -\frac{3}{7} \end{bmatrix}$

Example 2

13. Use the tables below to find the total number of tickets sold in each category for each type of performance. Write your answer as a table.

Saturday Number of Tickets

Performance	Adult	Child	Senior
Matinee	22	23	13
Evening	51	23	18

Sunday Number of Tickets

Performance	Adult	Child	Senior
Matinee	28	17	9
Evening	49	27	18

14. Use the tables below to find the total number of medals of each type won by each country. Write your answer as a table.

1994 Winter Olympic Games

Country	Gold	Silver	Bronze
Kenya	0	0	0
Japan	1	2	2
United States	6	5	2

Source: *The World Almanac 1995*

1992 Summer Olympic Games

Country	Gold	Silver	Bronze
Kenya	2	4	2
Japan	3	8	11
United States	37	34	37

Source: *The World Almanac 1995*

Practice 1-8

Mixed Exercises

Add each pair of matrices. Then subtract the second matrix from the first matrix in each pair.

1. $\begin{bmatrix} -2 & 3 \\ -4 & -8 \end{bmatrix}, \begin{bmatrix} 5 & 6 \\ -10 & -6 \end{bmatrix}$
   2. $\begin{bmatrix} 1 & -2 & 3 \\ 4 & -8 & 0 \end{bmatrix}, \begin{bmatrix} -1 & 5 & -9 \\ 4 & -5 & 1 \end{bmatrix}$
   3. $\begin{bmatrix} -\frac{4}{5} & \frac{2}{3} \end{bmatrix}, \begin{bmatrix} -\frac{1}{3} & \frac{1}{4} \end{bmatrix}$

Find the increase in population for each state. Write your answer in a table.

4.

**1950 Population
(rounded to the nearest hundred thousand)**

State	Population
Arkansas	1,900,000
Indiana	3,900,000
Michigan	6,400,000

**1990 Population
(rounded to the nearest hundred thousand)**

State	Population
Arkansas	2,400,000
Indiana	5,500,000
Michigan	9,300,000

Source: Bureau of the Census, U.S. Dept. of Commerce

Find each sum or difference.

5. $\begin{bmatrix} \frac{2}{3} & -6 \end{bmatrix} + \begin{bmatrix} -\frac{3}{4} & 10 \end{bmatrix}$
   6. $\begin{bmatrix} -3 & 2.5 & -6 \\ 10 & 3 & -4 \end{bmatrix} - \begin{bmatrix} 6 & -8 & 2 \\ 0 & -2 & 6 \end{bmatrix}$
   7. $\begin{bmatrix} \frac{7}{8} & -\frac{1}{2} \\ \frac{3}{5} & -\frac{1}{3} \end{bmatrix} + \begin{bmatrix} -\frac{1}{2} & \frac{4}{3} \\ -\frac{3}{4} & \frac{3}{2} \end{bmatrix}$

8. $\begin{bmatrix} -6 & 2 & -8 \\ 2 & 5 & -9 \\ 11 & 12 & -7 \end{bmatrix} - \begin{bmatrix} 4 & -8 & 11 \\ 5 & -6 & -8 \\ 1 & 15 & -8 \end{bmatrix}$
   9. $\begin{bmatrix} 2.8 & -3.7 & 9.4 \\ 0.5 & -5.2 & 0.9 \\ 3.7 & -1.9 & 2.2 \end{bmatrix} - \begin{bmatrix} 1.7 & -0.8 & 6.1 \\ 1.9 & 5.7 & -3.3 \\ 2.9 & -1.9 & -2.2 \end{bmatrix}$

10. Determine the change in the number of votes for each party from 1988 to 1992. Write your answer in the form of a matrix.

1988 Presidential Election

State	Democrat	Republican
Alabama	549,506	815,576
Colorado	621,453	728,177
Iowa	670,557	545,355
Minnesota	1,109,471	962,337

1992 Presidential Election

State	Democrat	Republican
Alabama	690,080	804,283
Colorado	629,681	562,850
Iowa	586,353	504,891
Minnesota	1,020,997	747,841

Source: Voter News Service; Federal Election Commission

Practice 1-9

Example Exercises

Example 1

Use the spreadsheet at right for Exercises 1–3.

1. Write the spreadsheet formulas for cells B2, C2, and D2.

2. Find the values for cells B2, C2, and D2.

3. Find the values for cells B3, C3, and D3.

	A	B	C	D
1	x	$x/2$	$x\wedge 2$	$4x$
2	2	▦	▦	▦
3	-4	▦	▦	▦

Use the spreadsheet at right for Exercises 4–6.

4. Write the spreadsheet formulas for cells B2, C2, D2.

5. Find the values for cells B2, C2, and D2.

6. Find the values for cells B3, C3, and D3.

	A	B	C	D
1	a	$3a$	$(a+2)/3$	$a\wedge 3 + 2$
2	7	▦	▦	▦
3	4	▦	▦	▦

Example 2

Evaluate each spreadsheet expression.

7. Area of a triangle: 0.5 * A2 * B2

   a. for A2 = 6 and B2 = 4

   b. for A2 = 12.7 and B2 = 4.8

8. Area of a square: A2^2

   a. for A2 = 5.4

   b. for A2 = 11.7

9. Cost of item plus tax: A2 + A2 * B2

   a. for A2 = $7.95 and B2 = 0.06

   b. for A2 = $15.95 and B2 = 0.08

10. Mean of three numbers: (A2 + B2 + C2)/3

    a. for A2 = 88, B2 = 93, and C2 = 89

    b. for A2 = 5.8, B2 = 19.2, and C2 = 15.8

Use the spreadsheet at right for Exercises 11–12.

11. A company uses a spreadsheet to calculate payroll. Determine the amount of pay for each employee.

12. Write the spreadsheet formula to calculate total pay.

	A	B	C	D
1	Name	Hours	Rate	Pay
2	Raul	38	$6.25	▦
3	Nhan	39.5	$7.50	▦
4	Sue	37	$6.75	▦
5			Totals	▦

Practice 1-9
• •
Mixed Exercises

1. Evaluate the spreadsheet expression (A3 + B3)/C3.

   a. for A3 = 6.8, B3 = 7.2, and C3 = 4

   b. for A3 = −12, B3 = 35 and C3 = −2

Use the spreadsheet at right for Exercises 2–4.

2. Write the spreadsheet formulas for cells B2 and C2.

3. Find the value for cells B2 and C2.

4. Find the value for cells B3 and C3.

	A	B	C
1	x	$x \wedge 3$	$(x + 4) / 5$
2	5	■	■
3	−1	■	■

5. Evaluate the spreadsheet expression (B2 + C2)^2.

   a. for B2 = 8 and C2 = 14

   b. for B2 = −12.6 and C2 = 8.6

   c. for B2 = −7 and C2 = 3

6. A teacher wishes to use these percents to compute grades.

Homework   20%
Quiz   35%
Test   45%

Use the spreadsheet at right to answer **a–b**.

   a. Write the formula for cell E2.

   b. Find the values for cells E2 and E3.

	A	B	C	D	E
1	Student	Homework	Quiz	Test	Grade
2	A. Garcia	90	96	94	■
3	C. Ho	94	92	88	■

7. Evaluate the spreadsheet expression 0.5 * B2 * (C2 + D2).

   a. for B2 = 10, C2 = 4, and D2 = 8

   b. for B2 = 4, C2 = −4, and D2 = −6

8. Evaluate the spreadsheet expression (A2 + 2 * B2)/4.

   a. for A2 = 2 and B2 = 8

   b. for A2 = 1.6 and B2 = −2.5

Use the spreadsheet at right for Exercises 9–11.

9. Write the spreadsheet formulas for cells B2, C2, D2.

10. Find the values for cells B2, C2, and D2.

11. Find the values for cells B3, C3, and D3.

	A	B	C	D
1	x	$x / 4$	$(2x) \wedge 2$	$x \wedge 2 + x$
2	2	■	■	■
3	6	■	■	■

Practice 2-1
Example Exercises

Example 1

Use the data in each table to draw a scatter plot.

1.

Minutes Studied	Test Score	Minutes Studied	Test Score
0	60	30	80
0	75	30	90
15	65	45	90
15	70	45	95
15	75	45	100

2.

Cost Ticket	Number Sold	Cost of Ticket	Number Sold
$2.50	100	$3.00	86
$2.50	95	$3.25	84
$2.50	92	$3.25	80
$2.75	96	$3.25	78
$2.75	94	$3.50	80

Example 2

Is there a *positive correlation*, a *negative correlation*, or *no correlation* between the two data sets in each scatter plot?

3.

4.
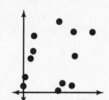

5.
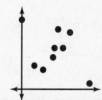

Use the scatter plot below for Exercises 6–9.

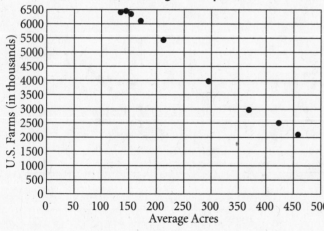

Source: *The Universal Almanac*

6. Sketch a trend line on the graph.

7. Is there a *positive correlation*, a *negative correlation*, or *no correlation* between the average acres and the number of farms?

8. As the average acres per farm increases what happens to the number of farms?

9. **Predict** the number of U.S. farms when the average acres value is 500.

Practice 2-1

Mixed Exercises

Use the data in each table to draw a scatter plot.

1. **Height and Hourly Pay of Ten People**

Height (inches)	Hourly Pay	Height (inches)	Hourly Pay
62	$6.00	72	$8.00
65	$8.50	72	$6.00
68	$6.50	73	$7.50
70	$6.00	74	$6.25
70	$7.50	74	$8.00

2. **Speed of Winds in Some U.S. Cities**

Station	Average Speed (mi/h)	Highest Speed (mi/h)
Atlanta, GA	9.1	60
Casper, WY	12.9	81
Dallas, TX	10.7	73
Mobile, AL	9.0	63
St. Louis, MO	9.7	60

Source: National Climatic Data Center

3. In Exercise 1, is there a *positive correlation*, a *negative correlation*, or *no correlation* between the height and the hourly pay?

4. In Exercise 2, is there a *positive correlation*, a *negative correlation*, or *no correlation* between average wind speed and highest wind speed?

Would you expect a *positive correlation*, a *negative correlation*, or *no correlation* between the two data sets? Why?

5. a person's age vs. the number of pets

6. number of times you brush your teeth vs. number of cavities

7. number of days a year it rains vs. number of umbrellas sold

Is there a *positive correlation*, a *negative correlation*, or *no correlation* between the two data sets in each scatter plot?

8.

9.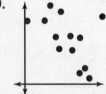

10.

Use the data in the table below for Exercises 11–13.

Years Employed	3	3	4	5	5	7	9	10	12
Salary ($)	24,000	25,000	26,000	28,000	29,000	30,000	33,000	34,000	40,000

11. Draw a scatter plot.

12. What type of correlation is there between the two data sets?

13. Predict the salary of an employee who has worked 6 yr.

© Prentice-Hall, Inc.

Practice 2-2

•••

Example Exercises

Example 1

The graph shows the relationship between time and total distance traveled by a teacher riding a bus.

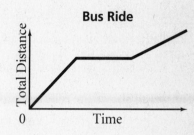

Bus Ride

1. What does the flat part of the graph represent?

2. The first section of the graph is steeper than the last section. Was the bus traveling faster in the first part of the trip or the last?

The graph shows the speed a student traveled on the way to school.

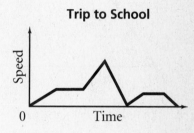

Trip to School

3. What do the flat parts of the graph represent?

4. Circle the sections of the graph that show speed decreasing.

Example 2

Sketch a graph to describe the following. Explain the activity in each section of the graph.

5. the height an airplane is above the ground flying from Dallas, TX to Atlanta, GA.

6. the speed of a person driving to the store and having to stop at two stoplights

Example 3

Classify the data as *continuous or discrete*. Explain your reasoning.

7. the floors an elevator stops on in a high-rise office building

8. the air temperature over a 24-h period

9. the class attendance each day for a week

10. the number of people eating in a restaurant each day for a week

11. the number of cars in a parking lot each day for a week

Practice 2-2
• •
Mixed Exercises

Classify the data as *continuous* or *discrete*. Explain your reasoning.

1. your body temperature over a 24-h period

2. daily movie attendance for a week

3. wind speed over a 24-h period

The graph shows the relationship between time and distance from home.

Your Bicycle Ride

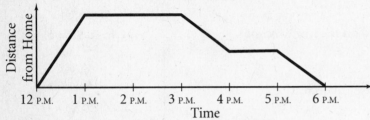

4. What do the flat parts of the graph represent?

5. What do the sections from 3 P.M. to 4 P.M. and from 5 P.M. to 6 P.M. represent?

6. What does the section from 12 P.M. to 1 P.M. represent?

Sketch a graph to describe the following. Explain the activity in each section of the graph.

7. your elevation above sea level as you hike in the mountains

8. your speed as you travel from home to school

Classify the data as *continuous or discrete*. Explain your reasoning.

9. the number of books checked out of the library each day for a month

10. the height above the ground as an airplane travels from New York to Los Angeles

The graph shows the relationship between time and speed for an airplane.

11. Circle the sections of the graph that show the speed increasing.

12. Circle the section of the graph that shows the plane not moving.

13. Circle the section of the graph that shows the plane moving at a constant speed.

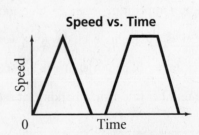

Speed vs. Time

Practice 2-3
· ·
Example Exercises

Example

Identify the independent and dependent variables.

1. total cost of gas, number of gallons of gas

2. perimeter of square, length of a side

3. total cost of item, change from ten-dollar bill

4. total calories, number of slices of bread

Choose scales and intervals that you could use to graph each table.

5.
x	y
−5	10
2	20
6	43
13	52

6.
x	y
−28	−50
−19	−10
−11	0
2	20

7.
x	y
1.0	−13.9
3.6	−6.7
12.9	1.2
25.7	2.4

Graph the data in each table.

8.
x	y
0	0
1	1
2	4
4	16
6	36

9.
x	y
−2	−8
−1	−6
2	0
5	6
7	10

10.
x	y
−2.6	2.76
−1.2	−2.56
0	−4
1.5	−1.75
3.5	8.25

11. The table to the right shows the effect of a 10 mi/h wind on the wind chill temperature.

   a. What are the independent and dependent variables?

   b. Graph the data.

   c. What will the wind chill be when the temperature is 15°F?

Temperature	Wind Chill
30°F	16°F
20°F	3°F
10°F	−9°F
0°F	−22°F
−10°F	−34°F

Source: National Weather Service

12. The table shows the interest earned on a savings account of $5000 at 5% interest compounded annually.

Length of Savings (yr)	1	2	4	7
Interest Earned ($)	250	512.50	1077.53	2035.50

   a. From the table, what can you say about the relationship between the length of savings and the interest earned?

   b. Identify the independent and dependent variables.

   c. Graph the data.

Practice 2-3
Mixed Exercises

Graph the data in each table.

1.

x	y
−4	18
−2	6
−1	3
2	6
3	11

2.

x	y
−3	−5
−1	−1
0	1
1	3
4	7

3.

x	y
−2.3	6.3
−1.7	5.1
0.5	0.7
1.2	−0.7
4.8	−7.9

Identify the independent and dependent variables.

4. cost of pencils, number of pencils

5. cost of item, change from twenty-dollar bill

6. speed of car, distanced travel

7. amount of sales tax, cost of items

Choose a scale that you could use to graph each table.

8.

x	y
−5	10
2	−6
6	−15
13	−23

9.

x	y
−18	−30
−13	−10
−5	25
2	75

10.

x	y
1.0	12.5
3.6	10.5
12.9	7.5
25.7	3.6

11. The table shows the cost for purchasing square yards of carpet.

Carpet (yd²)	10	15	20	30
Total Cost ($)	199.50	299.25	399.00	590.50

   a. From the table, what can you say about the relationship between the amount of carpet and the total cost?

   b. Identify the independent and dependent variables.

   c. Graph the data.

12. The table shows the cost to rent a car for one day at $20 plus mileage.

Miles Driven (mi)	50	100	150	200
Total Cost ($)	27.50	35.00	42.50	50.00

   a. Identify the independent and dependent variables.

   b. Graph the data.

   c. Use the graph to approximate the cost of renting the car and driving 120 mi.

   d. From the table, what can you say about the relationship between miles driven and total cost to rent the car?

Practice 2-4

Example Exercises

Example 1

Determine if each relation is a function.

1.

x	y
10	−5
15	1
27	6
29	7
36	8

2.

x	y
2	2
6	4
4	8
0	0
2	6

3.

x	y
−6	6
−3	6
4	6
8	6
9	6

4.

x	y
−6	2
−4	2
−2	4
−3	4
−4	4

Example 2

Evaluate each function rule.

5. $y = 5x - 2$ for $x = 3$

6. $y = x - 1$ for $x = -2$

7. $y = 2x - 13$ for $x = 8$

8. $y = 6(x - 6)$ for $x = 7$

9. $y = \frac{1}{2}x + 8$ for $x = 6$

10. $y = \frac{2}{3}x - 2$ for $x = 6$

11. $y = 6x - 4$ for $x = 1.5$

12. $y = \frac{3}{4}x$ for $x = -2$

13. $y = 3x + 2$ for $x = 5$

14. $y = 2(x + 9)$ for $x = -4$

15. $y = 2x^2 - 1$ for $x = 4$

16. $y = 3x^2 + 5$ for $x = 5$

Example 3

Find the range of each function when the domain is {−3, 0, 3}.

17. $t = 2s$

18. $m = 1.5n$

19. $y = \frac{1}{3}x$

20. $p = 4q - 6$

21. $m = 2.5n - 1.5$

22. $a = \frac{b + 15}{3}$

23. $y = x^2$

24. $y = \frac{1}{9}x^2$

Find the range of each function when the domain is {2, 4, 6}.

25. $f = 2g$

26. $s = 3t + 1$

27. $z = y^2$

28. $d = 4(8 - c)$

29. $a = \frac{3}{2}(b + 2)$

30. $y = \frac{12 - x}{2}$

31. $y = x^2 - 5$

32. $b = \frac{12}{c}$

33. $p = \frac{3(6 - q)}{2}$

Practice 2-4

• •

Mixed Exercises

Evaluate each function rule.

1. $y = 3x + 4$ for $x = 8$

2. $a = b - 6$ for $b = -2$

3. $m = n^2 + 8$ for $n = 5$

4. $s = -2t^2 + 3$ for $t = 4$

5. $p = 3q - 6$ for $q = 9$

6. $e = 15 - f$ for $f = 3$

Determine if each relation is a function.

7.

x	y
−2	2
0	4
2	6
3	6

8.

x	y
−5	3
2	−2
7	1
2	3

9.

x	y
−3	3
−1	5
0	2
−3	4

Find the range of each function when the domain is {−2, 0, 2}.

10. $j = 3k - 5$

11. $y = 3x^2 - 2x$

12. $d = -4.5e + 2.6$

13. $m = \frac{3}{2}n - 8$

Evaluate each function rule.

14. $y = 2x - \frac{1}{2}$ for $x = \frac{3}{4}$

15. $a = 3(8 + b)$ for $b = -3$

16. $d = 4.2e$ for $e = 3$

17. $g = -3(19 - h)$ for $h = 15$

18. $s = 2(t + 7)$ for $t = -5$

19. $m = 4n + 3$ for $n = 2.5$

Find the range of each function when the domain is {−1, 3, 5}.

20. $y = 3x + 2$

21. $a = 2(8 - b)$

22. $m = 25n$

23. $p = 2(q - 1)$

Evaluate each function rule.

24. $m = \frac{3}{4}(1 - n)$ for $n = \frac{1}{2}$

25. $y = \frac{2}{3}x$ for $x = \frac{9}{10}$

26. $a = b^2 + 2.2$ for $b = 3$

27. $c = 5(4d - 8)$ for $d = 2$

28. $a = \frac{2}{3}\left(\frac{3}{4} + b\right)$ for $b = \frac{1}{4}$

29. $y = x^2 - \frac{1}{4}$ for $x = \frac{1}{2}$

Find the range of each function when the domain is {−2, 2, 4}.

30. $y = \frac{3(6 - x)}{2}$

31. $a = \frac{20}{b}$

32. $m = \frac{1}{2}n + 3$

33. $y = \frac{2.5x}{2}$

Practice 2-5
Example Exercises

Example 1

Write a function rule for each table.

1.

x	f(x)
0	10
1	11
2	12
3	13

2.

x	f(x)
0	0
2	10
4	20
6	30

3.

x	f(x)
0	0
1	1
2	4
3	9

4.

x	f(x)
−4	−1
−2	1
2	5
4	7

5.

x	f(x)
0	0
3	6
6	12
9	18

6.

x	f(x)
−2	0
0	2
2	4
4	6

7.

x	f(x)
1	0
3	2
5	4
7	6

8.

x	f(x)
−3	−9
−1	−3
2	6
5	15

9. Find $f(5)$ for Exercise 1

10. Find $f(8)$ for Exercise 2

11. Find $f(6)$ for Exercise 3

12. Find $f(-1)$ for Exercise 4

13. Find $f(2)$ for Exercise 5

14. Find $f(7)$ for Exercise 6

Example 2

15. A car is 30 times larger than its scale model.

   a. Write a function rule to describe this relationship.

   b. If the model is 6 in. long, how long is the car?

   c. If the model is 2.5 in. wide, how wide is the car?

16. Pencils cost $.20 each.

   a. Write a function rule to calculate the total cost of any number of pencils.

   b. Use your rule to find the total cost of 12 pencils.

Example 3

17. You invest $209 to buy shirts and then sell them for $9.50 each.

   a. Write a function rule to determine your profit.

   b. Use your rule to find your profit after selling 24 shirts.

   c. How many shirts do you need to sell to get back your investment?

18. A car rental agency charges a fee of $25 plus $.20 for each mile driven.

   a. Write a function rule to determine the cost of renting a car.

   b. Use your rule to find the cost of renting a car and driving 150 miles.

Practice 2-5

Mixed Exercises

Write a function rule for each table.

1.

x	f(x)
0	3
2	5
4	7
6	9

2.

x	f(x)
0	0
1	3
3	9
5	15

3.

x	f(x)
5	0
10	5
15	10
20	15

4. **a.** Write a function rule to calculate the cost of buying bananas at $.39 a pound.

   b. How much would it cost to buy 3.5 pounds of bananas?

5. To rent a cabin, a resort charges $50 plus $10 per person.

   a. Write a function rule to calculate the total cost of renting the cabin.

   b. Use your rule to find the total cost for six people to stay in the cabin.

Find $f(2)$ for each function.

6. $f(x) = 6 - x$

7. $f(x) = 6x + 7$

8. $f(x) = x^2 + 5x$

9. $f(x) = -3x^2$

10. $f(x) = 2 + 4x$

11. $f(x) = 9 - x^2$

Write a function rule for each table.

12.

x	f(x)
−4	−2
−2	−1
6	3
8	4

13.

x	f(x)
−3	9
0	0
1	1
5	25

14.

x	f(x)
0	20
2	18
4	16
8	12

Find the range of each function when the domain is {0, 1, 5}.

15. $f(x) = 2x^2 - x$

16. $f(x) = 27 - 3x$

17. $f(x) = -x + 8$

18. Pens are shipped to the office supply store in boxes of 12 each.

   a. Write a function rule to calculate the total number of pens when you know the number of boxes.

   b. Calculate the total number of pens in 16 boxes.

19. **a.** Write a function rule to determine the change you would get from a twenty-dollar bill when purchasing items that cost $1.25 each.

   b. Calculate the change when five of these items are purchased.

   c. Can you purchase 17 of these items with a twenty-dollar bill?

Practice 2-6

Example Exercises

Example 1

Model each rule with a table of values and a graph.

1. $f(x) = x - 6$

2. $f(x) = 15 - x$

3. $f(x) = -5x$

4. $f(x) = \frac{1}{2}x + 2$

5. $f(x) = -\frac{2}{3}x + 4$

6. $f(x) = 5 - 3x$

7. $f(x) = 2x - 3$

8. $f(x) = -x - 2$

9. $f(x) = 3x - 8$

10. A motel charges $50 per night for a room. The total cost of a stay at the motel is a function of the number of nights stayed.

   a. Use the rule $C(n) = 50n$ to make a table of values and then a graph.

   b. What is the cost to spend 13 nights in the motel?

   c. Should the points on the graph be connected by a line? Explain why or why not.

11. The speed in ft/s that an object falls is a function of time in seconds.

   a. Use the rule $S(t) = 32t$ to make a table of values and then a graph.

   b. What is the speed when the time is 1.5 seconds?

   c. Should the points on the graph be connected by a line? Explain why or why not.

Example 2

Graph each function.

12. $y = x^2$

13. $y = 2x^2$

14. $f(x) = x^2 - 4$

15. $f(x) = -x^2 + 5$

16. $f(x) = x^2 - 1$

17. $f(x) = -x^2 + 1$

18. $y = x^2 - 2x + 1$

19. $f(x) = -3x^2 + 2x$

20. $f(x) = x^2 + 3x - 5$

Example 3

Make a table of values for each graph.

21.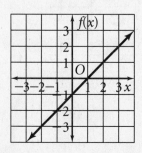

22.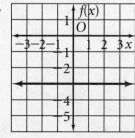

23.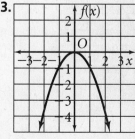

Practice 2-6
• •
Mixed Exercises

Model each rule with a table of values and a graph.

1. $f(x) = x + 1$

2. $f(x) = 2x$

3. $f(x) = 3x - 2$

4. $f(x) = \frac{3}{2}x - 2$

5. $f(x) = \frac{1}{2}x$

6. $f(x) = -\frac{2}{3}x + 1$

7. $f(x) = x^2 + 1$

8. $f(x) = -x^2 + 2$

9. $f(x) = x - 3$

10. Suppose a van gets 22 mi/gal. The distance traveled $D(g)$ is a function of the gallons of gas used.

  a. Use the rule $D(g) = 22g$ to make a table of values and then a graph.

  b. How far did the van travel when it used 10.5 gallons of gas?

  c. Should the points of the graph be connected by a line? Explain.

11. The admission to a fairgrounds is $3.00 per vehicle plus $.50 per passenger. The total admission is a function of the number of passengers.

  a. Use the rule $T(n) = 3 + 0.50n$ to make a table of values and then a graph.

  b. What is the admission for a car with six people in it?

  c. Should the points of the graph be connected by a line? Explain.

Model each rule with a graph.

12. $f(x) = 4x + 2$

13. $f(x) = x^2 - 2x + 1$

14. $f(x) = -3x + 7$

15. $f(x) = x^2 - 3$

16. $f(x) = 8 - \frac{3}{4}x$

17. $f(x) = \frac{2}{3}x - 7$

18. $f(x) = -\frac{2}{3}x + 6$

19. $f(x) = x^2 - 5$

20. $f(x) = -\frac{1}{2}x + 3$

21. $y = 5x - 10$

22. $y = 9 - x^2$

23. $y = 10 - 3x$

Make a table of values for each graph.

24.
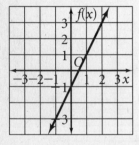

25.
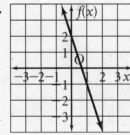

26.
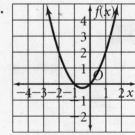

© Prentice-Hall, Inc.

Practice 2-7

· ·

Example Exercises

Example 1

What is the characteristic of the equation for each family of functions?

1. linear function   **2.** quadratic function   **3.** absolute value function

To what family of functions does each equation belong? Explain why.

4. $y = 3x + 3$ **5.** $y = -5x$ **6.** $y = x^2$ **7.** $y = |x - 2|$

8. $y = -\frac{1}{2}x$ **9.** $y = -2x^2 + 8$ **10.** $y = \left|\frac{2}{3}x + 9\right|$ **11.** $y = 2x^2 - 5x + 7$

12. Create two equations that belong to the linear family of functions.

13. Explain why the equation $y = x - |-8|$ is not an absolute value function.

Example 2

What is the characteristic of the graph for each family of functions?

14. linear function   **15.** quadratic function   **16.** absolute value function

To what family of functions does each graph belong? Explain why.

17.
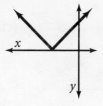

18.
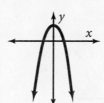

19.
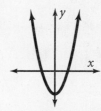

20.
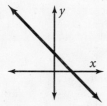

21.
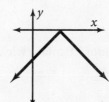

22.
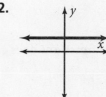

23. Sketch two graphs that belong to the quadratic family of functions.

Practice 2-7
Mixed Exercises

1. Create three equations that belong to the quadratic family of functions.

2. Create three equations that belong to the absolute value family of functions.

3. Sketch three graphs that belong to the linear family of functions.

To what family of functions does each equation belong? Explain why.

4. $y = 5 - |2x|$ 5. $y = 3x^2 - 2$ 6. $y = |x - 1|$

7. $y = 10x - 2$ 8. $y = |3x| + 2$ 9. $y = x^2 + 2x + 5$

10. $y = -\frac{2}{3}x^2 - 5$ 11. $y = -3x$ 12. $y = 7x + |-3|$

13. $y = 6 - 4x$ 14. $y = 3|x + 2|$ 15. $y = 4x + x^2$

To what family of functions does each graph belong? Explain why.

16.
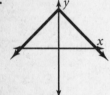

17.
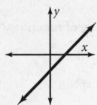

18.
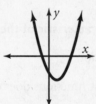

19.
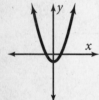

20.
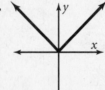

21.
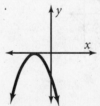

To what family of functions does each equation belong? Explain why.

22. $y = |x - 5|$ 23. $y = -\frac{2}{3}x - 5$ 24. $y = x + 4$

25. $y = 2 + 3x - x^2$ 26. $y = 4x^2 - x$ 27. $y = 3 + |2x|$

28. $y = \frac{1}{2}x^2$ 29. $y = -5x - 8$ 30. $y = 7x - 6$

31. $y = -6|x|$ 32. $y = -\frac{8}{9}x - 12$ 33. $y = -7x^2 + 7x - 6$

34. $y = 4 + x + x^2$ 35. $y = |\frac{2}{7}x| + 8$ 36. $y = -13 - x$

Practice 2-8

• •

Example Exercises

Example 1

Teresa has a pile of shoes: a pair of loafers, a pair of tennis shoes, one sandal, and one high-heel. Find each probability for picking one shoe out of the pile.

1. P(getting a sandal)   **2.** P(getting one of a pair)   **3.** P(cowboy boot)

One state is chosen at random from the 50 United States. Find each probability.

4. P(the state is Virginia)   **5.** P(the state begins with A)   **6.** P(the state touches the Pacific Ocean)

Example 2

7. There is a 25% chance of rain tomorrow. What is the probability that it will not rain?

8. On a multiple choice test question, the probability of guessing the wrong response is $\frac{3}{4}$. What is the probability of guessing correctly?

9. A bag of marbles contains two red, four blue, three green, and three yellow. One marble is chosen at random.

   a. What is P(red)?   **b.** What is P(not red)?   **c.** What is P(green or blue)?   **d.** What is P(red or yellow)?

Example 3

10. Draw a tree diagram to show the sample space for three coin tosses.

11. Use the sample space from Exercise 10 to find each probability.

   a. P(exactly 2 tails)   **b.** P(at least 2 heads)   **c.** P(exactly 1 tail)

12. Draw a tree diagram to show the sample space for forming 3-digit numbers with the digits 2, 5 and 7 if the digits may repeat.

13. Use the sample space from Exercise 12 to find each probability.

   a. P(2 appears 3 times)   **b.** P(5 appears at least once)   **c.** P(7 appears exactly once)

14. Use the sample space below for picking two coins out of a bank of one penny, two nickels, two dimes, and two quarters. Find each probability.

   a. P(total is 8¢)

   b. P(total is $\geq$ 15¢)

   c. P(total is 11¢)

   d. P(total is $\leq$ 15¢)

Sample Space for Picking Two Coins			
(5¢, 1¢)	(1¢, 5¢)	(1¢, 10¢)	(1¢, 25¢)
(10¢, 1¢)	(10¢, 5¢)	(5¢, 10¢)	(5¢, 25¢)
(25¢, 1¢)	(25¢, 5¢)	(25¢, 10¢)	(10¢, 25¢)

© Prentice-Hall, Inc.

Practice 2-8
•••
Mixed Exercises

1. One letter is chosen at random from the word *ALGEBRA*.

    a. What is P(the letter is *A*)?   **b.** What is P(letter is a vowel)?

    c. What is P(the letter is *A* or *G*)?

2. Patrice has a 40% chance of making a free throw. What is the probability
   that she will miss the free throw?

3. Jan is writing her name in color. She has a red pen and a blue pen. Jan
   can use either pen for each letter.

    a. Make a tree diagram to show the sample space.   **b.** What is P(the letter *n* is red)?

    c. What is P(either one or two letters are blue)?   **d.** What is P(her entire name is one color)?

4. A box of animal crackers contains five hippos, two lions, three zebras,
   and four elephants. One animal cracker is chosen at random.

    a. What is P(a hippo)?   **b.** What is P(not an elephant)?

    c. What is P(an elephant or a lion)?

5. Anthony is making a collage for his art class by picking shapes randomly.
   He has five squares, two triangles, two ovals, and four circles.

    a. What is P(circle is chosen first)?   **b.** What is P(a square is not chosen first)?

    c. What is P(a triangle or a square is chosen first)?

6. Find each probability for one roll of a number cube.

    a. $P(2)$ **b.** P(even)   **c.** P(not 2)

7. Your friend picks a letter of the alphabet. The probability of guessing the
   correct letter is $\frac{1}{26}$. What is the probability of guessing incorrectly?

8. Two different letter tiles are to be chosen from A, B, C, and D. Find the
   following probabilities.

    a. Draw a tree diagram to show the sample space.

    b. What is P(A and B are selected)?   **c.** What is P(one letter is C)?

    d. What is P(one letter is C and the other letter is A or D)?

9. One digit is chosen at random from the number 18,002,655,328.

    a. What is P(the digit is odd)?   **b.** What is P(the digit is greater than 4)?

    c. What is P(the digit is 0, 2, or 5)?

Practice 3-1
Example Exercises

Example 1

Solve and check.

1. $x + 8 = 12$ 2. $a + 15 = -28$ 3. $c - 12 = 19$

4. $y - 6 = -25$ 5. $39.3 = 13 + h$ 6. $-15 = b - 29$

7. $\frac{2}{3} = k + \frac{1}{3}$ 8. $x + \frac{1}{2} = \frac{3}{4}$ 9. $a - \frac{2}{3} = \frac{2}{3}$

Example 2

Solve and check.

10. $\frac{y}{3} = 5$ 11. $\frac{m}{13} = -3$ 12. $-10 = \frac{n}{-4}$

13. $-\frac{x}{7} = -10.4$ 14. $4y = 24$ 15. $3x = -21$

16. $-3d = -36$ 17. $\frac{d}{9} = -11.2$ 18. $\frac{a}{5} = 3.7$

19. $-7 = \frac{a}{4}$ 20. $\frac{s}{-6} = 9$ 21. $73.8 = 8.2x$

22. $-17.5 = 7d$ 23. $2.7f = -16.2$ 24. $-5p = -85$

Example 3

Write an equation to model. Then solve each problem.

25. Two packages of meat have a combined weight of 5.75 kg. If one package weighs 3.28 kg, how much does the other package weigh?

26. Alma caught a largemouth bass that measured $17\frac{1}{2}$ in. long. Her father caught one $14\frac{1}{2}$ in. long. How much longer was Alma's fish than her father's?

27. You ran a 5-mile race in 45 minutes. What was your average time per mile?

28. The normal July high temperature in Phoenix, AZ is 106°F. This is about 2.36 times that of Barrow, AK. What is the normal high temperature in Barrow? Round your answer to the nearest integer.

29. A chef cooks $1\frac{1}{2}$ potatoes for each serving of mashed potatoes. How many servings can he make from 18 potatoes?

30. The perimeter of an equilateral triangle is 25.5 cm. How long is each side?

Practice 3-1

••

Mixed Exercises

Solve and check.

1. $g - 6 = 2$

2. $15 + b = 4$

3. $8 = h + 24$

4. $63 = 7x$

5. $x + 7 = 17$

6. $-2n = -46$

7. $\frac{c}{14} = -3$

8. $\frac{x}{2} = 13$

9. $\frac{a}{5} = 3$

10. $r - 63 = -37$

11. $5 + d = 27$

12. $2b = -16$

13. $4y = 48$

14. $c - 25 = 19$

15. $a + 4 = 9.6$

16. $x + 29 = 13$

17. $-3d = -63$

18. $3f = -21.6$

19. $-\frac{x}{8} = 12$

20. $a - \frac{1}{3} = \frac{2}{3}$

21. $n - 3 = -3$

Write an equation to model. Then solve each problem.

22. A stack of 12 bricks is 27 in. high. How high is each brick?

23. The sum of Juanita's age and Sara's age is 33 yr. If Sara is 15 years old, how old is Juanita?

24. The tallest player on the basketball team is $77 \frac{3}{4}$ in. tall. This is $9 \frac{1}{2}$ in. taller than the shortest player. How tall is the shortest player?

25. The diameter of Jupiter is 88,000 mi. This is about 11.1 times the diameter of the Earth. What is the diameter of the Earth? Round your answer to the nearest integer.

26. The distance from Baltimore to New York is 202 mi. This is 205 mi less than the distance from Baltimore to Boston. How far is Baltimore from Boston?

Solve and check.

27. $y - 8 = -15$

28. $a + 27.7 = -36.6$

29. $3x = 27$

30. $a + 5 = -19$

31. $m - 9.5 = -27.4$

32. $-54 = -6s$

33. $x + \frac{1}{3} = \frac{5}{6}$

34. $-\frac{s}{3} = 7$

35. $\frac{m}{12} = -4.2$

36. $\frac{a}{3} = -11$

37. $\frac{z}{-8} = -3.7$

38. $\frac{y}{-11} = -6.1$

39. $-17.5 = 2.5d$

40. $b - 48 = -29$

41. $96 = -3h$

42. $-4.2x = 15.96$

43. $s + 87.8 = 38.1$

44. $-5x = 85$

45. $\frac{x}{-5} = 4.8$

46. $d + \frac{2}{3} = -\frac{1}{2}$

47. $-\frac{t}{2} = -9$

48. $45.6 = 6x$

49. $19.5 = -39.5 + f$

50. $m - 21 = -43$

Practice 3-2
· ·
Example Exercises

Example 1

Use tiles to solve each equation.

1. $2a + 1 = 7$ **2.** $3x - 5 = 1$ **3.** $2t - 7 = 11$

4. $6c + 1 = 7$ **5.** $-10 = 2y + 6$ **6.** $4b + 5 = -11$

Use tiles to solve each problem.

7. Suppose you earned $15 from your job last week. You want to save $3 and buy some books that cost $4 each. To find how many books you can buy, solve the equation $15 = 3 + 4x$.

8. It costs $10 to rent a VCR and $2 for each videotape. If you have $18, how many videotapes can you rent? To find the number of videotapes, solve the equation $18 = 10 + 2v$.

Example 2

Solve each equation. Check your solutions.

9. $-x + 7 = -21$ **10.** $39 = -3x + 3$ **11.** $13 = 8 - x$

12. $6 = \frac{d}{15} + 2$ **13.** $\frac{k}{3} - 23 = -36$ **14.** $\frac{n}{6} - 6 = 0$

15. $7 = -\frac{t}{4} - 9$ **16.** $2 = \frac{x}{5} - 2$ **17.** $13 = -\frac{z}{8} + 9$

Example 3

Use an equation to model and solve each problem.

18. A computer repair bill was $225. This included $75 for parts and $50 for each hour of labor. Find the number of hours of labor.

19. Suppose you have a 75 ft roll of paper that you will use to decorate for a party. You need one piece 10 ft long. How many 4.5 ft-long pieces can you get from the paper that is left?

20. Suppose you have $15 to plant a garden. If you spend $6 on seeds, how many packs of vegetable plants could you buy for $0.75 each?

21. Suppose you make $126 selling popcorn. If your expenses were $22.50, how many $1.50 bags of popcorn did you sell?

· ·

Practice 3-2

Mixed Exercises

Use tiles to solve each equation.

1. $5a + 2 = 7$ **2.** $2x + 3 = 7$ **3.** $3b + 6 = 12$

4. $9 = 5 + 4t$ **5.** $4a + 1 = 13$ **6.** $t + 2 = 12$

Use an equation to model and solve each problem.

7. You want to buy a bouquet of yellow roses and baby's breath for $16. The baby's breath costs $3.50 per bunch and the roses cost $2.50 each. To find how many roses you can buy, solve the equation $3.50 + 2.50r = 16$.

8. Suppose you walk at the rate of 210 ft/min. You need to walk 10,000 ft. To find how long it will take you to finish if you have already walked 550 ft, solve the equation $210x + 550 = 10,000$.

9. Suppose you have shelled 6.5 lb of pecans and you can shell pecans at a rate of 1.5 lb per hour. To find out how much longer it will take you to shell 11 lb of pecans, solve the equation $6.5 + 1.5x = 11$.

Solve each equation. Check your solutions.

10. $5.8n + 3.7 = 29.8$ **11.** $67 = -3y + 16$ **12.** $-d + 7 = 3$

13. $\frac{m}{9} + 7 = 3$ **14.** $6.78 + 5.2x = -36.9$ **15.** $5z + 9 = -21$

16. $3x - 7 = 35$ **17.** $36.9 = 3.7b - 14.9$ **18.** $4s - 13 = 51$

19. $9f + 16 = 70$ **20.** $11.6 + 3a = -16.9$ **21.** $-9 = -\frac{h}{12} + 5$

22. $-c + 2 = 5$ **23.** $-67 = -8n + 5$ **24.** $22 = 7 - 3a$

25. $\frac{k}{3} - 19 = -26$ **26.** $-21 = \frac{n}{3} + 2$ **27.** $3x + 5.7 = 15$

28. $\frac{a}{5} - 2 = -13$ **29.** $2x + 23 = 49$ **30.** $\frac{x}{2} + 8 = -3$

Use an equation to model and solve each problem.

31. The Postal Service charges $.32 for the first ounce to mail a first class letter. It charges $.23 for each additional ounce. It costs $1.01 to mail your letter. How many ounces did your letter weigh?

32. Suppose you want to buy a pair of pants and several pairs of socks. The pants cost $24.95 and the socks are $5.95 per pair. How many pairs of socks can you buy if you have $50.00 to spend?

Practice 3-3
Example Exercises

Example 1

Simplify each expression.

1. $6d - e + 3d - 2e$
2. $3 + 2c + 5c + 2$
3. $2a + 3b - 5b + 7a$
4. $6c - 7 + d + 4 - 6d$
5. $b - 3n + 12 - 6b + 2n$
6. $9c - 4 - 13c + 6$
7. $23 + 8m + 4n - 5m - 27$
8. $8x - 2y + 3x + 5y$
9. $11a - 3b + 6a - 7b$

Example 2

Solve and check each equation.

10. $3n + 4n = 63$
11. $-a + 5a = -52$
12. $6h - 8h + 9 = 37$
13. $2 = 6f - 3 - f$
14. $4b - 4 - 8b = 12$
15. $-8 = 5y - 3y$
16. $99 - 4s - 6s = -1$
17. $3t + 2t + 7 = 32$
18. $2t + 10 - t = -7$
19. $-2x - 3 + 8x = -45$
20. $5a - 2 - 4a = 0$
21. $8g + 4 - 5g = -5$

Use each equation to solve each problem.

22. Ian drove 1500 mi to New York in two days. He traveled 150 mi more the first day than he did the second day. To find how far he traveled the second day, solve the equation $150 + x + x = 1500$.

23. An amusement park added two new roller coasters totaling $2,800,000. One coaster is 800 m long and the other is 600 m long. To find the price per meter to build the coasters, solve the equation $2,800,000 = 800x + 600x$.

Example 3

Use an equation to solve each problem.

24. Suppose you need to put a fence around a rectangular garden that has a perimeter of 64 ft. The width is 12 ft less than the length. Find the length and width of the garden.

25. You buy 2.5 lb of pistachios and 3.5 lb of almonds. The total cost is $11.94. Pistachios and almonds sell for the same price. Find the cost per pound.

26. An apartment building contains 250 apartments. There are 50 more two-bedroom apartments than one-bedroom apartments. How many apartments of each type are there?

Practice 3-3

Mixed Exercises

Simplify each expression.

1. $7x - 5y - 4x + 3y$ 　　**2.** $7 - 5c - d + 9c + 2$ 　　**3.** $5a + 2b - 5b + 9a$

4. $2c - 3 + 9d + 7 - 6d$ 　　**5.** $j - 4k + 7 + 2j - 3k$ 　　**6.** $4c + 7 - 3c + 8$

Solve and check each equation.

7. $2n + 3n + 7 = -41$ 　　**8.** $2x - 5x + 6.3 = -14.4$ 　　**9.** $2z + 9.75 - 7z = -5.15$

10. $3h - 5h + 11 = 17$ 　　**11.** $2t + 8 - t = -3$ 　　**12.** $6a - 2a = -36$

13. $3c - 8c + 7 = -18$ 　　**14.** $7g + 14 - 5g = -8$ 　　**15.** $2b - 6 + 3b = 14$

Use each equation to solve each problem.

16. Consecutive even integers are even integers that differ by two as they increase in value. To find three consecutive even integers with sum -318, solve the equation $x + 2 + x + 4 + x = -318$.

17. Suppose a dealer sells cars and trucks. In the past month the dealer sold 12 more cars than trucks. If the dealer sold 48 vehicles, to find how many of each the dealer sold, solve the equation $t + 12 + t = 48$.

Solve and check each equation.

18. $5x + 4x - 27 = 81$ 　　**19.** $x + 24 - 9x = -8$

20. $25.66 = 3.8b + 1.9b + 9.7$ 　　**21.** $2a + 3a - 11.4 = 6.8$

Simplify each expression.

22. $28 - 6x + 7y + 5x - 23$ 　　**23.** $21 + 11m + 2n - 8m - 27$

24. $d - e + 5d + 7 - 3e$ 　　**25.** $19a - 13b - 4a + 7b$

Use an equation to solve each problem.

26. The total toll charge for one car and five bicycles to cross a bridge is $7.50. The toll for a car is $1.50 more than for a bicycle. Find the cost for a car to cross the bridge.

27. Consecutive integers are integers that differ by one as they increase in value. To find four consecutive integers with sum 138, solve the equation $m + m + 1 + m + 2 + m + 3 = 138$.

28. There were three times as many adults as students attending a school play. If the attendance was 480, how many adults and how many students attended the play?

Practice 3-4

••
Example Exercises

Example 1

Model each equation with tiles and solve.

1. $2(a + 3) = -4$ **2.** $3(t + 2) = 3$ **3.** $2(m - 1) = 8$

4. $4 = 4(k + 3)$ **5.** $3(2 - y) = 12$ **6.** $4(s + 3) = 8$

7. $7(b - 2) = -7$ **8.** $5 = 5(2 - y)$ **9.** $2(k + 3) - 4 = -2$

Simplify each expression.

10. $2(x + 6)$ **11.** $-5(8 - b)$ **12.** $4(-x + 7)$

13. $(5c - 7)(-3)$ **14.** $-2.5(3a + 5)$ **15.** $-(3k - 12)$

16. $-\frac{3}{4}(12 - 16d)$ **17.** $\frac{2}{3}(6h - 9)$ **18.** $(-3.2x + 2.1)(-6)$

Example 2

Solve and check each equation.

19. $3(b + 5) = 12$ **20.** $5(4d + 8) = 40$ **21.** $3(2x + 7) = 27$

22. $\frac{1}{3}(9b - 36) = -9$ **23.** $\frac{3}{4}(4x + 8) = -12$ **24.** $\frac{1}{2}(4 - 6x) = 8$

25. $4(5h + 15) - 6h = 18$ **26.** $2(3.5n - 1) = 26$ **27.** $2(a - 1) + 5 = 13$

28. $3 + 5(c + 3) = 18$ **29.** $-3(n - 4) - 2n = 17$ **30.** $-5(2x - 1) + 6x = 21$

31. $\frac{1}{2}(8a + 12) - 27 = 15$ **32.** $3x + 2(x + 4) = -7$ **33.** $-3d + \frac{1}{3}(6 + 3d) = -10$

Use an equation to model and solve each problem.

34. Suppose you are selling stuffed animals for $6 each to raise money for your club. You sold six more rabbits than monkeys. If you sold $120 worth of stuffed animals, how many of each type did you sell?

35. April buys eight books for $44. Paperback books cost $4 and hardback books cost $8. How many of each type of book did she buy?

36. You and a friend decide to meet at a park. You travel 2 mi farther to get to the park than your friend. Three times the distance you travel is 12 mi. How far did your friend travel to get to the park?

37. Suppose you have a coin collection of dimes and quarters containing 46 coins. If you have $6.70, how many of each type of coin do you have?

Practice 3-4
• •
Mixed Exercises

Solve and check each equation.

1. $4(2r + 8) = 88$

2. $-3(b - 5) = -21$

3. $3(f + 2) = -15$

4. $6h + 5(h - 5) = 52$

5. $-5d + 3(2d - 7) = -5$

6. $7 + 2(4x - 3) = 33$

7. $2(3h + 2) - 4h = -16$

8. $-3(4 - y) = -27$

9. $3(2n - 4) - 2n = 24$

10. $-w + 4(w + 3) = -12$

11. $4 = 0.4(3d - 5)$

12. $-4d + 2(3 + d) = -14$

13. $2x + \frac{3}{4}(4x + 16) = 7$

14. $2(3a + 2) = -8$

15. $5(t - 3) - 2t = -30$

16. $5(b + 4) - 6b = -24$

17. $\frac{2}{5}(5k + 35) - 8 = 12$

18. $0.4(2s + 4) = 4.8$

19. $\frac{2}{3}(9b - 27) = 36$

20. $\frac{1}{2}(12n - 8) = 26$

21. $0.5(2x - 4) = -17$

Simplify each expression.

22. $3.5(3x - 8)$

23. $4(x + 7)$

24. $-2.5(2a - 4)$

25. $\frac{2}{3}(12 - 15d)$

26. $-(2k - 11)$

27. $-\frac{1}{3}(6h + 15)$

28. $(2c - 8)(-4)$

29. $-3(4 - 2b)$

30. $2(3x - 9)$

Use an equation to model and solve each problem.

31. The attendance at a ball game was 400 people. Student tickets cost $2 and adult tickets cost $3. If $1050 was collected in ticket sales, how many of each type of ticket were sold?

32. Find two consecutive integers such that the sum of the first and 3 times the second is 55.

33. An angle and its complement always have a sum of 90°. The sum of the measures of an angle and five times its complement is 298°. What is the measure of the angle?

34. The perimeter of a pool table is 30 ft. It is twice as long as it is wide. What is the length of a pool table?

35. Suppose you have a coin collection of nickels and dimes containing 63 coins. If you have $5.05, how many of each type of coin do you have?

Solve and check each equation.

36. $2(a - 4) + 15 = 13$

37. $7 + 2(a - 3) = -9$

38. $13 + 2(5c - 2) = 29$

39. $5(3x + 12) = -15$

40. $4(2a + 2) - 17 = 15$

41. $2(m + 1) = 16$

42. $-4x + 3(2x - 5) = 31$

43. $-6 - 3(2k + 4) = 18$

44. $3(t - 12) = 27$

Practice 3-5

Example Exercises

Example 1

Solve each equation. Check your answers.

1. $\frac{3}{4}x = 9$ **2.** $\frac{3}{5}y = 12$ **3.** $\frac{2}{3}a = 14$ **4.** $4 = -\frac{1}{2}x$

5. $-\frac{2}{7}n = -6$ **6.** $-\frac{3}{8}k = 12$ **7.** $\frac{1}{3}(2x + 5) = 7$ **8.** $\frac{1}{2}(3k + 7) = -4$

Use an equation to solve.

9. In your class, $\frac{4}{5}$ of the students are right-handed. If there are 20 right-handed students, what is the total number of students in the class?

Example 2

Solve each equation. Check your answers.

10. $\frac{3a + 1}{5} = 2$ **11.** $\frac{s + 6}{2} = 12$

12. $\frac{7 - 4b}{7} = -3$ **13.** $-8 = \frac{h - 5}{3}$

14. $\frac{5a + 7 - 3a}{3} = -9$ **15.** $\frac{-t + 5 - 3t}{5} = -11$

16. $6 = \frac{x + 9 - 4x}{4}$ **17.** $\frac{9 + 4x - 15}{6} = 7$

Use an equation to solve.

18. Three members of a tug-of-war team weigh 163 lb, 148 lb, and 143 lb. What must the fourth member weigh if the average weight is 150 lb?

Example 3

Solve each equation. Check your answers.

19. $\frac{2}{3}l = \frac{3}{4}$ **20.** $\frac{1}{4}h + \frac{1}{2} = 1$

21. $\frac{1}{2}a + \frac{1}{3}a = 5$ **22.** $-\frac{3}{4}x + 2 = \frac{1}{2}$

23. $-\frac{3}{4} = \frac{2}{3}x - \frac{1}{4}$ **24.** $\frac{3}{4}b - \frac{1}{2}b = -8$

25. $\frac{3}{5}x + \frac{1}{2} = 4\frac{1}{10}$ **26.** $4x - \frac{2}{3} = 1$

Use an equation to solve.

27. Cliff took some money to the movies. He spent $\frac{1}{2}$ of the money on the ticket and $\frac{1}{3}$ of the money on snacks. He spent $10 total. How much money did he bring to the movies?

Name _____ Class _____ Date _____

Practice 3-5
• •

Mixed Exercises

Solve each equation. Check your answers.

1. $\frac{s+6}{3} = 9$

2. $-\frac{2}{5}n = -10$

3. $\frac{1}{2}a - \frac{1}{3}a = -2$

4. $\frac{1}{6} = \frac{2}{3}v - \frac{1}{2}$

5. $\frac{3}{5}s = -15$

6. $\frac{5-4b}{5} = -3$

7. $\frac{2}{3}x - 9 = \frac{1}{3}$

8. $\frac{2}{5}y = -8$

9. $\frac{2a+5}{9} = -3$

10. $\frac{2}{3}r - \frac{1}{2}r = -5$

11. $\frac{1}{5}(3x - 6) = 6$

12. $-\frac{2}{3}k = 10$

13. $8 = -\frac{2}{5}(d + 4)$

14. $6 = -\frac{3}{4}f$

15. $\frac{1}{3}h - \frac{1}{2} = \frac{1}{6}$

16. $\frac{7k + 6 - 4k}{3} = -11$

17. $\frac{1}{4}(6 - 2z) = -5$

18. $\frac{3}{8}b - \frac{1}{4}b = 3$

19. $-\frac{3}{4}m = -6$

20. $\frac{5d - 7 - 3d}{5} = -7$

Use an equation to solve.

21. Suppose you buy $1\frac{2}{3}$ lb of bananas for $.65. How much do bananas cost per pound?

22. Lopez spent $\frac{1}{3}$ of his vacation money for travel and $\frac{2}{5}$ of his vacation money for lodging. He spent $1100 for travel and lodging. What is the total amount of money he spent on his vacation?

23. On the first four days of the week, Ella took 30 min, 28 min, 34 min, and 31 min to get to school. If the average time for the week was 31 min, how long did Ella take to get to school on Friday?

24. Suppose you spent $\frac{1}{2}$ of your money buying clothes and $\frac{1}{4}$ of your money for a gift. If you spent $24, how much money did you have?

25. Victoria weighs $\frac{5}{7}$ as much as Mario. If Victoria weighs 125 lb, how much does Mario weigh?

Solve each equation. Check your answers.

26. $18 = \frac{c+5}{2}$

27. $\frac{2}{9}s = -6$

28. $\frac{1}{3}x = \frac{1}{2}$

29. $\frac{2}{3}g + \frac{1}{2}g = 14$

30. $\frac{3x+7}{2} = 8$

31. $\frac{2x-6}{4} = -7$

32. $\frac{2}{3}k + \frac{1}{4}k = 22$

33. $-\frac{4}{7}h = -28$

34. $-8 = \frac{4}{5}k$

35. $\frac{3}{4} - \frac{1}{3}z = \frac{1}{4}$

36. $-9 = \frac{3}{4}m$

37. $\frac{5}{6}c - \frac{2}{3}c = \frac{1}{3}$

38. $\frac{4}{5} = -\frac{4}{7}g$

39. $\frac{9x + 6 - 4x}{2} = 8$

40. $-\frac{1}{6}d = -4$

© Prentice-Hall, Inc.

Practice 3-6
· ·
Example Exercises

Example 1

1. Suppose you have a coin jar containing two nickels, three dimes, and five quarters. You pick a coin, replace it, and then pick a second coin. Find each probability.

   a. P(nickel and dime) **b.** P(nickel and quarter) **c.** P(two dimes)

   d. P(dime and quarter) **e.** P(two nickels) **f.** P(two quarters)

Example 2

2. Suppose you draw two marbles from a bag containing six red, three green, two yellow, and four blue. You pick the second one without replacing the first one. Find each probability.

   a. P(red and green) **b.** P(green and blue) **c.** P(yellow and red)

   d. P(two reds) **e.** P(two blues) **f.** P(red and blue)

Example 3

A and B are independent events. Find the missing probability.

3. $P(A) = \frac{3}{4}$, $P(A \text{ and } B) = \frac{1}{2}$. Find $P(B)$.

4. $P(A) = \frac{3}{7}$, $P(B) = \frac{1}{6}$. Find $P(A \text{ and } B)$.

5. $P(B) = \frac{9}{10}$, $P(A \text{ and } B) = \frac{3}{5}$. Find $P(A)$

6. $P(B) = \frac{1}{4}$, $P(A \text{ and } B) = \frac{3}{20}$. Find $P(A)$.

Use an equation to solve each problem.

7. A bag contains green and yellow color tiles. You pick two tiles without replacing the first one. The probability that the first tile is yellow is $\frac{3}{5}$. The probability of drawing two yellow tiles is $\frac{12}{35}$. Find the probability that the second tile you pick is yellow.

8. A bag contains red and blue marbles. You pick two marbles without replacing the first one. The probability of drawing a blue and then a red is $\frac{4}{15}$. The probability that your second marble is red if your first marble is blue is $\frac{2}{3}$. Find the probability that the first marble is blue.

Practice 3-6

• •
Mixed Exercises

1. Suppose you have a dark closet containing seven blue shirts, five yellow shirts, and eight white shirts. You pick two shirts from the closet. Find each probability.

   a. P(blue and yellow shirts) with replacing   **b.** P(blue and yellow shirts) without replacing

   c. P(two yellow shirts) with replacing   **d.** P(two yellow shirts) without replacing

   e. P(yellow and white shirts) with replacing   **f.** P(yellow and white shirts) without replacing

   g. P(two blue shirts) with replacing   **h.** P(two blue shirts) without replacing

A and B are independent events. Find the missing probability.

2. $P(A) = \frac{3}{7}$, $P(A \text{ and } B) = \frac{1}{3}$. Find $P(B)$.

3. $P(B) = \frac{1}{5}$, $P(A \text{ and } B) = \frac{2}{13}$. Find $P(A)$.

4. $P(B) = \frac{15}{16}$, $P(A \text{ and } B) = \frac{3}{4}$. Find $P(A)$.

5. $P(A) = \frac{8}{15}$, $P(B) = \frac{3}{4}$. Find $P(A \text{ and } B)$.

6. Suppose you draw two tennis balls from a bag containing seven pink, four white, three yellow, and two striped balls. Find each probability.

   a. P(yellow and pink) with replacing   **b.** P(pink and striped) without replacing

   c. P(two pink) with replacing   **d.** P(two pink) without replacing

   e. P(two striped) with replacing   **f.** P(two striped) without replacing

   g. P(pink and white) with replacing   **h.** P(pink and white) without replacing

7. Two students are selected at random from a class. The probability that the first student selected is a girl is $\frac{4}{7}$. The probability of selecting a boy after the girl was selected is $\frac{4}{9}$. Find the probability of selecting a girl and then a boy.

8. A bag contains red pens and blue pens. You pick two pens without replacing the first one. The probability that the first pen is blue is $\frac{3}{8}$. The probability of drawing a blue pen and then a red pen is $\frac{1}{4}$. Find the probability that the second pen you pick is red.

9. A bag contains red, white and blue balloons. You pick two balloons without replacing the first one. The probability of drawing a blue and then a white is $\frac{7}{75}$. The probability that your second balloon is white if your first balloon is blue is $\frac{1}{3}$. Find the probability that the first balloon is blue.

© Prentice-Hall, Inc.

Practice 3-7

•••

Example Exercises

Example 1

Model with an equation and solve.

1. What is 20% of 120?
2. What is 75% of 60?
3. What is 150% of 8?

4. What is 10.5% of 460?
5. What is 9% of 1000?
6. What is 5% of 180?

7. Suppose you are reading a book. You have read 40% of the book. If the book has 780 pages, how many pages have you read?

8. Kelli has decided to save 15% of her monthly income. If her monthly income is $2450, how much will she save?

Example 2

Model with an equation and solve.

9. 12% of what is 15?
10. 200% of what is 36?
11. 145% of what is 174?

12. 60% of what is 24?
13. 35.5% of what is 92.3?
14. 75% of what is 36?

15. Three students in the class received an A on a test. The three students represents 15% of the class. How many students are in the class?

16. Suppose 12% of the students are involved in drama. If 66 students are in drama, how many students are in the school?

Example 3

Model with an equation and solve.

17. What percent of 50 is 36?
18. What percent of 12 is 18?
19. What percent of 320 is 8?

20. What percent of 24 is 90?
21. What percent of 30 is 54?
22. What percent of 12 is 6.6?

23. Hans is required to make 50 sales per month. This month he has made 62 sales. What percent of the requirement has he fulfilled?

Example 4

Model using the equation $I = prt$ and solve.

24. You invest $700 for three years. Find the amount of simple interest you earn at an annual rate of 5%.

25. You invested $500 at a interest rate of 4.5%. How many years would it take to earn $90 in interest?

Practice 3-7
●●
Mixed Exercises

Model with an equation and solve.

1. 25% of what is 28?   **2.** What percent of 72 is 18?   **3.** 60% of what is 45?

4. What percent of 12 is 6?   **5.** What is 60% of 12?   **6.** 75% of what is 48?

7. What is 20% of 650?   **8.** What percent of 150 is 90?   **9.** What percent of 90 is 63?

10. What is 38% of 60?   **11.** 22.5% of what is 42?   **12.** 45% of what is 99?

13. What percent of 210 is 10.5?   **14.** 160% of what is 124?   **15.** What is 39% of 1500?

16. What is 250% of 14?   **17.** What percent of 20 is 36?   **18.** What is 8.25% of 160?

Model with an equation and solve.

19. Pablo has a goal to lose 25 lb. He has lost 16 lb. What percent of his goal has he reached?

20. You spent 16% of your vacation money on food. If you spent $48 on food, how much money did you spend on your vacation?

21. A writer earns $3400 a month. Last month she spent $204 on food. What percent of her income was spent on food?

22. Kiko spends 30% of her monthly income on rent. If she pays $810 for rent each month, what is her monthly income?

23. Suppose that 62.5% of freshmen entering a college graduate from it. If there are 2680 freshmen, how many will graduate from that college?

The formula for determining simple interest is $I = prt$. Using this formula, solve the following problems.

24. You invest $1500 for three years. Find the amount of simple interest you earn at an annual rate of 8.25%.

25. Suppose you invested $1200 for four years. You earned $312 in simple interest. What is the interest rate?

26. Suppose you invested some money at 8% simple interest for five years. If you received $500 in interest, how much money did you invest?

Model with an equation and solve.

27. What is 7% of 480?   **28.** What percent of 80 is 48?   **29.** 90% of what is 27?

30. What is 150% of 26?   **31.** 125% of what is 175?   **32.** What is 10.25% of 280?

33. What is 35% of 360?   **34.** What percent of 36 is 9?   **35.** 75% of what is 90?

36. 45% of what is 36?   **37.** What is 80% of 120?   **38.** What percent of 20 is 8?

39. 25% of what is 92?   **40.** What percent of 30 is 90?   **41.** What is 39% of 800?

© Prentice-Hall, Inc.

Practice 3-8

Example Exercises

Example 1

Find each percent of increase. Round your answers to the nearest whole number.

1. 10 to 14   **2.** 6 to 8   **3.** 60 to 100   **4.** 28 to 36

5. 230 m to 250 m   **6.** 36 ft to 45 ft   **7.** $8.50 to $10.75   **8.** 12,000 lb to 18,000 lb

9. $1200 to $1240   **10.** 15 to $16\frac{1}{2}$ **11.** 125 mi to 140 mi   **12.** $12\frac{3}{4}$ to $15\frac{1}{2}$

13. A store raised shirt prices from $24 to $27. Find the percent of increase.

14. In 1960, the average American generated 2.7 lb of garbage daily. In 1993, the amount had increased to 4.4 lb. What is the percent of increase? Round your answer to the nearest whole number.

15. Annual poultry consumption, from 1980 to 1993, increased from 40.6 lb to 61.1 lb per person. Find the percent of increase. Round your answer to the nearest whole number.

16. From 1990 to 1993, Girl Scout numbers increased from 2.48 million to 2.61 million. What is the percent of increase? Round your answer to the nearest whole number.

17. In 1980, California had 45 U.S. Representatives. That number increased to 52 in 1990. Find the percent of increase. Round your answer to the nearest whole number.

Example 2

Find each percent of decrease. Round your answers to the nearest whole number.

18. 150 to 125   **19.** $39.95 to $33.95   **20.** 380 yd to 300 yd   **21.** $8 to $6.50

22. 48 ft to 30 ft   **23.** 190 in. to 40 in.   **24.** 540 mi to 160 mi   **25.** 16.8 to 12

26. 25 g to 22 g   **27.** 150 ft to 137 ft   **28.** $54\frac{1}{8}$ to $36\frac{1}{4}$ **29.** $10\frac{1}{2}$ to $9\frac{1}{4}$

30. In 1980, annual red meat consumption was 126.4 lb per person. In 1993, the amount had decreased to 111.9 lb per person. What is the percent of decrease?

31. Between 1980 and 1993, the amount of milk drunk by the average American decreased from 27.6 gal to 24.8 gal annually. Find the percent of decrease.

32. The number of U.S. Representatives from New York decreased from 34 in 1980 to 31 in 1990. What is the percent of decrease?

© Prentice-Hall, Inc.

Practice 3-8
• •
Mixed Exercises

Find each percent of change. Describe the percent of change as a percent of increase or decrease. Round your answers to the nearest whole number.

1. 36 g to 27 g
2. 40 cm to 100 cm
3. 90 in. to 45 in.
4. 500 lb to 1500 lb

5. $90 to $84.50
6. $100 to $140
7. $15 to $5.50
8. 100 mi to 175 mi

9. 280 m to 320 m
10. 58 to 76
11. 60 to 150
12. 600 mi to 480 mi

13. 18 to 27
14. 290 yd to 261 yd
15. 64 ft to 48 ft
16. $8.50 to $12.75

17. $36\frac{1}{2}$ to $29\frac{1}{4}$
18. $74\frac{3}{4}$ to $66\frac{1}{2}$
19. $6\frac{3}{4}$ to $8\frac{1}{4}$
20. $15\frac{1}{2}$ to $18\frac{1}{4}$

21. 238 ft to 207 ft
22. 350 to 310
23. 18 ft to 50 ft
24. 26.2 to 22.8

Find each percent of change. Describe the percent of change as a percent of increase or decrease. Round your answers to the nearest whole number.

25. In 1985, the average price for gasoline was $1.19. In 1986, the average price for gasoline was $.93 cents. Find the percent of change.

26. The number of Boy Scouts in 1990 was 4.29 million. In 1993, the number of Boy Scouts was 4.17 million. What is the percent of change?

27. In 1980, Texas had 27 U.S. Representatives. That number increased to 30 in 1990. Find the percent of change.

28. A car dealer raised the price of a car from $10,500 to $11,000. Find the percent of change.

29. Between 1980 and 1990, the population of Atlanta, GA, went from 425,022 to 394,017. What is the percent of change?

30. The number of bowlers in 1990 was 71 million. In 1993, the number of bowlers was 79 million. Find the percent of change.

31. In 1980, the average annual tuition charge for a four-year public university was $840. The average annual tuition charge in 1993 was $2352. What is the percent of change?

32. In 1980, the average American drank 2.4 gal of bottled water annually. That changed to 9.2 gal of bottled water annually by 1993. What is the percent of change?

33. In 1980, 419,007 people rode a motorcycle to work. The number of people riding a motorcycle to work in 1990 was 237,404. Find the percent of change.

34. The United States imported 6,365,000 barrels of oil per day in 1980. In 1990, the United States imported 7,161,000 barrels of oil per day. What is the percent of change?

Practice 4-1
....
Example Exercises

Example 1

Solve using the multiplication property of equality.

1. $\frac{a}{3} = \frac{6}{9}$ 2. $\frac{f}{4} = \frac{1}{2}$ 3. $\frac{t}{5} = \frac{6}{10}$ 4. $-\frac{3}{5} = -\frac{k}{20}$ 5. $\frac{2}{3} = \frac{x}{18}$

6. $\frac{m}{2} = \frac{3}{5}$ 7. $-\frac{5}{8} = -\frac{c}{12}$ 8. $\frac{s}{6} = \frac{5}{8}$ 9. $\frac{z}{12} = \frac{7}{10}$ 10. $\frac{1}{6} = \frac{p}{9}$

Example 2

Which pairs of ratios could form a proportion? Justify your answer.

11. $\frac{3}{5}, \frac{6}{10}$ 12. $\frac{1}{5}, \frac{3}{20}$ 13. $-\frac{16}{20}, \frac{4}{5}$ 14. $\frac{25}{10}, \frac{5}{2}$ 15. $-\frac{11}{16}, \frac{16.4}{24}$

Solve using cross products.

16. $\frac{16}{a} = \frac{8}{9}$ 17. $\frac{g}{4} = \frac{6}{10}$ 18. $\frac{7}{5} = \frac{k}{15}$ 19. $\frac{4}{5} = \frac{10}{r}$ 20. $-\frac{1.6}{4} = -\frac{m}{10}$

21. $-\frac{7.5}{5} = -\frac{x}{2}$ 22. $\frac{6}{y} = \frac{3}{7}$ 23. $-\frac{1.5}{4} = -\frac{4.5}{t}$ 24. $\frac{2}{h} = \frac{6}{19.2}$ 25. $\frac{x}{54} = \frac{26}{3}$

Example 3

Use a proportion to solve.

26. $\triangle ABC$ is similar to $\triangle XYZ$. The length AB is 10. The length BC is 7. Find the length XY if the length YZ is 14.

27. Marty has a scale model of a car. The scale is 1 in. : 32 in. If the model is 6.75 in. long, how long is the actual car?

28. A blueprint scale is 1 in. : 12 ft. The width of a building is 48 ft. What is the width of the building on the blueprint?

Example 4

Use a proportion to solve.

29. Find 40% of 125.   30. What percent of 60 is 25?   31. 24 is 30% of what number?

32. Find 32.5% of 60.   33. 35 is 65% of what number?   34. 35 is what percent of 40?

35. A teacher spent $235.20 on classroom supplies. This was 80% of his classroom budget. How much was his budget?

Practice 4-1
....
Mixed Exercises

Which pairs of ratios could form a proportion? Justify your answer.

1. $\frac{10}{24}, \frac{7}{18}$ 2. $\frac{6}{9}, \frac{10}{15}$ 3. $\frac{3}{4}, \frac{18}{24}$ 4. $\frac{16}{2}, \frac{8}{1}$ 5. $\frac{-4.8}{4}, \frac{-6.4}{5}$

Solve each proportion.

6. $\frac{g}{5} = \frac{6}{10}$ 7. $\frac{z}{4} = \frac{7}{8}$ 8. $\frac{13.2}{6} = \frac{m}{12}$ 9. $-\frac{m}{5} = -\frac{2}{5}$

10. $\frac{5.5}{11} = \frac{x}{5}$ 11. $-\frac{2}{3} = -\frac{10}{t}$ 12. $\frac{4}{6} = \frac{x}{24}$ 13. $\frac{s}{3} = \frac{7}{10}$

14. $\frac{4}{9} = \frac{10}{r}$ 15. $\frac{x}{4.8} = \frac{6}{3.2}$ 16. $\frac{5}{4} = \frac{c}{12}$ 17. $-\frac{32}{h} = -\frac{1}{3}$

18. $\frac{2}{6} = \frac{p}{9}$ 19. $\frac{f}{6} = \frac{3}{4}$ 20. $\frac{15}{a} = \frac{3}{8}$ 21. $\frac{3}{4} = \frac{k}{24}$

22. $\frac{a}{6} = \frac{3}{9}$ 23. $\frac{4}{5} = \frac{k}{9}$ 24. $\frac{3}{y} = \frac{5}{8}$ 25. $\frac{t}{7} = \frac{9}{21}$

Use a proportion to solve each problem. Round your answers to the nearest tenth or to the nearest tenth of a percent.

26. 45 is 75% of what number? 27. Find 62% of 70. 28. 5 is what percent of 60?

29. 21.28 is 28% of what number? 30. Find 85% of 240. 31. What percent of 90 is 35?

32. In 1993, there were 14,331,000 workers 16–24 years old who were paid an hourly wage. Of this number, 1,153,000 earned $10 or more per hour. What percent of the workers earned $10 or more per hour?

33. Angie is using similar triangles to find the height of a tree. A stick that is 5 ft tall casts a shadow that is 4 ft long. The tree casts a shadow that is 22 ft long. How tall is the tree?

34. △*ABC* is similar to △*XYZ*. The length *AC* is 10. The length *BC* is 16. What is the length *XZ* if the length *YZ* is 12?

35. A map has a scale of 1 in. : 25 mi. Two cities are 175 mi apart. How far apart are they on the map?

Solve each proportion.

36. $\frac{t}{4} = \frac{15}{10}$ 37. $-\frac{6}{8} = -\frac{p}{12}$ 38. $\frac{3}{a} = \frac{6}{27}$

39. $\frac{8}{7} = \frac{c}{14}$ 40. $\frac{2.1}{6} = \frac{x}{4}$ 41. $\frac{z}{24} = \frac{3}{10}$

42. $\frac{2}{1.2} = \frac{5}{k}$ 43. $\frac{4}{7} = \frac{d}{28}$ 44. $-\frac{5}{p} = -\frac{6}{12}$

45. $\frac{f}{8} = \frac{9}{18}$ 46. $\frac{g}{20} = \frac{12}{48}$ 47. $\frac{2}{x} = \frac{8}{28}$

48. $\frac{2}{9} = \frac{10}{b}$ 49. $\frac{v}{15} = \frac{3}{4}$ 50. $\frac{18}{11} = \frac{49.5}{n}$

Practice 4-2

•••

Example Exercises

Example 1

Model each equation with tiles and solve.

1. $4x - 3 = 2x + 5$ **2.** $5y + 8 = 2y + 2$ **3.** $3a + 2 = -6 - a$

Example 2

Solve and check.

4. $3d + 5 = 2d + 6$ **5.** $-5s - 7 = 3s + 41$ **6.** $2h + 4 = 25 - h$

7. $\frac{1}{3}x + \frac{1}{3} = \frac{2}{3}x$ **8.** $2.3 - n = 4n - 3.2$ **9.** $8 - 7a = -a - 16$

Example 3

Solve and check.

10. $4g + 7 - 2g = 5g - 2$ **11.** $4v - 8 = 8 + 4v - v$ **12.** $3(7 - 2d) = 22 - 8d$

13. $-8t = 4(t + 5) + 2t$ **14.** $-6y + 15 = 3(y - 1)$ **15.** $\frac{1}{2}(2x - 5) = -2x$

16. A passenger train travels at 60 mi/h and a freight train travels at 40 mi/h. It takes the passenger train 1.5 h less time to cover the same distance as the freight train. How long does it take each train to make the trip?

17. Hans needs to rent a moving truck. Suppose Company A charges a rate of \$40/d and Company B charges \$60 plus \$20/d. How many days must Hans rent the moving truck to justify using Company B?

18. May rides her bike the same distance that Leah walks. May rides her bike 10 km/h faster than Leah walks. If it takes May 1 h and Leah 3 h, how fast does each travel?

Example 4

Solve each equation. If an equation has no solution, write *no solution*.

19. $3x + 2 - x = 2x + 1$ **20.** $5z - 3 = -3 + 4z$ **21.** $5t + 4 = 3(2 - t) + 8t$

Example 5

Solve each equation. Write *identity* or *no solution*.

22. $3(2b - 1) = -3 + 6b$ **23.** $4(n - 2) = 6n + 5 - 2n$ **24.** $8(3f - 4) = 4(6f - 8)$

Practice 4-2
• •
Mixed Exercises

Solve each equation. If appropriate, write *identity* or *no solution*.

1. $7 - 2n = n - 14$ **2.** $2(4 - 2r) = -2(r + 5)$ **3.** $3d + 8 = 2d - 7$

4. $6t = 3(t + 4) - t$ **5.** $8z - 7 = 3z - 7 + 5z$ **6.** $7x - 8 = 3x + 12$

7. $3(n - 1) = 5n + 3 - 2n$ **8.** $2(6 - 4d) = 25 - 9d$ **9.** $2y + 18 = 5y + 3$

10. $6h = 54 - 3h$ **11.** $4s - 12 = -5s + 51$ **12.** $8(2f - 3) = 4(4f - 8)$

13. $6k - 25 = 7 - 2k$ **14.** $3v - 9 = 7 + 2v - v$ **15.** $4(b - 1) = -4 + 4b$

16. $\frac{1}{4}x + \frac{1}{2} = \frac{1}{4}x - \frac{1}{2}$ **17.** $6 - 4d = 16 - 9d$ **18.** $\frac{2}{3}a - \frac{3}{4} = \frac{3}{4}a$

19. $2s - 12 + 2s = 4s - 12$ **20.** $3.6y = 5.4 + 3.3y$ **21.** $4.3v - 6 = 8 + 2.3v$

22. $5(f - 4) = 4(f + 6)$ **23.** $4b - 1 = -4 + 4b + 3$ **24.** $3k - 7 = 8 - 2k$

Solve and check.

25. Mari and Brice are picking oranges. Mari has picked 2 boxes of oranges and is picking 5 boxes per hour. Brice has picked 5 boxes of oranges and is picking at 3 boxes per hour. In how many hours will they have picked the same number of boxes?

26. Lois rides her bike to visit a friend. She travels at 10 mi/h. While she's there, it starts to rain. Her friend drives her home in a car traveling at 25 mi/h. It takes Lois 1.5 h longer to go to her friend's than it does to return home. How many hours did it take Lois to ride to her friend's house?

27. Suppose a video store charges non-members $4 to rent a video. A membership costs $21 and then videos cost only $2.50 to rent. How many videos would you need to rent in order to justify a membership?

28. Suppose your club is selling candles to raise money. It costs $100 to rent a spot to sell the candles. If the candles cost your club $1 each and are being sold for $5 each, how many candles must be sold to equal the expenses?

Solve each equation. If appropriate, write *identity* or *no solution*.

29. $5a + 12 = 6 - 3a$ **30.** $\frac{2}{3}(6x + 3) = 4x + 2$ **31.** $6.5 - 7a = 2a + 2$

32. $6y + 9 = 3(2y + 3)$ **33.** $4g + 7 = 5g - 1 - g$ **34.** $3x + 2 + x = x - 1$

35. $2(n + 2) = 5n - 5$ **36.** $6 - 3d = 5(2 - d)$ **37.** $2k + 18 = 5k$

38. $6.1h = 9.3 - 3.2h$ **39.** $-4.4s - 2 = -5.5s - 4.2$ **40.** $3(2f + 4) = 2(3f - 6)$

41. $\frac{3}{4}t - \frac{5}{6} = \frac{2}{3}t$ **42.** $3v + 8 = 8 + 2v + v$ **43.** $\frac{1}{2}d - \frac{3}{4} = \frac{3}{5}d$

44. $3h + 7 = 5h - 1$ **45.** $5(r + 3) = 2r + 6$ **46.** $8 - 3(p - 4) = 2p$

Practice 4-3
Example Exercises

Example 1

Use a number line to solve.

1. $|a| = 5$ 2. $|x| = 5.8$ 3. $|d| = 3.2$ 4. $12 = |k|$ 5. $8.2 = |n|$

6. $|m| = 13$ 7. $\frac{3}{4} = |t|$ 8. $|w| = 6$ 9. $|u| = 8$ 10. $3\frac{3}{4} = |f|$

Example 2

Solve and check each equation. If there is no solution, explain.

11. $|v| + 2 = 7$ 12. $|d| - 15 = -7$ 13. $5|h| = 25$

14. $8 = 12 + |s|$ 15. $\frac{|t|}{3} = 2$ 16. $36 = 9|r|$

17. $-5 = \frac{|z|}{-5}$ 18. $\frac{1}{2} = \frac{|c|}{10}$ 19. $-3|y| = -27$

20. $7 + |a| = 10$ 21. $-13 = |n| - 8$ 22. $7|m| = 35.7$

Example 3

Solve and check each equation. If there is no solution, explain.

23. $|d + 2| = 5$ 24. $|4f| = 24$ 25. $15 = |k - 3|$

26. $8 = |2h|$ 27. $-9 = |3 + n|$ 28. $|6v| = 12$

29. $|3z| + 7 = 10$ 30. $4|r - 4| = 12$ 31. $17 = 12 + |n + 2|$

32. $|2c| - 17 = -11$ 33. $2|5 + d| = 14$ 34. $|4w| - 11 = -3$

Example 4

Model with an equation and solve.

35. The length of a metal rod was measured to be 25.5 cm. The measured length may vary from the actual length by 0.025 cm. Find the maximum and minimum actual lengths.

36. A scale may vary by 0.4 lb when weighing objects. If the reading on the scale is 125.2 lb, what are the maximum and minimum weights of the object?

37. The median score on a test was 84. The high and low scores vary from the median by 8. What are the high and low scores on the test?

38. One poll reported that the approval rating of the President of the United States was 63%. The poll was accurate to within 3.8%. What are the maximum and minimum approval ratings for the President?

Practice 4-3
• •
Mixed Exercises

Solve and check each equation. If there is no solution, explain.

1. $13 = |n + 3|$ **2.** $|a| = 9.5$ **3.** $|d| - 25 = -13$ **4.** $|6z| + 3 = 21$

5. $|d| = 8.1$ **6.** $|3v| = 39$ **7.** $\frac{|t|}{9} = 3$ **8.** $6.8 = |4h|$

9. $|3c| - 45 = -18$ **10.** $|7w| + 15 = 36$ **11.** $3.8 = |k|$ **12.** $-32 = |n| - 38$

13. $-2 = \frac{|z|}{-7}$ **14.** $|u| = 2.7$ **15.** $12 + |a| = 19$ **16.** $7\frac{1}{8} = |f|$

17. $-4|7 + d| = -44$ **18.** $|x| = -0.8$ **19.** $|d + 18| = 12$ **20.** $11.3 = |n|$

Model with an equation and solve.

21. The average number of seeds in a package of cucumber seeds is 25. The number of seeds in the package can vary by three. What are the maximum and minimum number of seeds that could be in a package?

22. The mean distance of the earth from the sun is 93 million mi. The distance varies by 1.6 million mi. What are the maximum and minimum distances of the earth from the sun?

23. Leona was in a golf tournament last week. All of her four rounds of golf were within 2 strokes of par. If par was 72, what are the maximum and minimum scores that Leona could have made in the golf tournament?

24. Victor has a goal of making $75 per week at his after-school job. Last month he was within $6.50 of his goal. What are the maximum and minimum amounts that Victor might have made last month?

25. Members of the track team can run 400 m in an average time of 58.2 s. The fastest and slowest times varied from the average by 6.4 s. What were the maximum and minimum times for the track team?

Solve and check each equation. If there is no solution, explain.

26. $\frac{3}{4} = \frac{|c|}{12}$ **27.** $-44 = -4|r|$ **28.** $\frac{3}{8} = |t|$ **29.** $41 = |k + 32|$

30. $|13 + n| = 15$ **31.** $0.6|y| = 4.2$ **32.** $|r + 3| = 5$ **33.** $|11h| = 55$

34. $6.4 = 1.6|r|$ **35.** $15|m| = 45$ **36.** $7 = |s| - 3$ **37.** $19 = |k + 13|$

38. $6\frac{3}{7} = |t|$ **39.** $|v| + 17 = 29$ **40.** $|9f| = 81$ **41.** $|m| = 9\frac{1}{9}$

42. $19 = |-23 + k|$ **43.** $1.6|y| = 8.8$ **44.** $|k - 3| = 4$ **45.** $|h| - 6 = -5$

46. $|w| = -7\frac{2}{3}$ **47.** $5|m| = 5$ **48.** $17 = |s| - 8$ **49.** $|v| = \frac{7}{9}$

Practice 4-4

⋯⋯⋯⋯⋯⋯⋯⋯⋯⋯⋯⋯⋯⋯⋯⋯⋯⋯

Example Exercises

Example 1

The formula $A = \frac{1}{2}bh$ gives the area A for a triangle.

1. Solve this formula for h.

2. Find h if $b = 4$ in., $A = 16$ in.^{2}.

3. Solve this formula for b.

4. Find b if $h = 5$ in., $A = 50$ in.^{2}.

5. Find h if $b = 10$ in., $A = 80$ in.^{2}.

6. Find b if $h = 10$ in., $A = 75$ in.^{2}.

Example 2

The formula $P = 2(l + w)$ gives the perimeter P of a rectangle for length l and width w.

7. Solve this formula for l.

8. Find l if $P = 64$ cm, $w = 6$ cm.

9. Solve this formula for w.

10. Find w if $P = 36$ in., $l = 7$ in.

11. Find w if $P = 150$ cm, $l = 20$ cm.

12. Find l if $P = 100$ in., $w = 25$ in.

Example 3

The formula $R = \frac{V}{I}$ gives electrical resistance R, in ohms, for a voltage V, in volts, and a current I, in amps.

13. Solve this formula for I.

14. Find I if $V = 120$ volts and $R = 24$ ohms.

15. Solve this formula for V.

16. Find V if $I = 2.5$ amps and $R = 96$ ohms.

17. Find I if $V = 24$ volts and $R = 48$ ohms.

18. Find V if $I = 15$ amps and $R = 120$ ohms.

Example 4

Solve each equation for the given variable.

19. $2x + y = 6$; y

20. $5a - b = 7$; b

21. $d + 2e = f$; d

22. $12 + 3y = z$; y

23. $r = \frac{d}{t}$; t

24. $de = f$; e

25. $\frac{x}{3} = \frac{y}{6}$; y

26. $y = mx + b$; m

27. $3(a + b) = 7$; a

28. $3d + g = 9$; g

29. $V = lwh$; w

30. $n + 5 = p$; n

31. $xy + z = 5$; y

32. $A = \frac{1}{2}bh$; h

33. $4(m - 2n) = p$; m

Practice 4-4

• •

Mixed Exercises

Solve each equation for the given variable.

1. $ad = f; a$ **2.** $n + 3 = q; n$ **3.** $2(j + k) = m; k$ **4.** $2s + t = r; t$

5. $m + 2n = p; n$ **6.** $\frac{2}{w} = \frac{x}{5}; w$ **7.** $5a - b = 7; a$ **8.** $h = \frac{p}{n}; p$

9. $5d - 2g = 9; g$ **10.** $x + 3y = z; x$ **11.** $y = mx + b; x$ **12.** $V = lwh; l$

The formula $A = 2h(l + w)$ gives the lateral area A of a rectangular
solid with length l, width w, and height h.

13. Solve this formula for h.   **14.** Find h if $A = 144$ cm^2, $l = 7$ cm and $w = 5$ cm.

15. Solve this formula for l.   **16.** Find l if $A = 729.8$ in.^{2}, $h = 17.8$ in., and $w = 6.4$ in.

17. Find h if $A = 37.4$ ft^2, $l = 4.3$ ft and $w = 6.7$ ft.

18. Find l if $A = 9338$ m^2, $h = 29$ m, and $w = 52$ m.

The formula $P = \frac{F}{A}$ gives the pressure P for a force F and an area A.

19. Solve this formula for A.   **20.** Find A if $P = 14.8$ lb/in.^{2} and $F = 2960$ lb.

21. Solve this formula for F.   **22.** Find F if $P = 240$ lb/in.^{2} and $A = 20$ in.^{2}.

23. Find A if $P = 46.8$ lb/in.^{2} and $F = 2340$ lb.

24. Find F if $P = 24.5$ lb/in.^{2} and $A = 33.8$ in.^{2}.

Solve each equation for the given variable.

25. $3n - t = s; t$ **26.** $\frac{b + 3}{e} = \frac{f}{2}; e$ **27.** $w = 2xyz; y$ **28.** $k = 3mh + 3; h$

29. $ab = 6 + cd; a$ **30.** $2a + 4b = d; b$ **31.** $4xy + 3 = 5z; y$ **32.** $-2(3a - b) = c; b$

The formula $V = \frac{1}{3}lwh$ gives the volume V of a rectangular pyramid
with length l, width w, and height h.

33. Solve this formula for w.   **34.** Find w if $V = 64$ m^3, $l = 6$ m, and $h = 4$ m.

35. Solve this formula for h.   **36.** Find h if $V = 30.45$ ft^3, $l = 6.3$ ft, and $w = 2.5$ ft.

37. Find w if $V = 2346$ in.^{3}, $l = 17$ in., and $h = 18$ in.

38. Find h if $V = 7$ ft^3, $l = \frac{7}{4}$ ft, and $w = \frac{3}{4}$ ft.

Solve each equation for the given variable.

39. $2m - 3p = 1; p$ **40.** $a = b + cd; b$ **41.** $a + b = 2xz; z$ **42.** $x = 2y + 3z; y$

43. $\frac{a}{b} = \frac{c}{d}; d$ **44.** $2ab + 4 = d; a$ **45.** $\frac{5}{2} = \frac{1}{2}(b - c); b$ **46.** $d(a - b) = c; a$

Practice 4-5
Example Exercises

Example 1

Graph each inequality on a number line.

1. $b > 2$
2. $x \le -3$
3. $m \ne 2$
4. $0 > d$
5. $-4 \le t$
6. $h \ne 5$

Solve each inequality. Graph the solutions on a number line.

7. $a + 4 > 3$
8. $y - 3 > -2$
9. $4 + d < 2$
10. $f + 7 \ge 9$

11. $4.6 > t - 2.2$
12. $s + 2 \le -2$
13. $g + 2.7 < 1.8$
14. $6.2 < r + 2.2$

15. $b + \frac{1}{4} > \frac{1}{2}$
16. $\frac{2}{3} \ne m - \frac{1}{3}$
17. $n - 6 \ge 4$
18. $d - 9 \ne -7$

19. $7 \ge y + 6$
20. $9 \le 4 + z$
21. $v + 2\frac{3}{4} > -5\frac{1}{4}$
22. $5 < k - 2\frac{1}{3}$

23. $6 + s + 3 > 5$
24. $k - 3.5 < 9$
25. $-12 < p - 8$
26. $-7.1 > u - 2.8$

27. $d + 3 \le -5$
28. $6 + t - 8 \ge -7$
29. $-5 \ne w - 4$
30. $15 \ge 8 + b - 12$

Example 2

Model each problem with an inequality and solve.

31. Pat is on a diet and wants to lose more than 5 lb. So far he has lost 2 lb. How many more pounds must he lose?

32. The temperature at 6 A.M. is 56°F. The forecast is for a high of at most 75°F. What is the maximum amount that the temperature is forecast to increase during the day?

33. Suppose you are working for a trucking company. Your job is to load a truck with at least 5000 lb of freight. You have loaded 2395 lb of freight, but you had to unload 50 lb that was loaded by mistake. How many more pounds do you need to load?

34. Will wants to bowl at least 600 for a three game series. In the first two games, Will bowled a 203 and a 192. What is the minimum score that Will must have in the third game to get a 600?

35. You want to buy a new jacket that costs no more than $50. From your part-time job you have saved $23.95. How much more money do you need to buy the jacket?

36. This spring, you have already planted 78 bulbs, but a squirrel has dug up 10 of these bulbs. Your goal is to plant at least 110 bulbs. How many more bulbs do you need to plant to reach your goal?

Practice 4-5

Mixed Exercises

Solve each inequality. Graph the solutions on a number line.

1. $n - 7 \geq 2$ **2.** $y > 2$ **3.** $3.2 < r + 4.7$ **4.** $7 + b > 13$

5. $h + \frac{3}{4} > \frac{1}{2}$ **6.** $-\frac{5}{7} \neq c + \frac{2}{7}$ **7.** $g + 4.6 < 5.9$ **8.** $0 > d - 2.7$

9. $f + 4 \geq 14$ **10.** $x + 1 \leq -3$ **11.** $d - 13 \neq -8$ **12.** $m - 7 \neq -8$

13. $12 + v < 19$ **14.** $-4 \leq t + 9$ **15.** $6 < y - 3$ **16.** $a + 15 > 19$

17. $8 + d < 9$ **18.** $s + 3 \leq 3$ **19.** $9 + h \neq 5$ **20.** $7.6 > t - 2.4$

Model each problem with an inequality and solve.

21. It will take at least 360 points for Kiko's team to win the math contest. The scores for Kiko's teammates were 94, 82, and 87, but one of Kiko's teamates lost 2 points for an incomplete answer. How many points must Kiko get for her team to win the contest?

22. This season, Nora has 125 at bats in softball. She wants to have at least 140 at bats this season. What is the minimum number of at bats that Nora needs to reach her goal?

23. The average wind speed increased 19 mi/h from 8 A.M. to noon. The average decreased 5 mi/h from noon to 4 P.M. At 4 P.M., the average was at least 32 mi/h. What is the minimum value of the average wind speed at 8 A.M.?

24. Suppose it takes no more than 25 min for you to get to school. After you have traveled for 13.5 min, how much longer at most will it take you to get to school?

25. Joan has started a physical fitness program. One of her goals is to be able to run at least 5 mi without stopping. She can now run 3.5 mi without stopping. How many more miles does she have to run without stopping to achieve her goal?

26. Suppose you can get a higher interest rate on your savings if you maintain a balance of at least $1000 in your savings account. The balance in your savings account is now $1058. You deposit $44.50 into your account. What is the largest amount that you can withdraw and still get the higher interest rate?

Solve each inequality. Graph the solutions on a number line.

27. $\frac{3}{4} + z \geq -\frac{3}{4}$ **28.** $12 + d + 3 \leq 10$ **29.** $v - \frac{3}{4} > 1\frac{1}{4}$ **30.** $8 + m > 4$

31. $2 + f > -3$ **32.** $-27 \neq w - 24$ **33.** $9 \geq y + 4$ **34.** $12 + t < 4 - 15$

35. $-14 > -16 + u$ **36.** $-7 \leq -11 + z$ **37.** $38 \geq 33 + b$ **38.** $k - 27 < -29$

39. $a + 8 \leq 10$ **40.** $b + 6 < -4$ **41.** $13 < 8 + k - 6$ **42.** $j + 1.3 > 2.8$

© Prentice-Hall, Inc.

Practice 4-6

● ●

Example Exercises

Example 1

Solve each inequality. Graph the solutions on a number line.

1. $\frac{w}{2} > 5$ 2. $\frac{t}{4} < -2$ 3. $\frac{a}{4} \le 1$ 4. $\frac{n}{3} \ge -3$

5. $-3 \le \frac{x}{7}$ 6. $12 > \frac{y}{9}$ 7. $-2 \ge \frac{d}{2}$ 8. $7 < \frac{p}{8}$

9. $\frac{1}{2} < \frac{n}{6}$ 10. $\frac{c}{9} < \frac{2}{3}$ 11. $\frac{f}{8} < -\frac{1}{4}$ 12. $-\frac{3}{2} > \frac{k}{4}$

Example 2

Solve each inequality. Graph the solutions on a number line.

13. $-\frac{1}{2}p > 4$ 14. $\frac{1}{3}w \ge 1$ 15. $-y \ge 10$ 16. $-\frac{1}{6}h > -4$

17. $\frac{3}{4}r < 6$ 18. $-m < 12$ 19. $-\frac{2}{5}b \ge 2$ 20. $-\frac{2}{3}x \le \frac{4}{3}$

21. $\frac{1}{6}f < 1$ 22. $-\frac{5}{2}h < 10$ 23. $\frac{15}{4} < \frac{5}{4}s$ 24. $\frac{7}{8}q > 14$

Example 3

Solve each inequality. Graph the solutions on a number line.

25. $3c < 12$ 26. $6d > -18$ 27. $-4z > 20$ 28. $0.7v > 1.4$

29. $18 \le 3b$ 30. $3.0 \le 1.2g$ 31. $8 < -2k$ 32. $-8n \ge -16$

Model with an inequality and solve.

33. Suppose you earn $7.50 for every lawn that you mow. You need to earn at least $120 to pay for camp. How many lawns must you mow?

34. A gallon jug of milk costs $1.20. What is the greatest number of jugs of milk that you can buy with $6?

35. The student council is picking up litter along the highway. When they are halfway done, they have collected at least 5 bags of liter. If their rate of collection remains constant, what is the total number of bags they will have when they are finished?

36. A gallon of paint will cover 600 ft². If you have at least 2400 ft² to paint, what is the least number of gallons of paint that you will need?

37. Suppose you worked 18 h last week. Your pay was at least $111.60. What is your hourly rate of pay?

Practice 4-6
• •
Mixed Exercises

Solve each inequality. Check your solutions. Graph the solutions on a number line.

1. $\frac{15}{8} \le \frac{5}{2}s$ **2.** $60 \le 12b$ **3.** $\frac{4}{5}r < 8$ **4.** $\frac{5}{2} < \frac{n}{8}$

5. $-9n \ge -36$ **6.** $\frac{n}{7} \ge -6$ **7.** $7c < 28$ **8.** $16d > -64$

9. $\frac{t}{3} < -5$ **10.** $54 < -6k$ **11.** $\frac{w}{7} > 0$ **12.** $2.6v > 6.5$

13. $-4 < \frac{2}{5}m$ **14.** $17 < \frac{p}{2}$ **15.** $2.7 \le 1.8v$ **16.** $-5 \le \frac{x}{9}$

17. $-1 \ge \frac{d}{7}$ **18.** $-\frac{2}{3}x \le \frac{8}{9}$ **19.** $\frac{c}{12} < \frac{3}{4}$ **20.** $\frac{a}{4} \le -1$

Model with an inequality and solve.

21. Suppose you and a friend are working for a nursery planting trees. You can plant 8 trees per hour. What is the greatest number of hours that it would take you to plant at most 40 trees?

22. Suppose the physics club is going on a field trip. They will be riding in vans that will hold 7 people. At least 28 people will be going on the field trip. What is the least number of vans needed to make the trip?

23. You need to buy stamps to mail some letters. The stamps cost $.32 each. What is the maximum number of stamps that you can buy with $3.84?

24. The Garcias are putting down a brick border along their flower garden. The flower garden is no more than 31 ft long. If the bricks are 6 in. long, what is the greatest number of bricks needed?

25. Janet needs to travel 275 mi for a conference. She needs to be at the conference in no more than 5.5 h. What is the slowest average speed that she can drive and still make the conference?

Solve each inequality. Graph the solutions on a number line.

26. $\frac{1}{4}h < 4.9$ **27.** $\frac{7}{3}x < 21$ **28.** $-\frac{1}{9}f > 9$ **29.** $\frac{4}{5}b \le 12$

30. $\frac{3}{5}q > 15$ **31.** $84 \le 21b$ **32.** $\frac{f}{12} > -\frac{5}{6}$ **33.** $80.6 \le 6.5b$

34. $-\frac{1}{9}p > \frac{1}{3}$ **35.** $-9z > 63$ **36.** $\frac{1}{7}y \le 6$ **37.** $-\frac{5}{7} > \frac{k}{14}$

38. $6.8 > \frac{y}{5}$ **39.** $75 \le 15b$ **40.** $39 < -13k$ **41.** $7d > -29.4$

42. $8.5v > 61.2$ **43.** $-11n \ge -55$ **44.** $\frac{1}{4}y < 17$ **45.** $92 < -23k$

Practice 4-7

Example Exercises

Example 1

Solve each inequality.

1. $3x + 12 < 18$ 2. $15 + 4a > -1$ 3. $7 < -2p + 13$ 4. $-8 > 3h - 8$

5. $5t - 3t > -6$ 6. $2 \le \frac{1}{2}y - \frac{1}{4}y$ 7. $\frac{3}{4} + 3d \le 6\frac{3}{4}$ 8. $-n + 7 + 2n > 5$

Model with an inequality and solve.

9. Doreen has started a part-time business making and selling bird feeders. Her equipment cost her $75. If she makes a profit of $6 on each bird feeder, how many must Doreen sell to make a total profit of more than $135?

10. Suppose you want to order greeting cards. A box of greeting cards cost $4.95. There is a shipping and handling fee of $5.25 for the entire order. How many boxes of cards can you order if you want to spend no more than $30?

11. Tickets to a museum cost $5 for adults and $2.50 for children. There are five adults in the group. The total cost for the group was no more than $57.50. What is the greatest possible number of children in the group?

Example 2

Solve each inequality. Graph the solutions on a number line.

12. $3(f - 4) < -15$ 13. $4(5 + 2k) > 44$ 14. $-5 < 5(3 - 2b)$

15. $14 > 2(3d + 10)$ 16. $2(5g - 4) - 6g \ge 12$ 17. $-15 < -6(t + 1) + 9t$

18. $7h + 2(3h - 11) \le 17$ 19. $3(6 - z) < 45$ 20. $2(5y + 13) - 5.7 < 20.3$

21. $\frac{2}{3}(3x - 9) \ge 8$ 22. $15 > \frac{3}{4}(4 - 8g)$ 23. $6(u - 11) - 4u < -72$

Example 3

Solve each inequality. Graph the solutions on a number line.

24. $5z + 6 < 3z + 10$ 25. $6f + 30 > 4f + 28$

26. $7b - 6 < 5b + 8$ 27. $3m - 4 \ge 6 + 4m$

28. $\frac{3}{4}k < \frac{1}{4}k - \frac{1}{4}$ 29. $6t - 9 \ge 3 + 2t$

30. $-2.5 + 3.7v < 5.9 - 0.5v$ 31. $r > 6 - 2r + 9$

32. $5 - 2(4 - c) \le 9 - c$ 33. $3(g - 2) \ge 2g - 2$

34. $4n + 4 < 5 + 3n$ 35. $12.6 + 5.4y < 1.4y + 2$

Practice 4-7

Mixed Exercises

Solve each inequality. Graph the solutions on a number line.

1. $2z + 7 < z + 10$ **2.** $4(k - 1) > 4$ **3.** $1.5 + 2.1y < 1.1y + 4.5$

4. $h + 2(3h + 4) \geq 1$ **5.** $r + 4 > 13 - 2r$ **6.** $6u - 18 - 4u < 22$

7. $2(3 + 3g) \geq 2g + 14$ **8.** $2h - 13 < -3$ **9.** $-4p + 28 > 8$

10. $8m - 8 \geq 12 + 4m$ **11.** $5 + 6a > -1$ **12.** $\frac{1}{2}(2t + 8) \geq 4 + 6t$

13. $-5x + 12 < -18$ **14.** $2(3f + 2) > 4f + 12$ **15.** $13t - 8t > -45$

16. $2(c - 4) \leq 10 - c$ **17.** $\frac{1}{2}t - \frac{1}{3}t > -1$ **18.** $3.4 + 1.6v < 5.9 - 0.9v$

Model with an inequality and solve.

19. Ernest works in the shipping department loading shipping crates with boxes. Each empty crate weighs 150 lb. How many boxes weighing 35 lb can Ernest put in the crate if the total weight is to be no more than 850 lb?

20. Beatriz is in charge of setting up a banquet hall. She has five tables that will seat six people each. If no more than 62 people will attend, how many tables seating four people each will she need?

21. Suppose it costs $5 to enter a carnival. Each ride costs $1.25. You have $15 to spend at the carnival. What is the greatest number of rides that you can go on?

22. The cost to rent a car is $19.50 plus $.25 per mile. If you have $44 to rent a car, what is the greatest number of miles that you can drive?

23. The student council is sponsoring a concert as a fund raiser. Tickets are $3 for students and $5 for adults. The student council wants to raise more than $1000. If 200 students attend, how many adults must attend?

Solve each inequality.

24. $-18 < 2(12 - 3b)$ **25.** $5n + 3 - 4n < -5 - 3n$ **26.** $36 > 4(2d + 10)$

27. $2(5t - 25) + 5t < -80$ **28.** $3j + 2 - 2j < -10$ **29.** $\frac{2}{5}(5x - 15) \geq 4$

30. $7(2z + 3) > 35$ **31.** $2(3b - 2) < 4b + 8$ **32.** $\frac{1}{2}y + \frac{1}{4}y \geq -6$

33. $8(3f - 6) < -24$ **34.** $\frac{3}{4}k < \frac{3}{4} - \frac{1}{4}k$ **35.** $3(4g - 6) \geq 6(g + 2)$

36. $\frac{1}{2}(2g + 4) > -7$ **37.** $4(1.25y + 4.2) < 16.8$ **38.** $38 + 7t > -3(t + 4)$

39. $4(2d + 1) > 28$ **40.** $4(n - 3) < 2 - 3n$ **41.** $\frac{3}{4}d - \frac{1}{2} \leq 2\frac{1}{2}$

Practice 4-8

•••

Example Exercises

Example 1

Solve each inequality and graph the solution on a number line.

1. $5 \le x + 4 < 8$

2. $2 > h + 6 > -3$

3. $4.4 \le b - 2.1 \le 5.9$

4. $4d > -8$ and $6 > 2d$

5. $-2g > -12$ and $3g > 6$

6. $-2 < 3x + 4 < 13$

Example 2

Model each situation with an inequality and solve.

7. Javier is on a diet. He is supposed to eat at least 1500 but no more than 1800 calories per day. Before his last meal of the day he has had 1150 calories. What number of calories should Javier eat at his last meal of the day?

8. To get an A in class your total points must be between 540 and 600, inclusive. Suppose you have 503 points before the last test. What possible values for the last test will still give you an A in the class?

9. The art club is sponsoring an art show. They want the average attendance to be between 100 and 120 inclusive for their four shows. The attendance for the first three shows was 100, 105, and 91. What possible values for the attendance of the fourth show will allow them to reach their goal?

Example 3

Solve each inequality and graph the solution on a number line.

10. $d + 4 > 15$ or $d - 7 < -3$

11. $3f < -12$ or $2f > 6$

12. $2a + 3 > 11$ or $4a < 12$

13. $4h + 6 < 2$ or $-6h < -18$

14. $b + 4 > 15$ or $5b < 45$

15. $5m + 8 > 23$ or $7m < 7$

Example 4

Express each absolute value inequality as a compound inequality. Solve and graph the solution on a number line.

16. $|d| > 2$

17. $|h| < 6$

18. $|2k| > 8$

19. $|s + 4| < 2$

20. $|3c - 6| \ge 3$

21. $|2n + 3| \le 5$

22. $|3.8z| > 17.1$

23. $|\frac{2}{3}x| \le 4$

24. $9 > |6 + 3t|$

25. $|j| - 2 \ge 6$

26. $5 > |v + 2| + 3$

27. $|4y + 11| < 7$

© Prentice-Hall, Inc.

Practice 4-8
• •
Mixed Exercises

Solve each inequality and graph the solution on a number line.

1. $|s + 5| < 5$ **2.** $1 < 3x + 4 < 10$

3. $|k - 3| + 7 > 8$ **4.** $b - 2 > 18$ or $3b < 54$

5. $-4d > 8$ and $2d > -6$ **6.** $|t + 2| < 4$

7. $-3 < 3 + s < 7$ **8.** $|3j| + 4 \geq 10$

9. $\left|\frac{1}{2}x\right| < 1$ **10.** $g + 2 > -1$ or $g - 6 < -9$

11. $|9 + 3y| < 6$ **12.** $3f > 15$ or $2f < -4$

13. $|d| > 1$ **14.** $1 > 2h + 3 > -1$

15. $7 + 2a > 9$ or $-4a > 8$ **16.** $|4.4z| > 6.6$

17. $|c - 1| \geq 2$ **18.** $h < -1$ or $h > 2$

Model each situation with an inequality and solve.

19. The crowd that heard the President speak was estimated to be 10,000 people. The actual crowd could be 750 people more or less than this. What are the possible values for the actual crowd size?

20. Susie has designed an exercise program for herself. One part of the exercise program is that she plans on walking between 25 and 30 miles, inclusive, each week. She plans to walk the same distance each day. If Susie walks five days a week, what is the range in miles that she should walk each day?

21. A box of cereal should weigh more than 629.4 g and less than 630.6 g to pass inspection. The box that the cereal is packaged in weighs 5.5 g. What are the possible weights for the cereal?

22. Carmen works in a sporting goods store. Her goal is to sell between $500 and $600 worth of sporting equipment every week. So far this week she has sold $395 worth of equipment. What possible dollar amount of sales should Carmen make the rest of the week to reach her goal?

Solve each inequality and graph the solution on a number line.

23. $|2n - 1| \geq 1$ **24.** $|2k - 3| > 3$ **25.** $|h - 2| < 1$

26. $2.3 + p > 1$ and $1.5p < 12.3$ **27.** $9 < x + 2 < 11$ **28.** $5m + 8 < 23$ or $6m > 48$

29. $\left|\frac{3}{2}x\right| \leq 3$ **30.** $-2 < x < -1$ **31.** $\left|\frac{1}{2}x + 1\right| > 1$

32. $|s - 4| + 7 \leq 9$ **33.** $|w - 3| > 4$ **34.** $6 > 4x - 2 > -6$

35. $t + 5 < 2$ or $3t + 1 > 10$ **36.** $2g > 12$ and $3g < 24$ **37.** $|6x - 3| \geq 3$

Practice 4-9

•••

Example Exercises

Example 1

Graph each inequality on a number line. Use integers as a replacement set. If there are no solutions, write *no solution*.

1. $3d > 9$ **2.** $f + 4 < 3$ **3.** $3k < 2$ **4.** $|r + 2| < 3$

5. $4 < x + 2 < 8$ **6.** $2n < -3$ or $3n > 5$ **7.** $|4t + 2| \geq 6$ **8.** $\frac{p}{3} \geq \frac{2}{3}$

Graph each inequality on a number line. Use negative integers as a replacement set. If there are no solutions, write *no solution*.

9. $t - 3.5 > -6.5$ **10.** $14 < p - 5$ **11.** $t - 1 \geq -5$ **12.** $y - 11 > -11$

13. $\frac{t}{4} < -2$ **14.** $\frac{3}{2}h < -6$ **15.** $-0.6v < -1.8$ **16.** $-1 < 2x + 5 < 9$

Graph each inequality on a number line. Use $\{-2, 0, 1, 3, 5\}$ as a replacement set. If there are no solutions, write *no solution*.

17. $y - 4 > 0$ **18.** $n - 5 > 0$ **19.** $8c < 16$ **20.** $4.5 \geq -1.8g$

21. $5t - 3t > 4$ **22.** $5(p - 5) < -20$ **23.** $3f < -3$ or $2f > 5$ **24.** $|b| + 11 \geq 12$

Example 2

Model each situation with an inequality and solve.

25. Ken wants to buy a CD player for $150. He received $40 of this amount as a gift. He plans to earn the rest baby-sitting at $4.25 per hour. What is the least number of whole hours that he must baby-sit to earn enough money?

26. A group of students are going on a field trip. It will cost $100 for the transportation plus $3.75 for each student for a meal. The students have raised $210 to pay for the trip. What is the maximum number of students that can go on the trip?

27. You are making a beaded necklace that is at least 45 cm long. Each bead is 2 cm long. How many beads do you need?

28. The drama department is putting on a play. They pay a royalty fee of $300 plus $1.50 per ticket sold. The tickets sell for $5 each. How many tickets must they sell in order to cover their expenses?

Practice 4-9
• •
Mixed Exercises

Graph each inequality for the given replacement set. If there are no solutions, write *no solution*.

1. $5d > 10$, for the set of positive integers

2. $f + 8 < 8$, for the set of positive real numbers

3. $-3k \leq 9$, for the set of negative integers

4. $|z - 5| < 2$, for the set of positive integers

5. $1 < x - 3 < 4$, for $\{-2, -1, 0, 4, 5, 7\}$

6. $3n < -9$ or $7n > 35$, for $\{-5, 0, 5, 10, 15\}$

7. $|4g + 7| < 15$, for the set of positive integers

8. $|k + 4| < 2$, for the set of positive integers

9. $m - 2.3 > 1.7$, for the set of real numbers

10. $4 < p + 3 < 10$, for $\{2, 4, 6, 8, 10\}$

11. $n - 1 \geq 2$, for the set of negative integers

12. $s - 4 > -8$, for the set of negative integers

13. $\frac{t}{4} > 3$, for the set of positive real numbers

14. $\frac{n}{-4} \geq \frac{3}{4}$, for the set of real numbers

15. $-1.6v < 3.2$, for $\{-1, 0, 1, 2, 3, 4\}$

16. $1 < 2x + 3 < 5$, for the set of real numbers

Model each with an inequality and solve. Graph each solution on a number line. If there are no solutions, write *no solution*.

17. Fasul wants to buy a $14 belt he saw at the mall. He also wants to buy some T-shirts priced at $9 each. He has $55 to spend. How many T-shirts can he buy?

18. Suppose a music store pays $800 a month in rent. The bookkeeper has determined that other expenses average $8 for each item sold and income averages $14.50 for each item sold. How many items must the music store sell to make a profit?

19. Suppose you want to order some books. The books cost $5.95 each and there is a shipping and handling fee of $2.45 for the entire order. How many books can you order for $25?

20. Lara is a self-employed computer programmer. Her computer system cost her $5000. She charges $500 for each application she writes. She also has expenses of $75 for each application she writes. How many applications must she write to show a profit?

Graph each inequality for the given replacement set. If there are no solutions, write *no solution*.

21. $y - 4 > 0$, for the set of positive integers

22. $y + 5 \leq 8$ for the set of positive integers

23. $8c > -24$, for the set of negative integers

24. $-2g \leq -4$, for the set of negative real numbers

25. $9t - 6t > 6$, for $\{-3, 1, 3, 5, 7\}$

26. $2(x - 6) < -20$, for $\{-7, -5, -3, 1, 3, 5\}$

27. $4h < -8$ or $2h > 5$, for $\{-4, -3, -2, -1, 0\}$

28. $3 \geq |j + 4|$, for the set of positive integers

© Prentice-Hall, Inc.

Practice 5-1
Example Exercises

Example 1 and Example 2

Find the slope of each line.

1.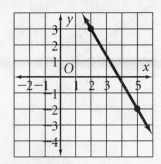

2.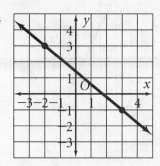

3.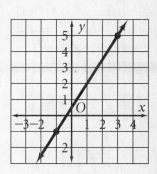

Example 3

Find the slope of the line passing through each pair of points.

4. $(3, 4), (6, 9)$ 5. $(-2, 7), (3, -8)$ 6. $(-1, -6), (4, -2)$

7. $(5, 0), (10, 5)$ 8. $(-2, -2), (-4, -12)$ 9. $(1, 1), (-3, -7)$

10. $(\frac{1}{2}, 3), (\frac{5}{2}, 11)$ 11. $(0, 9,), (9, 0)$ 12. $(-8, \frac{1}{4}), (8, \frac{1}{4})$

Example 4

Find the slope of each line using the points shown.

13.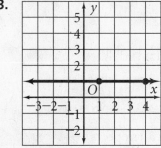

14.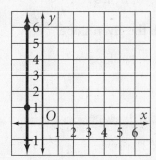

15.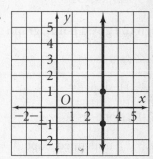

Example 5

Through the given point, graph a line with the given slope.

16. $(5, 2)$; slope $= 3$ 17. $(-2, 1)$; slope $= -2$

18. $(1, -1)$; slope $= \frac{2}{3}$ 19. $(3, -2)$; slope $= -\frac{3}{2}$

20. $(3, -1)$; slope $= 0$ 21. $(-2, -1)$; undefined slope

Practice 5-1

· ·

Mixed Exercises

Find the slope of each line.

1.
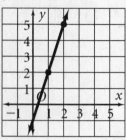

2.
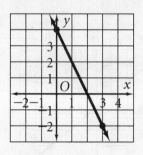

3.
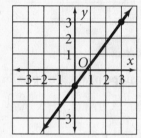

4.
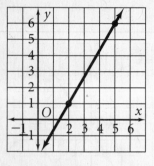

5.
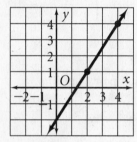

6.
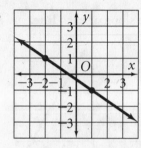

Find the slope of the line passing through each pair of points.

7. $(1, 2), (4, 3)$

8. $(7, 2), (3, 5)$

9. $(0, 2), (4, 6)$

10. $(-2, 5), (3, -4)$

11. $(2, 4), (6, 7)$

12. $(-2, -5), (4, 5)$

13. $(-3, -2), (4, -2)$

14. $(4, -2), (4, 9)$

15. $(5, 2), (8, -4)$

Through the given point, graph a line with the given slope.

16. $(1, 2)$; slope $= -3$

17 $(2, -1)$; slope $= 2$

18. $(-2, 1)$; slope $= 0$

19. $(1, -1)$; slope $= -\frac{3}{2}$

20. $(1, 1)$; slope $= \frac{2}{3}$

21. $(2, 3)$; undefined slope

22. $(2, 1)$; slope $= 1$

23. $(-3, 0)$; slope $= -\frac{2}{3}$

24. $(-2, 3)$; slope $= 0$

25. $(1, -2)$; undefined slope

26. $(4, 2)$; slope $= \frac{1}{2}$

27. $(1, 3)$; slope $= -\frac{4}{3}$

Find the slope of the line passing through each pair of points.

28. $(0, 0), (3, 7)$

29. $(-2, 4), (4, -1)$

30. $(-3, 6), (1, -2)$

31. $(2, 4), (4, -4)$

32. $(2, -10), (5, -6)$

33. $(5, 1), (11, 1)$

34. $(3, 7), (3, 5)$

35. $(7, 9), (2, 9)$

36. $(-5, -2), (-5, 3)$

Practice 5-2
• •
Example Exercises

Example 1

Find the rate of change. Explain what each rate of change means.

1.

2.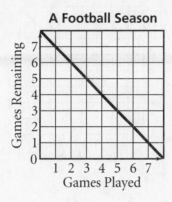

3.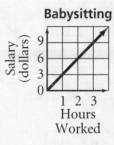

Example 2

Find the rate of change for each table. Graph the data.

4.

Years Employed	Weekly Salary
1	$500
2	$550
3	$600
4	$650

5.

Number of Days	Car Rental Charge
1	$50
2	$75
4	$125
8	$225

6.

Hours Worked	Salary
1	$6
2	$12
5	$30
10	$60

Example 3

Tell if the relationship between the data is linear.

7.

x	y
2	6
3	4
4	2
5	0

8.

x	y
1	3
3	8
5	14
7	21

9.

x	y
0	−2
4	−4
8	−6
12	−8

10.

x	y
−2	6
1	1
4	−4
7	−9

Practice 5-2
· ·
Mixed Exercises

Find the rate of change. Explain what each rate of change means.

1.

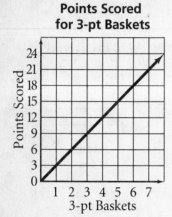

2.

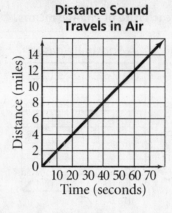

3.

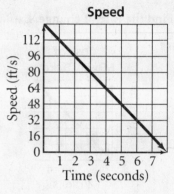

Tell if the relationship between the data is linear.

4.

x	y
1	10
2	14
3	18
4	22

5.

x	y
3	−2
6	3
9	8
12	13

6.

x	y
−6	30
−1	24
4	17
9	9

7.

x	y
13	−20
20	−8
27	4
34	16

Find the rate of change for each table. Graph the data.

8.

Touchdowns Made	Points Scored
1	6
2	12
3	18
4	24

9.

Hours of Labor	Plumber's Charge
1	$45
3	$85
5	$125
7	$165

10.

Hours	Equipment Rental
1	$75
4	$225
7	$375
10	$525

Practice 5-3

• •

Example Exercises

Example 1

Is each equation a direct variation? If it is, find the constant of variation.

1. $y = \frac{2}{3}x$ **2.** $7x + 4y = 2$ **3.** $3x - y = 0$ **4.** $-x + 2y = 0$

5. $4x + 2y = 7$ **6.** $y = \frac{1}{5}x + 3$ **7.** $-5x + y = 0$ **8.** $y = -\frac{3}{2}x$

9. $6x - 5y = 0$ **10.** $y = \frac{4}{5}x$ **11.** $9x + 3y = -3$ **12.** $2x + 3y = 0$

Example 2

13. The distance that you travel at a constant speed varies directly with the time spent traveling. It takes you 2 h to travel 100 mi.

     a. Write an equation for the relationship between time and distance.

     b. How far would you travel in 3.5 h?

14. The money you earn varies directly with the number of lawns you mow. You earn $36 for mowing three lawns.

     a. Write an equation for the relationship between money earned and lawns mowed.

     b. How much money would you earn for mowing seven lawns?

Example 3

For each table, tell whether *y* varies directly with *x*. If it does, write a function rule for the relationship between the data.

15.

x	y
4	2
8	4
14	7

16.

x	y
2	6
5	13.5
8	21

17.

x	y
−2	−5
4	4
8	10

18.

x	y
3	5.7
5	9.5
9	17.1

Example 4

Suppose the ordered pairs in each exercise are for the same direct variation. Find each missing value.

19. $(2, 1)$ and $(6, y)$ **20.** $(2, 1)$ and $(x, 3)$ **21.** $(5, y)$ and $(15, 12)$ **22.** $(x, 2)$ and $(6, 4)$

23. $(8, 2)$ and $(x, -3)$ **24.** $(x, 8)$ and $(1.5, 6)$ **25.** $(-2, -3)$ and $(x, 9)$ **26.** $(\frac{3}{2}, -3)$ and $(x, -8)$

27. $(3, y)$ and $(6, -8)$ **28.** $(1.4, 2.8)$ and $(x, 9)$ **29.** $(2, y)$ and $(-4, 14)$ **30.** $(2.6, 1)$ and $(1.3, y)$

Practice 5-3

Mixed Exercises

Is each equation a direct variation? If it is, find the constant of variation.

1. $y = 5x$ **2.** $8x + 2y = 0$ **3.** $y = \frac{3}{4}x - 7$ **4.** $y = 2x + 5$

5. $3x - y = 0$ **6.** $y = \frac{3}{5}x$ **7.** $-3x + 2y = 0$ **8.** $-5x + 2y = 9$

9. $8x + 4y = 12$ **10.** $6x - 3y = 0$ **11.** $x - 3y = 6$ **12.** $9x + 5y = 0$

Suppose the ordered pairs in each exercise are for the same direct variation. Find each missing value.

13. $(3, 2)$ and $(6, y)$ **14.** $(-2, 8)$ and $(x, 12)$ **15.** $(4, y)$ and $(16, 12)$ **16.** $(x, 8)$ and $(6, -16)$

17. $(3, y)$ and $(9, 15)$ **18.** $(2, y)$ and $(10, 15)$ **19.** $(-4, 3)$ and $(x, 6)$ **20.** $(3, y)$ and $(1.5, 6)$

21. $(\frac{2}{3}, 2)$ and $(x, 6)$ **22.** $(2.5, 5)$ and $(x, 9)$ **23.** $(4.8, 5)$ and $(2.4, y)$ **24.** $(9, 3)$ and $(x, -2)$

For each table, tell whether y varies directly with x. If it does, write a function rule for the relationship between the data.

25.

x	y
4	8
7	14
10	20

26.

x	y
-3	-2
3	2
9	6

27.

x	y
4	3
5	4.5
11	13.5

28.

x	y
-2	-2.8
3	4.2
8	11.2

29. Charles's law states that at constant pressure, the volume of a fixed amount of gas varies directly with its temperature measured in Kelvins. A gas has a volume of 250 mL at 300°K.

  a. Write an equation for the relationship between volume and temperature.

  b. What is the volume if the temperature increases to 420°K?

30. Your percent grade varies directly with the number of correct answers. You got a grade of 80 when you had 20 correct answers.

  a. Write an equation for the relationship between percent grade and number of correct answers.

  b. What would your percent grade be with 24 correct answers?

31. The amount of simple interest earned in a savings account varies directly with the amount of money in the savings account. You have $1000 in your savings account and earn $50 in simple interest. How much interest would you earn if you had $1500 in your savings account?

Practice 5-4

• •

Example Exercises

Example 1

Graph each equation.

1. $y = 2x + 1$ **2.** $y = 3x$ **3.** $y = -2x + 3$ **4.** $y = 4x + 2$

5. $y = \frac{2}{3}x + 3$ **6.** $y = -\frac{3}{2}x$ **7.** $y = -x - 2$ **8.** $y = -\frac{7}{3}x + 2$

9. $y = -4x + 1$ **10.** $y = x + 3$ **11.** $y = \frac{1}{3}x - 3$ **12.** $y = \frac{3}{5}x - 4$

Example 2

Rewrite each equation in slope-intercept form. Then graph each equation.

13. $y + 4 = 3x$ **14.** $y - 5x = 6$ **15.** $y = -5 + 2x$ **16.** $y + x = -4$

17. $y + \frac{4}{3}x = 1$ **18.** $y - \frac{1}{4}x = 3$ **19.** $y = -\frac{5}{2}x - 2$ **20.** $y - 5 = \frac{5}{4}x$

21. $y - 3x = 0$ **22.** $y - 5 = x$ **23.** $y + \frac{1}{4}x = 2$ **24.** $y - \frac{7}{4}x = -2$

Example 3

Write an equation of a line with the given slope and *y*-intercept.

25. $m = 3, b = 2$ **26.** $m = -4, b = -3$ **27.** $m = \frac{5}{3}, b = -7$ **28.** $m = -\frac{3}{7}, b = 5$

29. $m = -2, b = 0$ **30.** $m = \frac{1}{2}, b = 4$ **31.** $m = -\frac{1}{4}, b = 0$ **32.** $m = 6, b = -4$

Find the slope and *y*-intercept of each line. Write the equation of each line.

33. 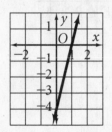   **34.** 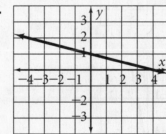   **35.**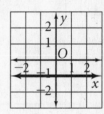

• •

Name_____ Class_____ Date_____

Practice 5-4

•••

Mixed Exercises

Graph each equation.

1. $y = x + 2$ **2.** $y + 3 = -\frac{1}{3}x$ **3.** $y = 2x - 1$ **4.** $y - \frac{3}{5}x = -1$

5. $y = \frac{1}{2}x - 4$ **6.** $y - 2x = -3$ **7.** $y = \frac{2}{5}x + 3$ **8.** $y + \frac{1}{3}x = -2$

9. $y = -x - 2$ **10.** $y - 6 = -2x$ **11.** $y = -5x - 2$ **12.** $y + x = 0$

13. $y + 4 = 2x$ **14.** $y = -5x + 5$ **15.** $y = -4 + x$ **16.** $y = -4x$

17. $y = \frac{4}{5}x + 2$ **18.** $y - \frac{3}{4}x = -5$ **19.** $y = -6$ **20.** $y - 3 = -\frac{2}{3}x$

21. $y = -\frac{7}{4}x + 6$ **22.** $y + 3x = 6$ **23.** $y + \frac{1}{5}x = -2$ **24.** $y = \frac{3}{7}x$

Write an equation of a line with the given slope and *y*-intercept.

25. $m = 4, b = 8$ **26.** $m = -2, b = -6$ **27.** $m = \frac{4}{3}, b = 0$

28. $m = -\frac{9}{5}, b = -7$ **29.** $m = -6, b = 1$ **30.** $m = \frac{3}{7}, b = -1$

31. $m = -\frac{1}{5}, b = -3$ **32.** $m = 9, b = 4$ **33.** $m = -8, b = 11$

34. $m = \frac{2}{9}, b = 0$ **35.** $m = -11, b = 13$ **36.** $m = -\frac{7}{2}, b = -6$

Find the slope and *y*-intercept of each line. Write the equation of each line.

37.
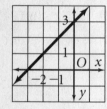

38.
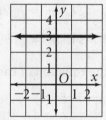

39.
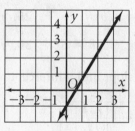

40.
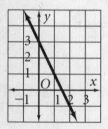

41.
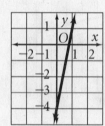

42.
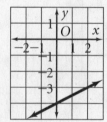

Name _____ Class _____ Date _____

Practice 5-5
Example Exercises

Example 1

Write the equation of a line through the given point with the given slope.

1. $(1, 4); m = 3$ **2.** $(-3, 1); m = -2$ **3.** $(-3, 2); m = 0$ **4.** $(5, -3); m = 5$

5. $(2, 0); m = \frac{3}{4}$ **6.** $(3, -5); m = -\frac{4}{3}$ **7.** $(9, -5); m = -1$ **8.** $(0, 6); m$ undefined

9. $(6, -6); m = -\frac{7}{3}$ **10.** $(7, 9); m = \frac{1}{2}$ **11.** $(1.5, 9.5); m = 0.5$ **12.** $(12, -7); m = \frac{5}{2}$

Example 2

Write an equation of a line through the given points.

13. $(2, 4), (5, 7)$ **14.** $(-1, 1), (2, 7)$ **15.** $(0, 4), (-2, -2)$ **16.** $(12, 18), (15, 12)$

17. $(-8, 7), (8, 15)$ **18.** $(50, 85), (60, 80)$ **19.** $(12, 9), (9, 17)$ **20.** $(0.5, 4), (3, 3.5)$

21. $(0, -5), (3, -2)$ **22.** $(-15, 9), (-10, 4)$ **23.** $(12, -4), (16, 1)$ **24.** $(6, 11), (3, 13)$

Write an equation of each line.

25. 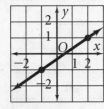   **26.** 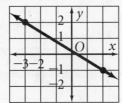   **27.**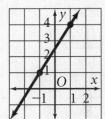

Example 3

Tell whether the relationship between the *x*- and *y*-values is linear. If it is, write an equation for the relationship between the values.

28.
x	y
-4	-4
0	4
2	8
6	16

29.
x	y
-3	3
6	6
12	8
21	11

30.
x	y
5	11
8	16
12	25
17	37

31.
x	y
-3	-13
-1	-5
0	-1
3	11

© Prentice-Hall, Inc.

Practice 5-5

• •
Mixed Exercises

Write the equation of a line through the given points or through the
given point with the given slope.

1. $(5, 7), (6, 8)$ **2.** $(-2, 3); m = -1$ **3.** $(1, 2), (3, 8)$ **4.** $(-2, 3); m = 4$

5. $(4, 7); m = \frac{3}{2}$ **6.** $(6, -2); m = -\frac{4}{3}$ **7.** $(0, 5), (-3, 2)$ **8.** $(8, 11), (6, 16)$

9. $(4, 2), (-4, -2)$ **10.** $(15, 16), (13, 10)$ **11.** $(0, -7); m = -4$ **12.** $(-3, 4), (1, 6)$

13. $(1, 2); m$ undefined   **14.** $(-6, 7); m = -\frac{1}{2}$ **15.** $(21, -2), (27, 2)$ **16.** $(7, 5); m = 0$

17. $(8, -2), (14, 1)$ **18.** $(4, 8), (2, 12)$ **19.** $(-5, 13), (-10, 9)$ **20.** $(6, 2); m = \frac{3}{4}$

21. $(5, -3); m = -2$ **22.** $(4, 3.5); m = 0.5$ **23.** $(-6, 2); m = \frac{5}{3}$ **24.** $(100, 90), (80, 120)$

25. $(-3, 6), (3, -6)$ **26.** $(11, 7), (9, 3)$ **27.** $(2, 7); m = \frac{5}{2}$ **28.** $(-9, 8); m = -\frac{5}{3}$

Tell whether the relationship between the *x*- and *y*-values is linear. If it is,
write an equation for the relationship between the values.

29.

x	y
2	3
3	7
4	11
5	15

30.

x	y
-3	4
-1	6
1	7
3	10

31.

x	y
-4	12
-1	8
5	-4
10	-8

32.

x	y
-2	5
3	-5
7	-13
11	-21

33.

x	y
-6	-5
-2	1
0	4
8	16

34.

x	y
-6	11
-3	9
6	3
15	-3

35.

x	y
-7	-3
-5	0
-1	3
3	7

36.

x	y
-4	1
2	4
6	6
14	10

Write an equation of each line.

37.
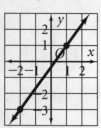

38.
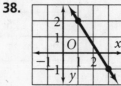

39.
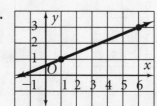

© Prentice-Hall, Inc.

Practice for 5-6

Example Exercises

Example 1

Decide if the data in each scatter plot follow a linear pattern. If they do, find the equation of a trend line.

1. 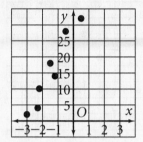   **2.** 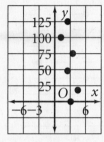   **3.**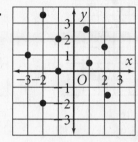

Draw a scatter plot. Write the equation of the trend line.

4.

x	y
1	25
2	28
3	27
4	31
5	30
6	34

5.

x	y
1	50
2	45
3	43
4	34
5	29
6	27

6.

Year	Mean SAT Score
1987	906
1988	904
1989	903
1990	900
1991	896
1992	899

Source: *World Almanac 1995*

7.

Year	Total Crimes (millions)
1987	13.5
1988	13.9
1989	14.3
1990	14.5
1991	14.9
1992	14.4

Source: *World Almanac 1995*

Example 2

Use a graphing calculator to find the equation of the line of best fit for the following data. Is there a strong correlation between the data?

8.

x	y
1	4
2	-3
3	6
4	9
5	15

9.

x	y
1	-4
2	8
3	3
4	12
5	9

10.

x	y
2	10
4	-3
7	8
9	-7
12	-15

11.

x	y
1	8
2	-4
3	15
5	20
9	6

Practice for 5-6

Mixed Exercises

Decide if the data in each scatter plot follow a linear pattern. If they do, find the equation of a trend line.

1.
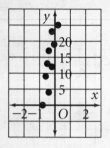

2.
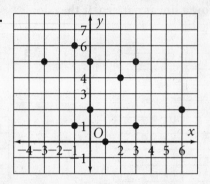

3.
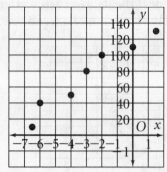

Use a graphing calculator to find the equation of the line of best fit for the following data. Is there a strong correlation between the data?

4.

x	y
1	7
2	5
3	−1
4	3
5	−5

5.

x	y
1	6
2	15
3	−5
4	1
5	−2

6.

x	y
1	5
4	8
8	3
13	10
19	13

7.

x	y
12	28
15	50
18	14
21	28
24	36

Draw a scatter plot. Write the equation of the trend line.

8.

x	y
1	17
2	20
3	22
4	26
5	28
6	31

9.

Year	U.S. Union Membership (millions)
1988	17.00
1989	16.96
1990	16.74
1991	16.57
1992	16.39
1993	16.60

Source: *World Almanac 1995*

10.

x	y
1	18
2	20
3	24
4	30
5	28
6	33

11.

Year	U.S. Luxury Car Sales (%)
1988	9.9
1989	11.6
1990	13.0
1991	13.9
1992	13.4
1993	12.8

Source: *World Almanac 1995*

Practice 5-7

Example Exercises

Example 1

Find the x- and y-intercept of each equation.

1. $2x + y = 4$ **2.** $x + 3y = 9$ **3.** $2x + 3y = 6$ **4.** $4x - 5y = 10$

Graph each equation.

5. $x + y = 5$ **6.** $x + 3y = -6$ **7.** $-5x + 3y = 15$ **8.** $3x - 2y = 12$

9. $-x + 4y = 8$ **10.** $3x + 2y = 6$ **11.** $-2x + 5y = 5$ **12.** $5x + 6y = 18$

Example 2

Graph each equation using a graphing calculator. Make a sketch of the graph. Include Xmin, Xmax, Ymin, Ymax, and the x- and y-intercepts.

13. $4x + 5y = 80$ **14.** $6x + 7y = 84$ **15.** $3x + 10y = 90$ **16.** $12x + 5y = 180$

17. $-5x + 16y = 160$ **18.** $8x - 6y = -192$ **19.** $7x - 5y = 70$ **20.** $9x + 7y = -126$

Example 3

21. You are buying $60 worth of a lawn seed mixture that consists of two types of seed. One type costs $5/lb and the other costs $6/lb.

     a. Write an equation to find the amount of each seed that you can buy.

     b. Graph your equation.

22. Suppose you have two summer jobs. You earn $4/h baby-sitting and $5/h weeding gardens. You want to earn $100.

     a. Write an equation to find the time you would need to work at each job.

     b. Graph your equation.

     c. Use your graph to find two different combinations of hours worked.

Example 4

Write an equation for a line through the given point with the given slope using the $Ax + By = C$ form.

23. $(2, 5); m = 3$ **24.** $(6, 1); m = 5$ **25.** $(-2, 4); m = -4$ **26.** $(7, -5); m = 2$

27. $(-2, 7); m = \frac{1}{2}$ **28.** $(4, 3); m = \frac{3}{2}$ **29.** $(-9, 4); m = -\frac{5}{3}$ **30.** $(-6, -2); m = -\frac{1}{4}$

Name _____ Class _____ Date _____

Practice 5-7
Mixed Exercises

Graph each equation.

1. $x + y = 3$ **2.** $x + 3y = -9$ **3.** $-2x + 3y = 6$ **4.** $5x - 4y = -20$

5. $3x + 4y = 12$ **6.** $7x + 3y = 21$ **7.** $3x - 5y = 15$ **8.** $2x - 3y = 4$

9. $x + 4y = 4$ **10.** $3x - 2y = -6$ **11.** $5x + 2y = 5$ **12.** $-7x + 2y = 14$

13. $3x + y = 3$ **14.** $-3x + 5y = 15$ **15.** $2x + y = 3$ **16.** $8x - 3y = 24$

Graph each equation using a graphing calculator. Make a sketch of the graph. Include Xmin, Xmax, Ymin, Ymax, and the x- and y-intercepts.

17. $6x + 5y = 90$ **18.** $4x + 7y = 84$ **19.** $9x + 5y = 180$ **20.** $3x + 8y = -120$

21. $7x - 10y = 140$ **22.** $-6x + 11y = 132$ **23.** $5x - 4y = -140$ **24.** $-11x + 3y = 165$

Write an equation for a line through the given point with the given slope using the $Ax + By = C$ form.

25. $(3, 1);\ m = 4$ **26.** $(5, 4);\ m = 2$ **27.** $(-3, 3);\ m = -2$ **28.** $(6, -2);\ m = 5$

29. $(2, -7);\ m = \frac{2}{3}$ **30.** $(9, 7);\ m = -4$ **31.** $(-1, 2);\ m = -\frac{4}{5}$ **32.** $(-5, 1);\ m = -\frac{1}{5}$

33. $(6, -7);\ m = \frac{5}{2}$ **34.** $(-4, -1);\ m = \frac{7}{3}$ **35.** $(-4, 2);\ m = -\frac{1}{3}$ **36.** $(-8, 10);\ m = -6$

37. The drama club sells 200 lb of fruit to raise money. They sell the fruit in 5-lb bags and 10-lb bags.

    a. Write an equation to find the number of each type of bag that they should sell.

    b. Graph your equation.

    c. Use your graph to find two different combinations of types of bags.

38. The student council is sponsoring a carnival to raise money. Tickets cost $5 for adults and $3 for students. They want to raise $450.

    a. Write an equation to find the number of each type of ticket they should sell.

    b. Graph your equation.

    c. Use your graph to find two different combinations of tickets sold.

39. Anna goes to a store to buy $70 worth of flour and sugar for her bakery. A bag of flour costs $5 and a bag of sugar costs $7.

    a. Write an equation to find the number of bags of each type Anna can buy.

    b. Graph your equation.

90 $Ax + By = C$ Form   Algebra Chapter 5

Practice 5-8

Example Exercises

Example 1

Find the slope of a line parallel to the graph of each equation.

1. $y = 3x - 8$ **2.** $y = \frac{2}{3}x + 6$ **3.** $y = -2x - 1.5$ **4.** $y = -\frac{5}{2}x + 11$

5. $9x + 3y = 6$ **6.** $y = -4$ **7.** $-8x + 6y = 4$ **8.** $0.5x - 6y = 4$

9. $x = 10$ **10.** $8x - 9y = 7$ **11.** $y = 0$ **12.** $-9x - 4y = 0$

Write an equation of a line that contains the given point and is parallel to the given line.

13. $(4, 1); y = 3x - 2$ **14.** $(2, 6); y = -2x + 5$ **15.** $(3, -4); y = 5x - 3$

16. $(8, 0); y = \frac{1}{2}x + 5$ **17.** $(-5, -8); y = -\frac{3}{5}x + 2$ **18.** $(8, -5); -5x - 4y = 3$

19. $(6, -2); 3x + 2y = 8$ **20.** $(-1, 7); 6x - 3y = 9$ **21.** $(0, 1); y = \frac{3}{7}x - 8$

Example 2

Write an equation of a line that contains the given point and is perpendicular to the given line.

22. $(5, 1); y = 5x - 2$ **23.** $(4, 1); y = -2x + 6$ **24.** $(3, 2); y = \frac{1}{4}x + 7$

25. $(6, 5); y = -\frac{1}{2}x + 1$ **26.** $(9, -3); y = 3x + 8$ **27.** $(0, 4); y = -\frac{5}{7}x - 2$

28.
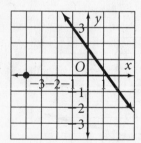

29.
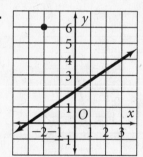

30.
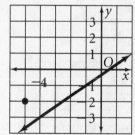

Practice 5-8

• ●

Mixed Exercises

Find the slope of a line parallel to the graph of each equation.

1. $y = 4x + 2$ **2.** $y = \frac{2}{7}x + 1$ **3.** $y = -9x - 13$ **4.** $y = -\frac{1}{2}x + 1$

5. $6x + 2y = 4$ **6.** $y - 3 = 0$ **7.** $-5x + 5y = 4$ **8.** $9x - 5y = 4$

9. $-x + 3y = 6$ **10.** $6x - 7y = 10$ **11.** $x = -4$ **12.** $-3x - 5y = 6$

**Write an equation of a line that contains the given point and is
perpendicular to the given line.**

13. $(6, 4); y = 3x - 2$ **14.** $(-5, 5); y = -5x + 9$ **15.** $(-1, -4); y = \frac{1}{6}x + 1$

16. $(1, 1); y = -\frac{1}{4}x + 7$ **17.** $(12, -6); y = 4x + 1$ **18.** $(0, -3); y = -\frac{4}{3}x - 7$

19.
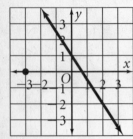

20.
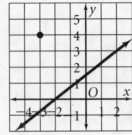

21.
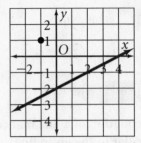

**Write an equation of a line that contains the given point and is parallel to
the given line.**

22. $(3, 4); y = 2x - 7$ **23.** $(1, 3); y = -4x + 5$ **24.** $(4, -1); y = x - 3$

25. $(4, 0); y = \frac{3}{2}x + 9$ **26.** $(-8, -4); y = -\frac{3}{4}x + 5$ **27.** $(9, -7); -7x - 3y = 3$

28.
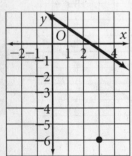

29.
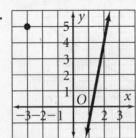

30.
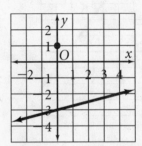

Practice 5-9
Example Exercises

Example 1

Solve each equation by graphing.

1. $3x + 9 = 0$　　**2.** $4x + 8 = 0$　　**3.** $-2x + 6 = 0$　　**4.** $2x + 8 = 10$

5. $4x - 8 = -12$　**6.** $\frac{1}{2}x + 25 = 23$　**7.** $-\frac{4}{3}x + 8 = 0$　**8.** $2(x + 1) = -2$

9. $\frac{2}{3}x + 8 = 0$　**10.** $4(x + 3) = -4$　**11.** $-x - 5 = -3$　**12.** $-\frac{3}{4}x + 9 = 6$

Example 2

Solve each equation by using a graphing calculator.

13. $4x + 11 = 0$　**14.** $5x - 23 = 0$　**15.** $8x + 5 = 0$　**16.** $-4x + 9 = 16$

17. $6x = 102$　　**18.** $\frac{x}{5} + 7 = 6$　**19.** $\frac{5}{6}x - 11 = 8$　**20.** $6(x - 2) = 3$

21. $\frac{3}{4}x + 6 = 0$　**22.** $-2x + 8 = -3$　**23.** $\frac{4x}{5} = 6$　　**24.** $5(x + 3) = 27$

Example 3

25. Suppose you invest $150.00 to start a business selling baby clothes and you make $9.50 on each set of baby clothes you sell.

　a. Write an equation relating income to expenses.

　b. Graph a related linear function to find the break-even point.

　c. How much profit would you make if you sold 20 sets of baby clothes?

26. Suppose you decide to make and sell silk flower arrangements. You spend $220.00 on materials. You sell each flower arrangement for $10.50 each.

　a. Write an equation relating income to expenses.

　b. Graph a related linear function to find the break-even point.

　c. How much profit would you make if you sold 23 silk flower arrangements?

27. Cheng invested $250.00 to start a business selling stuffed animals. He makes $8.50 on each stuffed animal he sells.

　a. Write an equation relating income to expenses.

　b. Graph a related linear function to find the break-even point.

　c. How much money would Cheng lose if he only sold 25 stuffed animals?

Name _____ Class _____ Date _____

Practice 5-9
· ·
Mixed Exercises

Solve each equation by graphing.

1. $2x + 8 = 0$ **2.** $7x + 7 = 0$ **3.** $-5x + 10 = 0$ **4.** $3x - 8 = 1$

5. $3x + 7 = 1$ **6.** $\frac{1}{3}x + 16 = 15$ **7.** $-\frac{3}{7}x + 3 = 0$ **8.** $4(x + 1) = 16$

9. $\frac{4}{3}x + 8 = 0$ **10.** $3(x + 7) = 6$ **11.** $-2x + 15 = 7$ **12.** $-\frac{5}{2}x - 2 = 3$

13. Suppose you invested \$180.00 to start a business selling boxes of dried fruit. You make \$5.75 on each box you sell.

   a. Write an equation relating income to expenses.

   b. Graph a related linear function to find the break-even point.

   c. How much profit would you make if you sold 40 boxes of dried fruit?

14. Suppose you want to start a business selling baseball caps. You spend \$175 on start-up costs and you make \$3.75 on each baseball cap you sell.

   a. Write an equation relating income to expenses.

   b. Graph a related linear function to find the break-even point.

   c. How much profit would you make if you sold 57 baseball caps?

15. Jami invested \$125 for materials to make 20 hanging plant holders. She makes \$12 on each plant holder she sells.

   a. Write an equation relating income to expenses.

   b. Graph a related linear function to find the break-even point.

   c. How much profit would Jami make if she sold all 20 plant holders?

16. Lorenzo decides to sell greeting cards. He spends \$80.00 on supplies and makes \$2.25 on each box of greeting cards that he sells.

   a. Write an equation relating income to expenses.

   b. Graph a related linear function to find the break-even point.

   c. How much money would Lorenzo lose if he only sold 25 boxes of greeting cards?

Solve each equation by using a graphing calculator.

17. $6x - 21 = 0$ **18.** $4x - 5 = 0$ **19.** $5x + 18 = 0$ **20.** $8x + 20 = -16$

21. $-4x = 33$ **22.** $\frac{x}{6} + 3 = 5$ **23.** $\frac{4}{3}x + 12 = 15$ **24.** $12(x - 3) = 9$

25. $\frac{8}{3}x + 4 = 0$ **26.** $-10x + 48 = -20$ **27.** $\frac{3x}{4} = 12$ **28.** $5(x - 5) = 17$

29. $6(x - 10) = 15$ **30.** $\frac{4}{7}x - 7 = 4$ **31.** $5x + 70 = 11$ **32.** $\frac{2}{3}x + 15 = 4$

Algebra Chapter 5

Practice 6-1

Example Exercises

Example 1

Solve each system of linear equations by graphing.

1. $y = 4x + 1$
$y = x + 4$

2. $y = 3x - 3$
$y = -x + 5$

3. $y = x - 5$
$y = -2x + 4$

4. $y = 2x + 10$
$y = -3x - 10$

5. $y = \frac{2}{3}x + 4$
$y = -\frac{1}{3}x - 2$

6. $y = \frac{1}{4}x - 8$
$y = -\frac{1}{2}x - 5$

7. $y = -3x + 5$
$-2x + y = -5$

8. $3x - y = 8$
$y = x + 2$

9. $5x + 6y = 12$
$3x - 2y = -4$

Example 2

Solve each system of linear equations by using a graphing calculator.

10. $y = x + 3$
$y = -x + 15$

11. $y = x - 8$
$y = -2x + 28$

12. $y = -2x + 8$
$y = -4x$

13. $y = 3x + 11$
$y = -5x + 11$

14. $y = 2x + 10$
$y = -3x + 85$

15. $y = -4x - 18$
$y = \frac{1}{2}x + 36$

16. $y = -2x - 60$
$y = 5x + 115$

17. $y = x - 85$
$y = \frac{1}{5}x - 33$

18. $y = \frac{3}{5}x + 2$
$2x + 5y = 85$

19. $2x + y = 50$
$5x - 2y = -10$

20. $6x + 5y = 0$
$2x + y = -36$

21. $12x + 5y = -78$
$-8x + 10y = -28$

Example 3

Solve each system by graphing. Write *no solution* or *infinitely many solutions* where appropriate.

22. $y = 3x - 4$
$y = 3x + 2$

23. $y = 5x - 1$
$y = 5x + 4$

24. $2y = -4x + 6$
$y = -2x + 3$

25. $y = \frac{1}{2}x + 6$
$-x + 2y = -4$

26. $6x + 3y = 12$
$y = -2x + 4$

27. $2x - y = 1$
$6x - 3y = 3$

28. $-5x + 10y = -20$
$2x + 4y = 8$

29. $y = \frac{4}{5}x - 2$
$4x - 5y = 10$

30. $8x + 2y = 4$
$y = -4x + 2$

Practice 6-1

Mixed Exercises

Solve each system by graphing. Write *no solution* or *infinitely many solutions* where appropriate.

1. $y = 3x - 1$
$y = -2x + 4$

2. $y = x - 1$
$y = -x + 7$

3. $y = \frac{3}{4}x + 2$
$\frac{3}{4}x - y = 4$

4. $y = 4x + 7$
$y = -3x$

5. $y = x - 3$
$y = \frac{1}{7}x + 3$

6. $y = -3x - 4$
$3x + y = -4$

7. $y = -x - 3$
$y = -2x - 8$

8. $y = -x + 2$
$3x + 3y = 12$

9. $y = x$
$y = 3x + 2$

10. $y = 4x - 3$
$y = -3x - 3$

11. $y = \frac{5}{3}x - 4$
$y = 2x - 6$

12. $y = 3x + 2$
$2x + y = -8$

13. $x = y + 4$
$y = x + 4$

14. $x + y = 2$
$y = -2x - 1$

15. $2x - y = 3$
$y = x + 4$

16. $3x - 6y = 12$
$2x - 4y = 8$

17. $x - y = 1$
$y = \frac{3}{4}x + 1$

18. $y = x$
$x = 2y + 2$

19. $3x - y = 9$
$y = x + 1$

20. $2x + y = 0$
$y = 2x - 4$

21. $y = 2x - 6$
$x + y = 9$

22. $y = -x$
$y = 3x + 12$

23. $4x + y = 6$
$y = -4x - 1$

24. $y = 4x$
$y = -3x$

Solve each system by using a graphing calculator. Write *no solution* or *infinitely many solutions* where appropriate.

25. $y = x + 6$
$y = 2x - 7$

26. $y = \frac{7}{2}x - 6$
$y = 3x - 2$

27. $y = 2x - 20$
$y = -x + 34$

28. $y = \frac{2}{3}x + 4$
$2x - 3y = 3$

29. $y = -x - 5$
$y = 3x - 105$

30. $x + y = -10$
$2x + 3y = -30$

31. $3x - 4y = 0$
$2x + y = 110$

32. $y = \frac{1}{7}x + 10$
$x - 2y = 0$

33. $2x + y = 6$
$3y = -6x + 9$

34. $y = \frac{5}{6}x + 12$
$y = \frac{4}{3}x - 6$

35. $2x - y = 8$
$3x - 2y = 0$

36. $x + 2y = 2$
$3x + 4y = 22$

Practice 6-2

Example Exercises

Example

Solve each system using substitution.

1. $y = 2x$
$y = 3x - 2$

2. $y = x$
$y = 2x - 4$

3. $y = -\frac{2}{5}x - 18$
$2x - 3y = 22$

4. $y = -2x + 19$
$y = x + 7$

5. $y = -\frac{4}{5}x - 10$
$2x + y = 20$

6. $x + 2y = -7$
$x = y + 23$

7. $x + 5y = 2$
$x = -4y + 5$

8. $3x + y = 9$
$y = -5x + 9$

9. $-2x + y = 6$
$y = 3x + 9$

10. $2x + y = 4$
$y = 4x + 1$

11. $x + y = 38$
$x = 2y - 25$

12. $y = x + 2.8$
$y = 2x - 4.6$

Example

Solve each system using substitution.

13. $x + y = 4$
$2x + 3y = 9$

14. $3x + y = 3$
$9x + 2y = 7$

15. $x - y = 1$
$2x + 4y = 26$

16. $3x + 5y = 3$
$x + y = -1$

17. $7x - y = 10$
$x = \frac{1}{3}y - 2$

18. $2x + 3y = 2$
$x + 6y = 4$

19. $x + y = 9.6$
$x = 2y - 7.2$

20. $x + 5y = 8$
$2x + y = 16$

21. $2x + 4y = 0$
$2x + 6y = 6$

22. $2x + 4y = 10$
$2x + 3y = 18$

23. $y = \frac{3}{2}x - 12$
$2x - y = 28$

24. $5x - 4y = -3$
$-2x + 3y = 18$

Example

Solve each system using substitution. Write *no solution* or *infinitely many solutions* where appropriate.

25. $y = x + 6$
$-x + y = 4$

26. $x + 2y = 8$
$x = -2y + 8$

27. $x + y = -4$
$2x + 2y = 6$

28. $x = -\frac{3}{2}y + 3$
$4x + 6y = 12$

29. $x - 3y = 4$
$2x - 6y = 8$

30. $y = -\frac{3}{4}x + 1$
$3x + 4y = 10$

31. $5x + y = 4$
$10x + 2y = 8$

32. $2x + 3y = 9$
$-4x - 6y = -12$

33. $6x + 3y = -6$
$2x + y = -2$

Practice 6-2
* *
Mixed Exercises

Solve each system using substitution. Write *no solution* or *infinitely many solutions* where appropriate.

1. $y = x$
$y = -x + 2$

2. $y = x + 4$
$y = 3x$

3. $y = 3x - 10$
$y = 2x - 5$

4. $x = -2y + 1$
$x = y - 5$

5. $y = 5x + 5$
$y = 15x - 1$

6. $y = x - 3$
$y = -3x + 25$

7. $y = x - 7$
$2x + y = 8$

8. $y = 3x - 6$
$-3x + y = -6$

9. $x + 2y = 200$
$x = y + 50$

10. $3x + y = 10$
$y = -3x + 4$

11. $y = 2x + 7$
$y = 5x + 4$

12. $3x - 2y = 0$
$x + y = -5$

13. $4x + 2y = 8$
$y = -2x + 4$

14. $6x - 3y = 6$
$y = 2x + 5$

15. $2x + 4y = -6$
$x - 3y = 7$

16. $5x - 3y = -4$
$x + y = -4$

17. $y = -\frac{2}{3}x + 4$
$2x + 3y = -6$

18. $2x + 3y = 8$
$\frac{3}{2}y = 4 - x$

19. $3x - y = 4$
$2x + y = 16$

20. $x + y = 0$
$x = y + 4$

21. $5x + 2y = 6$
$y = -\frac{5}{2}x + 1$

22. $2x + 5y = -6$
$4x + y = -12$

23. $4x + 3y = -3$
$2x + y = -1$

24. $y = -\frac{2}{3}x + 1$
$4x + 6y = 6$

25. $5x - 6y = 19$
$4x + 3y = 10$

26. $2x + y = 6.6$
$5x - 2y = 0.3$

27. $2x - 4y = 3.8$
$3x - y = 17.7$

28. $3x + 4y = 8$
$4.5x + 6y = 12$

29. $3x - 4y = -5$
$x = y + 2$

30. $y = \frac{1}{3}x + 10$
$x = 3y + 6$

31. $2x + 5y = 62$
$3x - y = 23.3$

32. $-5x + y = 6$
$2x - 3y = 60$

33. $x = \frac{3}{4}y - 6$
$y = \frac{4}{3}x + 8$

34. $5x + 6y = -76$
$x + 2y = -44$

35. $3x - 2y = 10$
$y = \frac{3}{2}x - 1$

36. $-3x + 2y = -6$
$-2x + y = 6$

37. $3x + 2y = 5$
$x + 4y = 0$

38. $2x + 5y = 16$
$x + 3y = 16$

39. $5x + 3y = 12$
$3y = -5x + 3$

40. $7x - 2y = 24$
$4x - y = 8$

41. $5x - y = -18$
$4x + 2y = 92$

42. $2x + y = 24$
$5x + 3y = 48$

Practice 6-3

Example Exercises

Example 1

Solve each system using elimination. Check your solution.

1. $x + y = 3$
$x - y = 1$

2. $x + y = 8$
$x - y = 10$

3. $2x + y = 7$
$3x - y = 3$

4. $x + 3y = 9$
$x - 3y = -3$

5. $5x + y = 16$
$-5x + 3y = 8$

6. $5x - 4y = -21$
$-2x + 4y = 18$

7. $4x + 8y = 18$
$-4x + 5y = 8$

8. $2x + 7y = 31$
$5x - 7y = -45$

9. $3x + 6y = 11$
$5x - 6y = 13$

10. $9x + y = 3$
$-9x + 3y = 9$

11. $x - 6y = 2$
$6x + 6y = 12$

12. $12x - 5y = -7$
$-10x + 5y = 5$

Example 2

Solve each system using elimination. Check your solution.

13. $2x + y = 5$
$x + y = 4$

14. $5x + y = 27$
$3x + y = 17$

15. $x + 6y = 20$
$x + 2y = 12$

16. $3x + 4y = 1$
$2x + 4y = -2$

17. $6x + 10y = 54$
$6x + 7y = 36$

18. $8x + 13y = -8$
$8x + 15y = -56$

19. $11x + 2y = 44$
$8x + 2y = 32$

20. $7x + 16y = 9$
$10x + 16y = 6$

21. $12x + 7y = 68$
$12x + 6y = 72$

22. $5x - 9y = 22$
$3x - 9y = 6$

23. $-3x + 5y = -1$
$2x + 5y = 4$

24. $8x - 2y = 0$
$4x - 2y = -1$

Example 3

Solve each system using elimination. Check your solution.

25. $2x + 5y = 34$
$x + 2y = 14$

26. $2x - y = 5$
$5x + 2y = 17$

27. $-2x + 5y = 9$
$x + y = 13$

28. $5x - 2y = 24$
$x + 2y = 12$

29. $6x + 3y = 33$
$4x + y = 15$

30. $12x - 9y = 45$
$2x + 3y = 3$

31. $2x + 2y = 8$
$3x + 2y = 12$

32. $4x - 3y = 17$
$5x + 4y = 60$

33. $8x + 5y = 6$
$3x - 2y = 10$

34. $-3x + 8y = 10$
$5x + 6y = 80$

35. $4x + 12y = -24$
$3x - 6y = -18$

36. $5x - 6y = 48$
$2x + 5y = -3$

Practice 6-3
• •
Mixed Exercises

Solve each system using elimination. Check your solution.

1. $x + 2y = 7$
$3x - 2y = -3$

2. $3x + y = 20$
$x + y = 12$

3. $5x + 7y = 77$
$5x + 3y = 53$

4. $2x + 5y = -1$
$x + 2y = 0$

5. $3x + 6y = 6$
$2x - 3y = 4$

6. $2x + y = 3$
$-2x + y = 1$

7. $9x - 3y = 24$
$7x - 3y = 20$

8. $2x + 7y = 5$
$2x + 3y = 9$

9. $x + y = 30$
$x - y = 6$

10. $4x - y = 6$
$3x + 2y = 21$

11. $x + 2y = 9$
$3x + 2y = 7$

12. $3x + 5y = 10$
$x - 5y = -10$

13. $2x - 3y = -11$
$3x + 2y = 29$

14. $8x - 9y = 19$
$4x + y = -7$

15. $2x + 6y = 0$
$-2x - 5y = 0$

16. $-2x + 3y = -9$
$x + 3y = 3$

17. $4x - 3y = 11$
$3x - 5y = -11$

18. $3x + 7y = 48$
$5x - 7y = -32$

19. $-2x + 3y = 25$
$-2x + 6y = 58$

20. $3x + 8y = 81$
$5x - 6y = -39$

21. $8x + 13y = 179$
$2x - 13y = -69$

22. $-x + 8y = -32$
$3x - y = 27$

23. $2x + 7y = -7$
$5x + 7y = 14$

24. $x + 6y = 48$
$-x + y = 8$

25. $6x + 3y = 0$
$-3x + 3y = 9$

26. $7x + 3y = 25$
$-2x - y = -8$

27. $3x - 8y = 32$
$-x + 8y = -16$

28. $4x - 7y = -15$
$-4x - 3y = -15$

29. $5x + 7y = -1$
$4x - 2y = 22$

30. $6x - 3y = 69$
$7x - 3y = 76$

31. $x + 8y = 28$
$-3x + 5y = 3$

32. $8x - 6y = -122$
$-4x + 6y = 94$

33. $2x + 9y = 36$
$2x - y = 16$

34. $-6x + 12y = 120$
$5x - 6y = -48$

35. $-x + 3y = 5$
$-x - 3y = 1$

36. $10x - 4y = 6$
$10x + 3y = 13$

37. $6x + 3y = 27$
$-4x + 7y = 27$

38. $6x - 8y = 40$
$5x + 8y = 48$

39. $3x + y = 27$
$-3x + 4y = -42$

40. $2x + 8y = -42$
$-x + 8y = -63$

41. $5x + 9y = 112$
$3x - 2y = 8$

42. $-3x + 2y = 0$
$-3x + 5y = 9$

43. $8x - 2y = 58$
$6x - 2y = 40$

44. $7x - 9y = -57$
$-7x + 10y = 68$

45. $9x + 3y = 2$
$-9x - y = 0$

46. $9x + 8y = 50$
$-3x + 5y = 14$

47. $2x - 7y = 9$
$8x + 5y = 69$

48. $9x + 7y = 157$
$12x + 7y = 193$

49. $3x + 5y = 18$
$12x - 3y = 3$

50. $2x + 6y = 54$
$2x - 6y = -18$

51. $3x - 9y = -51$
$3x - 7y = -37$

Practice 6-4

Example Exercises

Example 1

Use a system of linear equations to solve each problem.

1. Attendance at a concert was 480. The ratio of adults to students was 5 to 3. How many adults attended? How many students attended?

2. Tami has both a checking account and a savings account at the bank. She has a total of $850 in both accounts. The ratio of checking to savings is 3 to 7. How much money does Tami have in her checking account? How much does she have in her savings account?

3. You have a money jar containing nickels and quarters worth $1.55. The money jar contains 11 coins. How many of each coin do you have?

4. The ratio of right-handed students to left-handed students is 9 to 2. There are 352 students in the school. How many students are right-handed? How many students are left-handed?

5. Rinaldo and Brooke are picking up trash along the highway. Together they have collected 15 bags of trash. Brooke has collected 3 more bags than Rinaldo. How many bags has each collected?

Example 2

Use a system of linear equations to solve each problem.

6. A toy manufacturing company makes a doll that sells for $12. It costs $5 in labor to make each doll. The total cost for the materials is $420. How many dolls must they sell to break even?

7. Maria is starting a small business selling flowers. She has to pay $150 for a vendor's permit. Each bouquet costs her $7 and she sells them for $15. How many bouquets must Maria sell to break even?

8. Suppose you are going into business mowing lawns. You have purchased a lawn mower for $200. Gas and oil cost you $1.50 per lawn. You are charging $15 per lawn. How many lawns must you mow to break even?

9. Suppose you are selling crafts at a craft show. It costs you $100 to rent a table. Each item costs you $4 to make. You sell them for $10 each. How many must you sell to break even?

Practice 6-4
. . . .
Mixed Exercises

Use a system of linear equations to solve each problem.

1. Your teacher is giving you a test worth 100 points containing 40 questions. There are 2-point and 4-point questions on the test. How many of each type of question are on the test?

2. Suppose you are starting an office-cleaning service. You have spent $315 on equipment. To clean the office you use $4 worth of supplies. You charge $25. How many offices must you clean to break even?

3. The math club and the science club had fundraisers to buy supplies for a hospice. The math club spent $135 buying six cases of juice and one case of bottled water. The science club spent $110 buying four cases of juice and two cases of bottled water. How much did a case of juice cost? How much did a case of bottled water cost?

4. A sporting-goods manufacturer has spent $1000.00 researching a new product. It will cost them $4.50 to manufacture the item that they will sell for $12.00. How many items must they sell to break even?

5. Kay spends 250 min/wk exercising. Her ratio of aerobics to weight training is 3 to 2. How many min/wk does she spend on aerobics? How many min/wk does she spend on weight training?

6. Suppose you invest $1500 in equipment to put pictures on T-shirts. You buy each T-shirt for $3. After you have placed the picture on the shirt you sell it for $20. How many T-shirts must you sell to break even?

7. Christy has a coin collection consisting of nickels and dimes. She has 28 coins worth $2.25. How many of each coin does Christy have?

8. Suppose you are starting a daycare center. You have spent $1500 on equipment and materials for the children. You spend $10/da on food. Your total income is $50/da. How many days will it take you to break even?

9. Suppose you bought supplies for a party. Three rolls of streamers and 15 party hats cost $30. Later you bought 2 rolls of streamers and 4 party hats for $11. How much did each roll of streamers cost? How much did each party hat cost?

10. The new parking lot has spaces for 450 cars. The ratio of spaces for full-sized cars to compact cars is 11 to 4. How many spaces are for full-sized cars? How many spaces are for compact cars?

Practice 6-5
Example Exercises

Example 1

Graph each linear inequality.

1. $y > 3$ **2.** $y < 2$ **3.** $y > -1$

4. $x < 4$ **5.** $x > -3$ **6.** $y > x + 2$

7. $y < -2x + 3$ **8.** $y > 3x - 1$ **9.** $y < 4x + 5$

10. $y > \frac{2}{3}x - 1$ **11.** $y < -\frac{1}{2}x + 3$ **12.** $y > \frac{3}{2}x - 2$

13. $y > 5x - 2$ **14.** $y < -4x + 3$ **15.** $y > -x + 8$

Example 2

Graph each linear inequality.

16. $x + y \le 3$ **17.** $-x + y \ge -1$ **18.** $3x + y \ge 4$

19. $-2x + y \le 6$ **20.** $4x + 2y \le -4$ **21.** $-6x + 2y \ge -6$

22. $x + 3y \le -3$ **23.** $x + 4y \ge 4$ **24.** $-x + 3y \le -12$

25. $4x + 3y \ge -9$ **26.** $-2x + 5y \le 20$ **27.** $8x - 5y \le 15$

28. $-10x + 4y \ge 24$ **29.** $8x - 4y \ge 16$ **30.** $5x - 3y \le 9$

Example 3

Write the linear inequality described. Then graph the inequality.

31. Suppose you are responsible for recycling the metal cans and plastic bottles at your school. How many bags of each type can you send to the recycling center if the truck holds no more than nine bags?

   a. Write a linear inequality that describes the situation.

   b. Graph the linear inequality.

   c. Write three possible solutions to the problem.

32. Members of the school choir are going to see a musical. They will be riding in cars and vans. The cars will hold 5 students and the vans will hold 8 students. How many vehicles of each type will the choir use if no more than 40 students will be going?

   a. Write a linear inequality that describes the situation.

   b. Graph the linear inequality.

   c. Write three possible solutions to the problem.

Practice 6-5

Mixed Exercises

Graph each linear inequality.

1. $y \geq -4$

2. $x + y < -2$

3. $y < x$

4. $x > 2$

5. $4x + y > -6$

6. $-3x + y \leq -3$

7. $x + 4y \leq 8$

8. $y > 2x + 6$

9. $y > -x + 2$

10. $2x + 3y < -9$

11. $y \leq \frac{3}{7}x + 2$

12. $4x + 2y < -8$

13. $y \leq \frac{3}{4}x + 1$

14. $x - y > 4$

15. $y \geq -\frac{2}{5}x - 2$

Write the linear inequality described. Then graph the inequality.

16. Suppose your class is raising money for the Red Cross. You make $5 on each basket of fruit and $3 on each box of cheese that you sell. How many items of each type must you sell to raise more than $150?

  a. Write a linear inequality that describes the situation.

  b. Graph the linear inequality.

  c. Write two possible solutions to the problem.

17. Suppose you intend to spend no more than $60 buying books. Hardback books cost $12 and paperbacks cost $5. How many books of each type can you buy?

  a. Write a linear inequality that describes the situation.

  b. Graph the linear inequality.

  c. Write two possible solutions to the problem.

18. Suppose that for your exercise program you either walk 5 mi/da or ride your bicycle 10 mi/da. How many days will it take you to cover a distance of at least 150 mi?

  a. Write a linear inequality that describes the situation.

  b. Graph the linear inequality.

  c. Write two possible solutions to the problem.

Graph each linear inequality.

19. $6x - 4y > -16$

20. $y \geq -\frac{1}{4}x - 3$

21. $-5x + 4y < -24$

22. $y < -5x + 6$

23. $6x - 4y < -12$

24. $y \geq -\frac{9}{5}x + 7$

25. $y > \frac{5}{7}x - 3$

26. $y < -5x + 9$

27. $-7x + 3y < -18$

28. $y \geq \frac{6}{5}x - 8$

29. $-12x + 8y < 56$

30. $16x + 6y > 36$

Practice 6-6

. . . .

Example Exercises

Example 1

Solve each system of linear inequalities by graphing.

1. $x > 3$
$y < 2$

2. $x < 6$
$y > -1$

3. $y \geq -2$
$x \leq 5$

4. $y < 3x + 2$
$y < -2x + 1$

5. $y > -3x - 2$
$y < 4x + 5$

6. $y < 5x + 6$
$y > 2x - 2$

7. $-x + y > 6$
$3x + y \leq 4$

8. $5x + y < -8$
$y > \frac{5}{2}x + 3$

9. $x + 2y < 6$
$x + 2y > -6$

10. Two typists are working on a statistical report. To finish on time, together they need to type at least 30 pages per day. This is the first time typist A has typed material that contains mostly numbers, so she may be expected to type no more than $\frac{2}{3}$ as many pages as typist B. What are the acceptable combinations of typing output that the typists might produce in a day?

    a. Write a system of two inequalities that describes this situation.

    b. Graph the system to show all possible solutions.

    c. Name a point that is a solution of the system.

11. Some land on a farm is to be fenced as a feeder lot for cattle. The farmer wants the distance around the lot to be no more than 2600 ft. The length should be greater than 800 ft. What are the possible dimensions of the lot?

    a. Write a system of two inequalities that describes this situation.

    b. Graph the system to show all possible solutions.

    c. Name a point that is a solution of the system.

Example 2

Solve each system of linear inequalities by graphing.

12. $y > 3$
$y < 1$

13. $y > -3x + 1$
$y < -3x - 3$

14. $x + y > 4$
$y < -x + 2$

15. $-3x + y < -1$
$y > 3x + 3$

16. $5x + y > 1$
$y < -5x - 2$

17. $y > \frac{3}{5}x + 4$
$-3x + 5y \leq -5$

. . . .

Practice 6-6
· ·
Mixed Exercises

Solve each system of linear inequalities by graphing.

1. $y < 6$
   $y > 3$

2. $x < 7$
   $y > 2$

3. $x < 2$
   $x > 5$

4. $x + y > -2$
   $-x + y < 1$

5. $x + y < 2$
   $x + y > 5$

6. $y < -5x + 6$
   $y > 2x - 1$

7. $y < 2x - 3$
   $-2x + y > 5$

8. $-x + 3y < 12$
   $y \geq -x + 4$

9. $y \leq -\frac{1}{2}x + 3$
   $y \geq -\frac{5}{3}x + 2$

10. $y \geq \frac{3}{4}x + 1$
   $y \geq -\frac{2}{3}x - 1$

11. $6x + 4y > 12$
   $-3x + 4y > 12$

12. $3x + y < 6$
   $-2x + y < 6$

13. $-4x + 2y < -2$
   $-2x + y > 3$

14. $-5x + y > -2$
   $4x + y < 1$

15. $y < \frac{9}{5}x - 8$
   $-9x + 5y > 25$

16. $5x + 4y < 1$
   $8y \geq -10x + 24$

17. $6x + 8y < 32$
   $-4x + 6y < 24$

18. $x + 7y < 14$
   $x - 6y > -12$

19. In basketball you score 2 points for a basket and 1 point for a free throw. Suppose you scored no more than 15 points in a game. How many baskets and free throws could you have made?

   a. Write a system of three inequalities that describes this situation.

   b. Graph the system to show all possible solutions.

   c. Name a point that is a solution of the system.

20. Suppose you need to use at least $1.00 worth of stamps to mail a package. You have as many $.03 stamps as you need but only four $.32 stamps. How many of each stamp can you use?

   a. Write a system of two inequalities that describes this situation.

   b. Graph the system to show all possible solutions.

   c. Name a point that is a solution of the system.

Practice 6-7

Example Exercises

Example 1

Using linear programming, find the values of x and y that maximize the equation.

1. $x \geq 0$
$y \geq 0$
$y \leq 3$
$x + y \leq 5$
$P = 5x + 8y$

2. $x \geq 0$
$y \geq 0$
$x + y \leq 6$
$D = 30x + 6y$

3. $x \geq 2$
$y \geq 0$
$y \leq x$
$x \leq 10$
$F = 15x + 25y$

4. $x \geq 0$
$y \geq 0$
$x + y \leq 7$
$L = 18x + 15y$

Example 2

Evaluate each equation to find the minimum and maximum values.

5. $x \geq 0$
$x \leq 5$
$y \geq 1$
$y \leq 3$
$A = 2x + 4y$

6. $x \geq 0$
$y \geq 0$
$x + y \leq 8$
$B = 4x + y$

7. $x \geq 0$
$y \geq 0$
$y \leq 6$
$x + y \leq 12$
$C = 3x + 2y$

8. $x \geq 0$
$y \geq 0$
$x + y \leq 10$
$-x + y \leq 6$
$D = 6x + 5y$

Example 3

Use linear programming to solve each problem.

9. You have 30 a to grow strawberries and tomatoes. You want at least 10 a to grow strawberries. You want at least 5 a to grow tomatoes. The profit for strawberries is $80/a and the profit for tomatoes is $60/a. How many acres of each crop should you plant to maximize your profit? What is your maximum profit?

10. You are designing a concert hall that will seat no more than 1200 people. You want at least 400 seats that will cost $15 per ticket. You want no more than 700 seats that will cost $25 per ticket. How many of each type of seat should you design to maximize the income from ticket sales? What is the maximum income?

Practice 6-7

• •

Mixed Exercises

Evaluate each equation to find the minimum and maximum values.

1. $x \geq 2$
  $x \leq 9$
  $y \geq 3$
  $y \leq 7$
  $A = 5x + 2y$

2. $x \geq 0$
  $y \geq 0$
  $2x + y \leq 10$
  $B = x + 3y$

3. $x \geq 0$
  $y \geq 0$
  $y \leq 9$
  $x + y \leq 14$
  $C = 7x + 8y$

4. $x \geq 0$
  $y \geq 0$
  $3x + y \leq 12$
  $-2x + y \leq 7$
  $D = 2x + 4y$

Using linear programming, find the values of x and y that maximize the equation.

5. $x \geq -1$
  $x \leq 3$
  $y \leq 0$
  $x - 2y \leq 4$
  $A = 6x + 18y$

6. $x \geq 2$
  $y \geq 0$
  $x \leq 5$
  $y \leq 8$
  $F = 18x + 22y$

7. $y \geq |x|$
  $x \geq -y$
  $y \leq 5$
  $E = 10x + 13y$

8. $x \geq 0$
  $y \geq 0$
  $2x + 5y \leq 10$
  $D = 12x + 20y$

Use linear programming to solve each problem.

9. You are in charge of decorating the school gym for graduation. You need to buy gold and blue rolls of crepe paper. Gold crepe paper costs $5 per roll and blue crepe paper costs $3 per roll. You will need at least ten rolls of crepe paper. You want no more than seven rolls of blue and no more than six rolls of gold. How many rolls of each color crepe paper should you buy to minimize your cost? What is the minimum cost?

10. A small computer company manufactures two models of computers. One model is for business use and the other model is for personal use. The company can make no more than eight computers per day. They want to build no more than five business computers and no more than six personal computers per day. The company makes a profit of $75 on each personal computer and $100 on each business computer. How many of each type of computer should they make to maximize their profit? What is the profit?

11. You own a company that makes furniture. Your company makes end tables and coffee tables. Each week you must make at least 6 end tables and at least 4 coffee tables. Your company can make at most 16 tables per week. The profit on a coffee table is $40 and on an end table it is $30. How many tables of each should you make per week to maximize your profit? What is your maximum profit?

Practice 6-8

Example Exercises

Example 1

Solve each system of equations.

1. $y = |x|$
$y = 5$

2. $y = x + 2$
$y = x^2$

3. $y = 4x - 5$
$y = |x + 1|$

4. $x = -2$
$y = x^2 - 4$

5. $y = x^2 - 3$
$y = 2x$

6. $y = |x - 3|$
$y = -\frac{1}{2}x + 3$

7. $y = |2x|$
$y = x^2$

8. $y = |x|$
$y = |x - 2|$

9. $y = -x^2$
$y = -3x + 2$

Example 2

Solve each system of equations.

10. $y = |x|$
$y = |x| + 3$

11. $y = x^2$
$y = x - 7$

12. $y = |x| - 2$
$y = 4x^2$

13. $y = -2x^2$
$y = x + 1$

14. $y = |x - 2|$
$y = -x^2$

15. $y = x - 1$
$y = |2x| + 1$

16. $y = x^2 + 1$
$y = -x^2$

17. $y = |x - 3|$
$y = -x - 4$

18. $y = -2x - 2$
$y = x^2 + 3$

Example 3

Solve each system of equations using a graphing calculator.

19. $y = 2x^2$
$y = 2x + 12$

20. $y = |x + 1|$
$y = \frac{1}{2}x + 2$

21. $y = x^2 - 1$
$y = -x^2 + 1$

22. $y = x^2 + 1$
$y = 5x + 15$

23. $y = -x^2 - 6$
$y = 7x + 20$

24. $y = \frac{1}{20}x^2$
$-x + 2y = 20$

25. $10x - 3y = 12$
$y = 4x^2$

26. $y = |3x| - 4$
$y = -x^2$

27. $y = -\frac{1}{50}x^2 + 200$
$x + 3y = 596$

Practice 6-8

Mixed Exercises

Solve each system of equations.

1. $y = x^2$
   $y = 4$

2. $y = x^2$
   $y = -3$

3. $y = |x|$
   $y = x + 4$

4. $y = |x| + 1$
   $y = -\frac{7}{4}x + 1$

5. $y = x^2 - 2$
   $y = -x^2 - 2$

6. $y = |2x|$
   $y = x + 3$

7. $y = \left|\frac{1}{2}x\right|$
   $y = 2x + 5$

8. $y = 2x^2$
   $y = -2x + 12$

9. $y = \frac{1}{3}x^2$
   $y = \frac{3}{4}x - 4$

10. $y = |2x| - 1$
   $y = \frac{1}{2}x^2 + 4$

11. $y = x^2$
   $y = -x^2 + 8$

12. $y = |x + 2|$
   $y = 3x - 2$

13. $y = -x^2 + 6$
   $y = 2$

14. $y = |x - 3|$
   $y = \frac{5}{2}x + 3$

15. $y = 3x + 6$
   $y = 3x^2$

Solve each system of equations using a graphing calculator.

16. $y = -\frac{5}{3}x + 8$
   $y = |x|$

17. $y = \frac{7}{2}x - 6$
   $y = |4x| + 1$

18. $y = 2x^2$
   $y = -2x + 4$

19. $y = 2x^2 + 5$
   $y = |x|$

20. $y = |2x| - 1$
   $y = \frac{1}{2}x - 1$

21. $y = |2x - 3|$
   $y = 2x + 7$

22. $y = \frac{1}{2}x^2 + 2$
   $y = 2x + 8$

23. $y = x^2 - 3$
   $y = -3x + 1$

24. $y = \left|\frac{1}{2}x\right|$
   $y = -\frac{1}{4}x - 3$

25. $y = -x^2 + 3$
   $y = -3x - 1$

26. $y = -2x^2 - 6$
   $y = |x| - 6$

27. $y = \frac{1}{3}x^2 - 3$
   $y = x + 3$

28. $y = 3x^2 + 1$
   $y = \frac{1}{2}x^2 - 1$

29. $y = 3x + 11$
   $y = |3x + 1|$

30. $y = -\frac{1}{2}x - 10$
   $y = -\frac{1}{20}x^2$

Practice 7-1

••

Example Exercises

Example 1

Find the values of *a*, *b*, and *c* for each quadratic function.

1. $y = 5x^2 - 2x + 1$　　**2.** $y = 2x^2 + 6x - 7$　　**3.** $y = -x^2 + 4x - 3$

4. $y = \frac{5}{2}x^2 + \frac{2}{3}x + 8$　　**5.** $y = \frac{1}{2}x^2 + 3x - 5$　　**6.** $y = 4x^2 - 9x$

7. $y = \frac{3}{2}x^2 + 6$　　**8.** $y = -\frac{1}{3}x^2 + \frac{3}{4}x$　　**9.** $y = \frac{7}{3}x^2 + 4$

Make a table of values and graph each quadratic function.

10. $y = 3x^2$　　**11.** $y = -3x^2$　　**12.** $y = 2.5x^2$

13. $y = -2.5x^2$　　**14.** $y = -\frac{1}{4}x^2$　　**15.** $y = \frac{1}{4}x^2$

Tell whether each parabola opens upward or downward, and whether the *y*-coordinate of the vertex is a maximum or a minimum.

16. $y = -3x^2$　　**17.** $y = -7x^2$　　**18.** $y = 0.5x^2$

19. $y = 5x^2$　　**20.** $y = -4x^2$　　**21.** $y = \frac{3}{2}x^2$

22. $y = -\frac{7}{4}x^2$　　**23.** $y = -\frac{2}{3}x^2$　　**24.** $y = \frac{4}{3}x^2$

Example 2

Graph each quadratic function using a graphing calculator.

25. $y = x^2$　　**26.** $y = 4x^2$　　**27.** $y = -8x^2$

28. $y = \frac{3}{4}x^2$　　**29.** $y = -\frac{1}{6}x^2$　　**30.** $y = \frac{1}{8}x^2$

31. $y = -5x^2$　　**32.** $y = 3.5x^2$　　**33.** $y = -5.5x^2$

Order each group of quadratic functions from widest to narrowest graph.

34. $y = x^2, y = 5x^2, y = 3x^2$　　**35.** $y = -8x^2, y = \frac{1}{2}x^2, y = -x^2$

36. $y = 5x^2, y = -4x^2, y = 2x^2$　　**37.** $y = -\frac{1}{2}x^2, y = \frac{1}{3}x^2, y = -3x^2$

38. $y = 6x^2, y = -7x^2, y = 4x^2$　　**39.** $y = \frac{3}{4}x^2, y = 2x^2, y = \frac{1}{5}x^2$

Practice 7-1
Mixed Exercises

Find the values of a, b, and c for each quadratic function.

1. $y = -2x^2 - 9x + 12$ **2.** $y = 8x^2 - 11x + 7$ **3.** $y = -x^2 + 7x - 11$

4. $y = \frac{7}{4}x^2 + 6x - 1$ **5.** $y = -\frac{1}{4}x^2 - 5x + 8$ **6.** $y = 14x^2 - 10x$

7. $y = -\frac{3}{5}x^2 - \frac{1}{3}x + 1$ **8.** $y = \frac{8}{3}x^2$ **9.** $y = \frac{6}{5}x^2 + 15$

10. $y = 3x^2 - 2x$ **11.** $y = -7x^2 + 8$ **12.** $y = x^2 + 9x$

Order each group of quadratic functions from widest to narrowest graph.

13. $y = 3x^2, y = -2x^2, y = -4x^2$ **14.** $y = -7x^2 \ y = -18x^2, y = 13x^2$

15. $y = -\frac{1}{2}x^2, y = -\frac{1}{4}x^2, y = -\frac{1}{3}x^2$ **16.** $y = -9x^2, y = \frac{1}{5}x^2, y = -\frac{2}{3}x^2$

17. $y = -7x^2, y = -\frac{3}{2}x^2, y = -3x^2$ **18.** $y = 4x^2, y = 2x^2, y = 9x^2$

19. $y = x^2, y = -3x^2, y = 5x^2$ **20.** $y = \frac{9}{4}x^2, y = 11x^2, y = \frac{3}{4}x^2$

Tell whether each parabola opens upward or downward and whether the y-coordinate of the vertex is a maximum or a minimum.

21. $y = 6x^2$ **22.** $y = -8x^2$ **23.** $y = 2.5x^2$

24. $y = 9x^2$ **25.** $y = x^2$ **26.** $y = -\frac{1}{2}x^2$

27. $y = -\frac{1}{3}x^2$ **28.** $y = -\frac{1}{4}x^2$ **29.** $y = \frac{4}{5}x^2$

30. $y = -2x^2$ **31.** $y = 3x^2$ **32.** $y = -\frac{4}{9}x^2$

33. $y = 11x^2$ **34.** $y = -\frac{11}{4}x^2$ **35.** $y = 13x^2$

Graph each quadratic function. Use either a table of values or a graphing calculator.

36. $y = 2x^2$ **37.** $y = \frac{1}{2}x^2$ **38.** $y = -4x^2$

39. $y = 5x^2$ **40.** $y = 7x^2$ **41.** $y = \frac{3}{2}x^2$

42. $y = -\frac{1}{2}x^2$ **43.** $y = -\frac{1}{6}x^2$ **44.** $y = \frac{5}{2}x^2$

45. $y = -7x^2$ **46.** $y = -2x^2$ **47.** $y = -3.5x^2$

48. $y = -\frac{3}{5}x^2$ **49.** $y = -\frac{1}{5}x^2$ **50.** $y = 7.5x^2$

Practice 7-2

. . . .
Example Exercises

Example 1

Graph each quadratic function. Use either a table of values or a graphing calculator.

1. $y = x^2 + 3$ **2.** $y = x^2 - 1$ **3.** $y = -x^2 + 2$

4. $y = -x^2 - 4$ **5.** $y = 2x^2 - 2$ **6.** $y = 2x^2 + 3$

7. $y = \frac{1}{2}x^2 + 2$ **8.** $y = \frac{1}{2}x^2 - 3$ **9.** $y = \frac{1}{3}x^2 + 5$

10. $y = \frac{1}{3}x^2 - 4$ **11.** $y = 2.5x^2 + 3$ **12.** $y = 2.5x^2 + 5$

13. $y = 5x^2 + 8$ **14.** $y = 5x^2 - 8$ **15.** $y = -3.5x^2 - 4$

Example 2

16. The price of a stock on the NYSE is modeled by the function
$y = 0.005x^2 + 10$, where x is the number of months the stock
has been available.

   a. Graph the function.

   b. What values make sense for the domain? Explain why.

   c. What values make sense for the range? Explain why.

17. You are designing a poster. The poster is 24 in. wide by 36 in. tall. On
this poster you want to place a square photograph and some printing. If
each side of the photograph is x in., the function $y = 864 - x^2$ gives
the area of the poster available for printing.

   a. Graph the function.

   b. What values make sense for the domain? Explain why.

   c. What values make sense for the range? Explain why.

18. You are placing a circular drawing on a square piece of poster board.
The poster board is 15 in. wide. The part of the poster board not
covered by the drawing will be painted blue. If the radius of the drawing
is r, the function $A = 225 - 3.14r^2$ gives the area to be painted blue.

   a. Graph the function.

   b. What values make sense for the domain? Explain why.

   c. What values make sense for the range? Explain why.

Practice 7-2

· ·

Mixed Exercises

1. A rock falls from a cliff that is 80 ft high. The function
   $h = -16t^2 + 80$ gives the height of the rock after t seconds.

   a. Graph the function.

   b. What values make sense for the domain? Explain why.

   c. What values make sense for the range? Explain why.

2. You are going to place a square sand box in a garden that is 6 ft wide
   by 10 ft long. If each side of the sand box is x ft, the function
   $A = 60 - x^2$ gives the area of the garden.

   a. Graph the function.

   b. What values make sense for the domain? Explain why.

   c. What values make sense for the range? Explain why.

**Graph each quadratic function. Use either a table of values or
a graphing calculator.**

3. $y = x^2 - 6$

4. $y = -x^2 + 3$

5. $y = -2x^2 + 5$

6. $y = -3x^2 + 7$

7. $y = 1.5x^2 - 4$

8. $y = -1.5x^2 + 1$

9. $y = -3.5x^2 + 6$

10. $y = -\frac{3}{2}x^2 - 6$

11. $y = -\frac{3}{2}x^2 + 5$

12. $y = 0.25x^2 - 5$

13. $y = 3x^2 + 2$

14. $y = -0.5x^2 + 7$

15. $y = \frac{5}{2}x^2$

16. $y = -3x^2 - 3$

17. $y = -\frac{3}{5}x^2 + 4$

18. $y = -\frac{1}{4}x^2 + 3$

19. $y = -5x^2 + 10$

20. $y = \frac{4}{3}x^2$

21. A rope connects two poles that are 80 ft apart. The function
    $y = 0.02x^2 + 15$ models the height the rope is above the ground.

    a. Graph the function.

    b. What values make sense for the domain? Explain why.

    c. What values make sense for the range? Explain why.

22. You are painting a circle on a square piece of paper. Each side of the
    paper is 18 in. The function $A = 324 - 3.14r^2$ gives the area of the
    paper that you will not paint.

    a. Graph the function.

    b. What values make sense for the domain? Explain why.

    c. What values make sense for the range? Explain why.

© Prentice-Hall, Inc.

Practice 7-3

· ·

Example Exercises

Example 1

Find the equation of the axis of symmetry and the coordinates of the vertex of the graph of each function.

1. $y = x^2 + 4x + 4$ **2.** $y = x^2 - 6x + 7$ **3.** $y = x^2 + 8x - 9$

4. $y = -3x^2 + 12x - 6$ **5.** $y = 2x^2 - 8$ **6.** $y = 6x - 3x^2$

Make a table of values and graph each function. Label the axis of symmetry, the vertex, and the y-intercept.

7. $y = x^2 + 6x + 9$ **8.** $y = x^2 - 4x - 5$ **9.** $y = x^2 - 2x - 8$

10. $y = x^2 + 8x + 10$ **11.** $y = -x^2 - 2x - 1$ **12.** $y = -2x^2 + 12x - 10$

13. $y = -3x^2 - 6x + 2$ **14.** $y = 4x^2 - 8x + 1$ **15.** $y = -x^2 + 8x - 12$

Example 2

Find the vertex of each function. Determine if the vertex is a maximum or minimum.

16. $y = 4x^2 + 8x + 9$ **17.** $y = 5x^2 + 20x + 21$ **18.** $y = -3x^2 + 18x - 20$

19. You have 60 in. of molding to use as a frame around a picture you are painting. The area of the painting is given by the function $y = 30x - x^2$ where x is the width in inches. What width gives the maximum area for the painting? What is the maximum area?

20. You are trying to dunk a basketball. You need to jump 2.5 ft in the air in order to dunk the ball. The height that your feet are above the ground is given by the function $h = -16t^2 + 12t$. What is the maximum height your feet will be above the ground? Will you be able to dunk the basketball?

Example 3

Graph each quadratic inequality.

21. $y > x^2 - 3$ **22.** $y \geq x^2 + 2$ **23.** $y < -x^2 + 4$

24. $y > x^2 + 4x - 5$ **25.** $y < x^2 - 6x + 1$ **26.** $y < -x^2 + 8x + 1$

27. $y \geq -2x^2 + 4x - 1$ **28.** $y \leq -3x^2 + 6x - 2$ **29.** $y \geq 2x^2 + 10x - 3$

· ·

Practice 7-3
• •
Mixed Exercises

Find the equation of the axis of symmetry and the coordinates of the vertex of the graph of each function.

1. $y = x^2 - 10x + 2$ **2.** $y = x^2 + 12x - 9$ **3.** $y = -x^2 + 2x + 1$

4. $y = 3x^2 + 18x + 9$ **5.** $y = 3x^2 + 3$ **6.** $y = 16x - 4x^2$

7. $y = 0.5x^2 + 4x - 2$ **8.** $y = -4x^2 + 24x + 6$ **9.** $y = -1.5x^2 + 6x$

Graph each function. Use a graphing calculator or a table of values. Label the axis of symmetry, the vertex, and the y-intercept.

10. $y = x^2 - 6x + 4$ **11.** $y = x^2 + 4x - 1$ **12.** $y = x^2 + 10x + 14$

13. $y = x^2 + 2x + 1$ **14.** $y = -x^2 - 4x + 4$ **15.** $y = -4x^2 + 24x + 13$

16. $y = -2x^2 - 8x + 5$ **17.** $y = 4x^2 - 16x + 10$ **18.** $y = -x^2 + 6x + 5$

19. $y = 4x^2 + 8x$ **20.** $y = -3x^2 + 6$ **21.** $y = 6x^2 + 48x + 98$

Graph each quadratic inequality.

22. $y > x^2 + 1$ **23.** $y \geq x^2 - 4$ **24.** $y < -x^2 + 1$

25. $y > x^2 + 6x + 3$ **26.** $y < x^2 - 4x + 4$ **27.** $y < -x^2 + 2x - 3$

28. $y \geq -2x^2 - 8x - 5$ **29.** $y \leq -3x^2 + 6x + 1$ **30.** $y \geq 2x^2 - 4x - 3$

Find the vertex of each function. Determine if the vertex is a maximum or minimum.

31. $y = 2x^2 - 12x + 9$ **32.** $y = -2x^2 - 16x - 33$ **33.** $y = -4x^2 + 4x - 1$

34. $y = -3.5x^2 - 14x - 10$ **35.** $y = 0.05x^2 - 3.2x + 4$ **36.** $y = -1.8x^2 + 16.2x - 18.2$

37. You and a friend are hiking in the mountains. You want to climb to a ledge that is 20 ft above you. The height of the grappling hook you throw is given by the function $h = -16t^2 - 32t + 5$. What is the maximum height of the grappling hook? Can you throw it high enough to reach the ledge?

38. The total profit made by an engineering firm is given by the function $p = f(x) = x^2 - 25x + 5000$. Find the minimum profit made by the company.

Practice 7-4

• •

Example Exercises

Example 1

Simplify each expression.

1. $\sqrt{25}$ 2. $-\sqrt{81}$ 3. $\pm\sqrt{144}$ 4. $\sqrt{121}$

5. $\pm\sqrt{\frac{1}{4}}$ 6. $\sqrt{0.36}$ 7. $\sqrt{6.25}$ 8. $-\sqrt{\frac{25}{36}}$

Tell whether each expression is *rational* or *irrational*.

9. $-\sqrt{38}$ 10. $\sqrt{256}$ 11. $\pm\sqrt{169}$ 12. $\sqrt{140}$

Example 2

Between what two consecutive integers is each square root?

13. $\sqrt{19.4}$ 14. $-\sqrt{32.8}$ 15. $\sqrt{8.7}$ 16. $\sqrt{12.8}$

17. $-\sqrt{45.25}$ 18. $\sqrt{60.82}$ 19. $\sqrt{110.52}$ 20. $-\sqrt{91.87}$

Example 3

Use a calculator to simplify each expression. Round to the
nearest hundredth.

21. $\sqrt{40}$ 22. $\sqrt{53}$ 23. $-\sqrt{17}$ 24. $\sqrt{19.2}$

25. $\sqrt{58.7}$ 26. $-\sqrt{40.8}$ 27. $\sqrt{79.51}$ 28. $-\sqrt{161.54}$

Example 4

29. The velocity (in ft/s) an object will reach when dropped is given by the
formula $v = \sqrt{64s}$, where s is the distance (in feet) the object has
fallen. Find the velocity of an object that has fallen each distance.
Round to the nearest tenth.

   a. 9 ft   b. 12 ft   c. 40 ft   d. 50 ft   e. 100 ft

Name _____ Class _____ Date _____

Practice 7-4
Mixed Exercises

Tell whether each expression is *rational* or *irrational*.

1. $-\sqrt{64}$

2. $\sqrt{1600}$

3. $\pm\sqrt{160}$

4. $\sqrt{144}$

5. $\sqrt{125}$

6. $-\sqrt{340}$

7. $\sqrt{1.96}$

8. $-\sqrt{0.09}$

Use a calculator to simplify each expression. Round to the nearest hundredth.

9. $\sqrt{20}$

10. $\sqrt{73}$

11. $-\sqrt{38}$

12. $\sqrt{130}$

13. $\sqrt{149.3}$

14. $-\sqrt{8.7}$

15. $\sqrt{213.8}$

16. $-\sqrt{320.7}$

17. $\sqrt{113.9}$

18. $-\sqrt{840.6}$

19. $-\sqrt{1348.9}$

20. $\sqrt{928.2}$

Simplify each expression.

21. $\sqrt{49}$

22. $-\sqrt{2.25}$

23. $\sqrt{\frac{1}{16}}$

24. $\sqrt{400}$

25. $\sqrt{6.25}$

26. $\pm\sqrt{\frac{36}{25}}$

27. $\sqrt{196}$

28. $\sqrt{2.56}$

29. $\sqrt{0.25}$

30. $\pm\sqrt{\frac{9}{100}}$

31. $\sqrt{576}$

32. $\pm\sqrt{\frac{121}{36}}$

33. $\sqrt{1600}$

34. $-\sqrt{0.04}$

35. $\sqrt{2500}$

36. $\sqrt{4.41}$

Between what two consecutive integers is each square root?

37. $\sqrt{40}$

38. $\sqrt{139}$

39. $-\sqrt{75}$

40. $\sqrt{93}$

41. $-\sqrt{105.6}$

42. $-\sqrt{173.2}$

43. $\sqrt{1123.7}$

44. $\sqrt{216.9}$

Work each problem. Round to the nearest tenth if necessary.

45. You are to put a metal brace inside square shipping containers. The formula $d = \sqrt{2x^2}$ gives the length of the metal brace, where x is the length of the side of the container. Find the length of the brace for each distance.

   a. $x = 3$ ft

   b. $x = 4.5$ ft

   c. $x = 5$ ft

   d. $x = 8$ ft

46. You are designing a cone-shaped storage container. Use the formula $r = \sqrt{\frac{3v}{\pi h}}$ to find the radius of the storage container. Find the radius when $v = 10,000$ ft^3 and $h = 10$ ft.

Practice 7-5

Example Exercises

Example 1

Solve each equation.

1. $x^2 = 36$ **2.** $x^2 = 64$ **3.** $x^2 = 144$

4. $2x^2 = 8$ **5.** $3x^2 = 27$ **6.** $4x^2 = 64$

7. $x^2 - 81 = 0$ **8.** $x^2 - 196 = 0$ **9.** $x^2 - 400 = 0$

10. $x^2 - 10 = 26$ **11.** $x^2 - 52 = -3$ **12.** $x^2 - 6 = 75$

13. $4x^2 = 9$ **14.** $9x^2 - 25 = 0$ **15.** $2x^2 + 11 = 43$

16. $x^2 + 5 = 9$ **17.** $2x^2 - 19 = 31$ **18.** $25x^2 - 9 = 7$

Example 2

Solve each equation. Round solutions to the nearest tenth.

19. $a^2 = 8$ **20.** $x^2 = 15$ **21.** $x^2 = 30$

22. $x^2 - 12 = 0$ **23.** $d^2 - 20 = 0$ **24.** $4m^2 - 68 = 0$

25. $7n^2 - 77 = 0$ **26.** $2s^2 - 8 = 12$ **27.** $8x^2 - 40 = 8$

28. You are designing a cylindrical storage container for compost. You want it to hold 500 ft³ and be 8 ft high. Use the formula $V = \pi r^2 h$ to find the radius of the storage container.

29. The distance s in feet that an object falls when dropped is given by the formula $s = 16t^2$, where t is the elapsed time in seconds. How long will it take an object to fall 200 ft?

30. A landscape designer is planning a flower garden for a city park. The park has an area of 40,000 ft². He wants the flower garden to be a square and to be 10% of the park's area. What are the dimensions of the garden?

Example 3

Solve each equation by graphing the related function. If an equation has no solution, write *no solution*.

31. $x^2 - 9 = 0$ **32.** $x^2 - 1 = 0$ **33.** $x^2 + 3 = 0$

34. $x^2 + 1 = 17$ **35.** $x^2 = 0$ **36.** $x^2 - 3 = 46$

37. $x^2 + 1 = 0$ **38.** $x^2 + 6 = 42$ **39.** $x^2 - 30 = 51$

40. $x^2 + 3 = 3$ **41.** $x^2 - 25 = 0$ **42.** $x^2 + 8 = 6$

© Prentice-Hall, Inc.

Practice 7-5

•• ●

Mixed Exercises

Solve each equation by graphing, using mental math, or using paper and pencil. If the equation has no solution, write *no solution*. Round to the nearest hundredth if necessary.

1. $x^2 = 16$　　　　　**2.** $x^2 - 144 = 0$　　　　**3.** $3x^2 - 27 = 0$

4. $x^2 + 16 = 0$　　　**5.** $x^2 = 12$　　　　　　**6.** $x^2 = 49$

7. $x^2 + 8 = -10$　　　**8.** $3x^2 = 300$　　　　　**9.** $2x^2 - 6 = 26$

10. $x^2 = 80$　　　　　**11.** $81x^2 - 10 = 15$　　　**12.** $2x^2 = 90$

13. $x^2 = 300$　　　　　**14.** $4x^2 + 9 = 41$　　　　**15.** $2x^2 + 8 = 4$

16. $x^2 + 8 = 72$　　　**17.** $4x^2 + 6 = 7$　　　　**18.** $x^2 = 121$

19. $5x^2 + 20 = 30$　　**20.** $x^2 + 6 = 17$　　　　**21.** $3x^2 + 1 = 54$

22. $2x^2 - 7 = 74$　　　**23.** $x^2 + 1 = 0$　　　　**24.** $4x^2 - 8 = -20$

25. $9x^2 = 1$　　　　　**26.** $x^2 + 4 = 4$　　　　　**27.** $3x^2 = 1875$

28. $x^2 = 9$　　　　　　**29.** $5x^2 - 980 = 0$　　　**30.** $x^2 - 10 = 100$

31. $4x^2 - 2 = 1$　　　**32.** $3x^2 - 75 = 0$　　　**33.** $x^2 + 25 = 0$

34. $2x^2 - 10 = -4$　　**35.** $4x^2 + 3 = 3$　　　　**36.** $4x^2 - 8 = 32$

37. $7x^2 + 8 = 15$　　　**38.** $x^2 + 1 = 26$　　　　**39.** $6x^2 = -3$

40. $x^2 - 400 = 0$　　　**41.** $7x^2 - 8 = 20$　　　**42.** $2x^2 - 1400 = 0$

43. $5x^2 + 25 = 90$　　**44.** $x^2 + 4x^2 = 20$　　**45.** $5x^2 - 18 = -23$

46. $3x^2 - x^2 = 10$　　**47.** $2x^2 + 6 - x^2 = 9$　　**48.** $x^2 - 225 = 0$

49. $-3 + 4x^2 = 2$　　**50.** $7x^2 - 1008 = 0$　　**51.** $6x^2 - 6 = 12$

Solve each problem. Round to the nearest tenth if necessary.

52. You want to build a fence around a square garden that covers 506.25 ft². How many feet of fence will you need to complete the job?

53. The formula $A = 6s^2$ will calculate the surface area of a cube. Suppose you have a cube that has a surface area of 216 in.². What is the length of each side?

54. You drop a pencil out of a window that is 20 ft above the ground. Use the formula $V^2 = 64s$, where V is speed and s is distance fallen, to calculate the speed the pencil is traveling when it hits the ground.

55. You want to construct a circular fish pond in your garden. You want the pond to cover an area of 300 ft². What is the radius of the pond?

56. During the construction of a skyscraper a bolt fell from 400 ft. What was the speed of the bolt when it hit the ground? Use $V^2 = 64s$.

© Prentice-Hall, Inc.

Practice 7-6

Example Exercises

Example 1

Write each equation in standard form.

1. $4x^2 + 7x = 8$

2. $3x^2 - 4 = 9x$

3. $9x^2 = -6x + 13$

4. $x^2 + 6x = x - 10$

5. $5x^2 - 6 = -8x - 4$

6. $7x^2 + 10 = 4x + 12$

Use the quadratic formula to solve each equation.

7. $x^2 + 5x + 4 = 0$

8. $x^2 + x - 12 = 0$

9. $x^2 - 3x - 10 = 0$

10. $x^2 - 5x + 6 = 0$

11. $x^2 - 2x - 8 = 0$

12. $x^2 + 8x + 12 = 0$

13. $x^2 + 3x = -2$

14. $x^2 - 25 = 0$

15. $x^2 + 3x = 0$

Example 2

Use the quadratic formula to solve each equation. Round the solutions to the nearest hundredth.

16. $x^2 + 7x + 9 = 0$

17. $x^2 - 2x - 7 = 0$

18. $x^2 - 9x - 1 = 0$

19. $x^2 + 3x = 8$

20. $-x^2 - 7x = -11$

21. $x^2 - 13x = 10$

22. $-2x^2 + 9x + 15 = 0$

23. $5x^2 - 16x + 10 = 0$

24. $4x^2 - 30x + 45 = 0$

25. $3x^2 - x = 11$

26. $6x^2 + 33x = 50$

27. $-7x^2 = 23x - 10$

Example 3

Use the quadratic formula to solve each equation.

28. $2x^2 + 6x + 4 = 0$

29. $4x^2 - 4x - 8 = 0$

30. $3x^2 - 3x = 18$

31. $-x^2 + 16x = 60$

32. $-3x^2 - 27x = 42$

33. $2x^2 - 8x = 42$

34. You throw a ball up to a friend who is on a balcony 38 ft above the ground. You throw the ball with a starting velocity of 48 ft/s. The ball is 6 ft high when it leaves your hand. After how many seconds will your friend have a chance to catch the ball? Use the vertical motion formula $-16t^2 + vt + s = h$.

35. The path that a ball follows when thrown into the air from a height of 5 ft is given by the formula $h = -0.1d^2 + 1.5d + 5$, where h is the height of the ball and d is the distance traveled along the ground. How far has the ball traveled when it is 10 ft in the air?

Practice 7-6
• •
Mixed Exercises

Write each equation in standard form.

1. $6x^2 - x = -9$

2. $2x^2 + 8 = -3x$

3. $2x^2 = 7x - 11$

4. $x^2 + 3x = 5x + 1$

5. $8x^2 - 1 = 3x - 7$

6. $5x^2 + 16 = -5x$

7. $6 - 7x^2 = -2$

8. $-4x + 9 = -3x^2$

9. $5x + 7x^2 - 3 = -7$

Use the quadratic formula to solve each equation. Round solutions to the nearest hundredth when necessary.

10. $x^2 - 4x + 3 = 0$

11. $x^2 + 2x - 3 = 0$

12. $x^2 - x = 42$

13. $x^2 - 20x = -96$

14. $3x^2 + 11x - 8 = 0$

15. $3x^2 + 3x - 4 = 2$

16. $x^2 - 7x + 9 = 0$

17. $2x^2 - 22x - 52 = 0$

18. $2x^2 - x - 12 = 0$

19. $6x^2 - 24x - 192 = 0$

20. $x^2 + 5x = 66$

21. $x^2 + 4x - 437 = 0$

22. $x^2 - 20 = -2x + 60$

23. $4x^2 + 10x + 1 = 0$

24. $2x^2 + 42 = -20x$

25. $3x^2 - 15x = -10$

26. $x^2 = x - 182$

27. $7x^2 + 18x = 4$

28. $4x^2 = 28x - 72$

29. $5x^2 = 19x - 17$

30. $-6x^2 + 20 = 43x$

31. $-2x^2 = 11x - 8$

32. $3x^2 = 192$

33. $-x^2 - 15x = 56$

34. $4x^2 + 17x + 8 = 20$

35. $16x + 60 = -x^2$

36. $3x^2 + 7x = 13$

37. $15x = x^2 + 44$

38. $12x^2 = 11x - 2$

39. $x^2 - 3x + 10 = 50$

40. $x^2 - 40 = 2x + 80$

41. $-2x^2 + 8x = 3$

42. $2x^2 - 110x = -1500$

Use the quadratic formula to solve each problem.

43. You are standing on a bridge that is 64 ft above a river. You kick a small stone off the bridge into the water. After how many seconds will the stone hit the river? Use the vertical motion formula $-16t^2 + vt + s = h$.

44. The function $P = -5t^2 + 70t + 600$ models a company's profit in thousands of dollars, where t is the number of years since 1990.
   a. Estimate the company's profit in 2005.
   b. Use the function to predict in what year the company will break even.

45. You are on the roof of a building. You throw a ball into the air with a velocity of 32 ft/s. The ball is 48 ft above the ground when it leaves your hand. How many seconds will it take for the ball to reach the ground? Use the vertical motion formula $-16t^2 + vt + s = h$.

Practice 7-7

Example Exercises

Example 1

Find the number of solutions of each equation.

1. $x^2 + 5x + 2 = 0$ **2.** $x^2 - 3x - 5 = 0$ **3.** $x^2 + 4x + 4 = 0$

4. $x^2 - 6x + 9 = 0$ **5.** $x^2 - 7x + 5 = 0$ **6.** $x^2 - x + 8 = 0$

7. $4x^2 - 20x + 25 = 0$ **8.** $2x^2 + 8 = 0$ **9.** $3x^2 - 12x = 0$

10. $-2x^2 = 5x + 8$ **11.** $5x^2 = 6x - 1$ **12.** $9x^2 + 1 = 6x$

13. $8x^2 + 13x + 7 = 0$ **14.** $14x^2 - 9x - 5 = 0$ **15.** $-7x^2 - 21x + 40 = 0$

16. $18x^2 + 12x = -2$ **17.** $-10x^2 + 20x = 9$ **18.** $14x^2 - 15x = -5$

19. $0.5x^2 + 7.5x - 3 = 0$ **20.** $-4.2x^2 + 4.5x = -5$ **21.** $0.25x^2 + 6x = 0$

22. $2.5x^2 - 10.5x + 20 = 0$ **23.** $-4x^2 + 20x = 25$ **24.** $3.4x^2 - 7 = 0$

Example 2

25. You are trying to throw a ball over a wire that is 40 ft above the ground. The height of the ball is modeled by the equation $h = -16t^2 + 40t + 6$. Will you be able to throw the ball over the wire?

26. The area of a park is modeled by the equation $A = -2x^2 + 10x + 200$.

    a. What value of x, if any, will give an area of 200 ft^2?

    b. Is it possible for the park to have an area of 225 ft^2?

    c. Is it possible for the park to have an area of 250 ft^2?

27. The equation $E = 3t^2 - 50t + 900$ models a company's production expenses over the past 15 yr.

    a. Were the expenses ever $600?

    b. Were the expenses ever $700?

28. You are trying to hit a golf ball over a tree. The equation $h = -16t^2 + 120t$ models the height of the golf ball t seconds after it is hit.

    a. The tree is 35 ft tall. Will the golf ball go over the tree?

    b. The tree is 40 ft tall. Will the golf ball go over the tree?

Practice 7-7
· ·
Mixed Exercises

Find the number of solutions of each equation.

1. $x^2 + 6x + 10 = 0$ **2.** $x^2 - 4x - 1 = 0$ **3.** $x^2 + 6x + 9 = 0$

4. $x^2 - 8x + 15 = 0$ **5.** $x^2 - 5x + 7 = 0$ **6.** $x^2 - 4x + 5 = 0$

7. $3x^2 - 18x + 27 = 0$ **8.** $4x^2 - 8 = 0$ **9.** $-5x^2 - 10x = 0$

10. $-x^2 = 4x + 6$ **11.** $4x^2 = 9x - 3$ **12.** $8x^2 + 2 = 8x$

13. $7x^2 + 16x + 11 = 0$ **14.** $12x^2 - 11x - 2 = 0$ **15.** $-9x^2 - 25x + 20 = 0$

16. $16x^2 + 8x = -1$ **17.** $-16x^2 + 11x = 11$ **18.** $12x^2 - 12x = -3$

19. $0.2x^2 + 4.5x - 2.8 = 0$ **20.** $-2.8x^2 + 3.1x = -0.5$ **21.** $0.5x^2 + 0.6x = 0$

22. $1.5x^2 - 15x + 2.5 = 0$ **23.** $-3x^2 + 27x = -40$ **24.** $2.1x^2 + 4.2 = 0$

25. One of the games at a carnival involves trying to ring a bell with a ball by hitting a lever that propels the ball into the air. The height of the ball is modeled by the equation $h = -16t^2 + 39t$. If the bell is 25 ft above ground will it be hit by the ball?

26. You are placing a rectangular picture on a square poster board. You can enlarge the picture to any size. The area of the poster board not covered by the picture is modeled by the equation $A = -x^2 - 10x + 300$. Is it possible for the area not covered by the picture to be 100 in.^{2}?

27. The equation $h = -16t^2 + 58t + 3$ models the height of a baseball t seconds after it has been hit.

     a. Was the height ever 40 ft?

     b. Was the height ever 60 ft?

28. A firefighter is on the fifth floor of an office building. She needs to throw a rope into the window above her on the seventh floor. The function $h = -16t^2 + 36t$ models how high above her she is able to throw a rope. If she needs to throw the rope 40 ft above her to reach the seventh floor window, will the rope go into the window?

Find the number of x-intercepts of each function.

29. $y = x^2 + 10x + 16$ **30.** $y = x^2 + 3x + 5$ **31.** $y = x^2 - 2x - 7$

32. $y = 3x^2 - 3$ **33.** $y = 2x^2 + x$ **34.** $y = 3x^2 + 2x + 1$

35. $y = x^2 - 8x - 4$ **36.** $y = x^2 - 16x + 64$ **37.** $y = -2x^2 - 5x - 6$

38. $y = -4x^2 - 5x - 2$ **39.** $y = -x^2 + 12x - 36$ **40.** $y = -5x^2 + 11x - 6$

Practice 8-1
•••
Example Exercises

Example 1

Complete the table for each exercise.

1. The number of cells doubles every hour.

Time	Number of Cells
Initial	100
1 h	200
2 h	400
3 h	▧
4 h	▧
5 h	▧
6 h	▧

2. The investment doubles every 8 yr.

Time	Investment Worth
Initial	$500
8 yr	$1000
16 yr	$2000
24 yr	$4000
32 yr	▧
▧	▧
▧	▧

3. The number of insects triples every 2 mo.

Time	Number of Insects
Initial	20
2 mo	60
4 mo	180
6 mo	▧
8 mo	▧
▧	▧
▧	▧

Example 2

Evaluate each exponential function.

4. $y = 3^x$ for $x = 1, 2,$ and 4

5. $y = 2^x$ for $x = 2, 3,$ and 5

6. $y = 2.5^x$ for $x = 2, 3,$ and 4

7. $y = 0.3^x$ for $x = 1, 4,$ and 5

8. $y = 100 \cdot 2^x$ for $x = 4, 5,$ and 6

9. $y = 200 \cdot 0.5^x$ for $x = 1, 3,$ and 4

10. $y = 2000 \cdot 3^x$ for $x = 3$ and 5

11. $y = 25 \cdot 5^x$ for $x = 1, 3,$ and 4

12. $y = \left(\frac{1}{3}\right)^x$ for $x = 1, 2,$ and 4

13. $y = \left(\frac{2}{5}\right)^x$ for $x = 1, 2,$ and 3

14. $y = 4096\left(\frac{1}{2}\right)^x$ for $x = 3$

15. $y = 125\left(\frac{4}{5}\right)^x$ for $x = 2, 3,$ and 4

Example 3

Graph each function.

16. $y = 4^x$

17. $y = 8^x$

18. $y = 2.5^x$

19. $y = 5^x$

20. $y = 4 \cdot 1.5^x$

21. $y = 4 \cdot 2^x$

22. $y = \frac{1}{5} \cdot 5^x$

23. $y = \frac{1}{9} \cdot 3^x$

24. $y = 8\left(\frac{1}{2}\right)^x$

Practice 8-1
· ·
Mixed Exercises

Complete the table for each exercise.

1. Investment increases by
1.5 times every 5 yr.

Time	Value of Investment
Initial	$800
5 yr	$1200
10 yr	$1800
15 yr	$2700
20 yr	▦
25 yr	▦
▦	▦
▦	▦

2. The number of animals
doubles every 3 mo.

Time	Number of Animals
Initial	18
3 mo	36
6 mo	72
9 mo	▦
12 mo	▦
▦	▦
▦	▦
▦	▦

3. The amount of matter
halves every year.

Time	Amount of Matter
Initial	3200 g
1 yr	1600 g
2 yr	800 g
3 yr	▦
▦	▦
▦	▦
▦	▦
▦	▦

Evaluate each function for the domain {1, 2, 4, 5}.

4. $y = 2^x$

5. $y = 3.1^x$

6. $y = 0.8^x$

7. $y = 2 \cdot 4^x$

8. $y = 10 \cdot 3^x$

9. $y = 25 \cdot 5^x$

10. $y = \left(\frac{2}{3}\right)^x$

11. $y = 100\left(\frac{1}{10}\right)^x$

12. $y = \frac{1}{4} \cdot 8^x$

Graph each function.

13. $y = 3^x$

14. $y = 6^x$

15. $y = 1.5^x$

16. $y = 7^x$

17. $y = 10 \cdot 5^x$

18. $y = 16 \cdot 0.5^x$

19. $y = \frac{1}{8} \cdot 2^x$

20. $y = \frac{1}{2} \cdot 4^x$

21. $y = 8\left(\frac{5}{2}\right)^x$

Evaluate each function.

22. $y = 5.5^x$ for $x = 1, 3,$ and 4

23. $y = 4 \cdot 1.5^x$ for $x = 2, 4,$ and 5

24. $y = 3 \cdot 4^x$ for $x = 1, 3,$ and 5

25. $y = 6^x$ for $x = 2, 3,$ and 4

26. $y = 0.7^x$ for $x = 1, 3,$ and 4

27. $y = 3.1^x$ for $x = 1, 2,$ and 3

28. $y = 500 \cdot 0.5^x$ for $x = 1, 4,$ and 5

29. $y = 5000 \cdot 0.1^x$ for $x = 2, 4,$ and 8

30. $y = 5.5^x$ for $x = 2, 3,$ and 4

31. $y = 2^x$ for $x = 4, 8,$ and 10

32. $y = 128 \cdot 0.25^x$ for $x = 2, 3$ and 4

33. $y = 25 \cdot 4^x$ for $x = 3, 4,$ and 6

Practice 8-2
•••
Example Exercises

Example 1

Write an exponential function to model each situation. Find each amount after the specified time.

1. Suppose a new automobile currently costs $10,000. The cost of a new automobile increases 5% per year. Determine what the cost of a new car would be after each of the following years.

   a. 1 yr   **b.** 2 yr   **c.** 5 yr   **d.** 7 yr

2. The population of a city of 450,000 people increases 2.5% per year. Determine what the population of that city would be after each of the following years.

   a. 1 yr   **b.** 3 yr   **c.** 6 yr   **d.** 10 yr

Example 2

Write an exponential function to model each situation. Find each amount after the specified time.

3. Suppose you invest $1000 in an account paying 5.5% interest compounded annually. Find the account balance after each of the following years.

   a. 1 yr   **b.** 5 yr   **c.** 10 yr   **d.** 20 yr

4. Suppose you invest $2500 in an account paying 7.25% interest compounded annually. Find the account balance after each of the following years.

   a. 1 yr   **b.** 2 yr   **c.** 6 yr   **d.** 25 yr

Example 3

Write an exponential function to model each situation. Find each amount after the specified time.

5. Suppose you invest $5000 in an account paying 5.5% interest. Find the account balance after 15 yr with the interest compounded the following ways.

   a. annually   **b.** semi-annually   **c.** quarterly   **d.** daily

Practice 8-2
• •
Mixed Exercises

Write an exponential function to model each situation. Find each amount after the specified time.

1. Suppose one of your ancestors invested $500 in 1700 in an account paying 4% interest compounded annually. Find the account balance after each of the following dates.

   a. 1750 .
   b. 1800
   c. 1900
   d. 2000

2. Suppose you invest $1500 in an account paying 4.75% interest. Find the account balance after 25 yr with the interest compounded the following ways.

   a. annually
   b. semi-annually
   c. quarterly
   d. monthly

3. The starting salary for a new employee is $25,000. The salary for this employee increases by 8% per year. What is the salary after each of the following years?

   a. 1 yr
   b. 3 yr
   c. 5 yr
   d. 15 yr

4. Suppose you invest $750 in an account paying 5.25% interest compounded annually. Find the account balance after each of the following years.

   a. 3 yr
   b. 5 yr
   c. 7 yr
   d. 18 yr

5. The tax revenue that a small city receives increases by 3.5% per year. In 1980, the city received $250,000 in tax revenue. Determine the tax revenue after each of the following dates.

   a. 1985
   b. 1988
   c. 1990
   d. 1996

6. Suppose your grandmother invested $500 in 1960 at 7%. Find the account balance in 1995 with the interest compounded the following ways.

   a. semi-annually
   b. quarterly
   c. monthly
   d. daily

7. The population of a city of 120,000 people increases by 1.05% per year. Determine what the population of the city is after each of the following years.

   a. 1 yr
   b. 2 yr
   c. 4 yr
   d. 8 yr

8. Suppose you invest $1200 in an account paying 6% interest compounded quarterly. Find the account balance after each of the following years.

   a. 2 yr
   b. 5 yr
   c. 10 yr
   d. 25 yr

Practice 8-3

• •

Example Exercises

Example 1

Use the graph to answer each exercise.

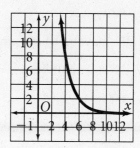

1. What is the value of the function when $x = 4$?

2. What is the value of the function when $x = 6$?

3. When is the value of the function 4?

Example 2

Use a table of values to graph each function.

4. $y = 10 \cdot 0.9^x$ 5. $y = 4.5 \cdot 0.95^x$ 6. $f(x) = 100 \cdot 0.1^x$

7. $y = 90 \cdot 0.8^x$ 8. $y = 30 \cdot 0.85^x$ 9. $g(x) = 100 \cdot 0.99^x$

10. $y = 512 \cdot \left(\frac{1}{2}\right)^x$ 11. $y = 64 \cdot \left(\frac{3}{4}\right)^x$ 12. $y = 27 \cdot \left(\frac{2}{3}\right)^x$

Example 3

Calculate the percent of decrease for each decay factor.

13. 0.9   14. 0.85   15. 0.09   16. 0.72

17. 0.58   18. 0.998   19. 0.53   20. 0.01

Calculate the decay factor for each percent of decrease.

21. 75%   22. 1.5%   23. 4%   24. 18.2%

25. 0.5%   26. 83%   27. 7.2%   28. 3.8%

Write an exponential function to model each situation. Find each amount after the specified time.

29. A city of 140,000 people has a 1% annual decrease in population. Determine the city's population after each of the following years.

   a. 2 yr   b. 5 yr   c. 10 yr   d. 20 yr

30. A $6000 investment has a 8.5% loss each year. Determine the value of the investment after each of the following years.

   a. 1 yr   b. 3 yr   c. 5 yr   d. 8 yr

• •

Practice 8-3

Mixed Exercises

Use the graph to answer each exercise.

1. What is the value of the function when $x = 3$?

2. What is the value of the function when $x = 4$?

3. When is the value of the function 2?

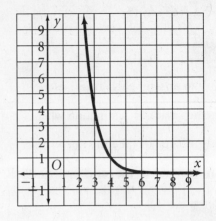

Find the percent of decrease for each decay factor.

4. 0.92   **5.** 0.75   **6.** 0.04   **7.** 0.995

8. 0.73   **9.** 0.18   **10.** 0.65   **11.** 0.025

Write an exponential function to model each situation. Find each amount after the specified time.

12. Suppose the acreage of forest is decreasing by 2% per year because of development. If there are currently 4,500,000 acres of forest, determine the amount of forest land after each of the following years.

    a. 3 yr   **b.** 5 yr   **c.** 10 yr   **d.** 20 yr

13. A \$10,500 investment has a 15% loss each year. Determine the value of the investment after each of the following years.

    a. 1 yr   **b.** 2 yr   **c.** 4 yr   **d.** 10 yr

14. A city of 2,950,000 people has a 2.5% annual decrease in population. Determine the city's population after each of the following years.

    a. 1 yr   **b.** 5 yr   **c.** 15 yr   **d.** 25 yr

15. A \$25,000 purchase has a 12% decrease in value per year. Determine the value of the purchase after each of the following years.

    a. 1 yr   **b.** 3 yr   **c.** 5 yr   **d.** 7 yr

Use a table of values to graph each function.

16. $y = 18 \cdot 0.98^x$ **17.** $y = 8.5 \cdot 0.998^x$ **18.** $f(x) = 48 \cdot 0.625^x$

19. $y = 50 \cdot 0.875^x$ **20.** $y = 6 \cdot 0.95^x$ **21.** $g(x) = 25 \cdot 0.2^x$

22. $y = 36 \cdot \left(\frac{1}{3}\right)^x$ **23.** $y = 15 \cdot \left(\frac{3}{5}\right)^x$ **24.** $y = 9 \cdot \left(\frac{8}{9}\right)^x$

Practice 8-4

•••

Example Exercises

Example 1

Simplify each expression.

1. 3^0 **2.** 6^0 **3.** -4^0 **4.** $(-9)^0$ **5.** 5.45^0

Evaluate each function for $t = 0$.

6. $f(t) = 75 \cdot 3^t$ **7.** $f(t) = 25 \cdot 7^t$ **8.** $f(t) = -6 \cdot 2.5^t$ **9.** $f(t) = 5.9 \cdot 10^t$

Example 2

Write each expression as a simple fraction.

10. 6^{-2} **11.** 5^{-4} **12.** 8^{-3} **13.** 10^{-2} **14.** 7^{-1}

15. 9^{-2} **16.** 8^{-1} **17.** $(-4)^{-2}$ **18.** $(-2)^{-2}$ **19.** $(-13)^{-1}$

20. -6^{-3} **21.** -3^{-2} **22.** 4^{-5} **23.** 11^{-2} **24.** -5^{-3}

Example 3

Rewrite each expression so that all exponents are positive.

25. $2x^{-3}$ **26.** $-4y^{-2}$ **27.** $6ab^{-2}$ **28.** $-3x^{-1}y$ **29.** $2v^{-2}w^{-3}$

30. $\dfrac{1}{x^{-4}}$ **31.** $\dfrac{3}{x^{-2}}$ **32.** $\dfrac{5}{st^{-2}}$ **33.** $\dfrac{6f}{g^{-1}}$ **34.** $\dfrac{-2k^3}{j^{-4}h^{-7}}$

35. $\dfrac{a^{-2}}{b^{-3}}$ **36.** $\dfrac{m^{-4}}{n^{-1}}$ **37.** $\dfrac{x^2y^{-3}}{z^{-5}}$ **38.** $\dfrac{4d^{-4}e^{-1}}{f^{-8}}$ **39.** $\dfrac{2}{a^2b^{-3}}$

Example 4

Use a graphing calculator to graph each function over the domain $\{-2 \le x \le 2\}$.

40. $y = 3^x$ **41.** $y = -3^x$ **42.** $y = \left(\dfrac{1}{3}\right)^x$ **43.** $y = -\left(\dfrac{1}{3}\right)^x$

44. $y = \left(\dfrac{3}{4}\right)^x$ **45.** $y = -\left(\dfrac{1}{2}\right)^x$ **46.** $y = \left(\dfrac{5}{2}\right)^x$ **47.** $y = -\left(\dfrac{3}{2}\right)^x$

48. $y = 2 \cdot 2^x$ **49.** $y = \dfrac{1}{2} \cdot 2^x$ **50.** $y = 2\left(\dfrac{1}{2}\right)^x$ **51.** $y = \dfrac{1}{4}\left(\dfrac{1}{2}\right)^x$

52. $y = 3 \cdot (1.5)^x$ **53.** $y = -2 \cdot (2.5)^x$ **54.** $y = 0.5 \cdot 4^x$ **55.** $y = 2.5 \cdot 2^x$

Practice 8-4

• •

Mixed Exercises

Write each expression as an integer or a simple fraction.

1. 16^0

2. 4^{-2}

3. 3^{-3}

4. 8^{-4}

5. $\frac{1}{2^{-5}}$

6. $\frac{4}{4^{-3}}$

7. $\frac{3}{6^{-1}}$

8. $\frac{1}{2^{-5}}$

9. $3 \cdot 8^0$

10. $16 \cdot 2^{-2}$

11. 12^{-1}

12. -7^{-2}

13. $16 \cdot 4^0$

14. 9^0

15. $\frac{32^{-1}}{8^{-1}}$

16. $\frac{9}{2^{-1}}$

17. $\frac{8^{-2}}{4^0}$

18. $\frac{9^{-1}}{3^{-2}}$

19. $5(-6)^0$

20. 3.7^0

21. $(-9)^{-2}$

22. $(-4.9)^0$

23. $-6 \cdot 3^{-4}$

24. $\frac{7^{-2}}{4^{-1}}$

Evaluate each expression for $m = 4, n = 5$, and $p = -2$.

25. m^p

26. n^m

27. p^p

28. n^p

29. $m^p n$

30. m^{-n}

31. p^{-n}

32. mn^p

33. p^{-m}

34. $\frac{m}{n^p}$

35. $\frac{1}{n^{-m}}$

36. $-n^{-m}$

Rewrite each expression so that all exponents are positive.

37. x^{-8}

38. xy^{-3}

39. $a^{-5}b$

40. $m^2 n^{-9}$

41. $\frac{1}{x^{-7}}$

42. $\frac{3}{a^{-4}}$

43. $\frac{5}{d^{-3}}$

44. $\frac{6}{r^{-5}s^{-1}}$

45. $3x^{-6}y^{-5}$

46. $8a^{-3}b^2c^{-2}$

47. $15s^{-9}t^{-1}$

48. $-7p^{-5}q^{-3}r^2$

49. $\frac{d^{-4}}{e^{-7}}$

50. $\frac{3m^{-4}}{n^{-8}}$

51. $\frac{6m^{-8}n}{p^{-1}}$

52. $\frac{a^{-2}b^{-1}}{cd^{-3}}$

Use a graphing calculator to graph each function over the domain $\{-2 \le x \le 2\}$.

53. $y = 2^x$

54. $y = -2^x$

55. $y = \left(\frac{1}{2}\right)^x$

56. $y = -\left(\frac{1}{2}\right)^x$

57. $y = 2 \cdot 4^x$

58. $y = \frac{1}{2} \cdot 4^x$

59. $y = -\left(\frac{3}{4}\right)^x$

60. $y = -3 \cdot 2^x$

61. $y = (1.1)^x$

62. $y = \frac{3}{4} \cdot 3^x$

63. $y = -2 \cdot 3^x$

64. $y = -4\left(\frac{1}{2}\right)^x$

65. $y = 2(3.5)^x$

66. $y = \left(\frac{2}{5}\right)^x$

67. $y = 5(0.5)^x$

68. $y = 7\left(\frac{1}{4}\right)^x$

Practice 8-5
Example Exercises

Example 1

Write each number in scientific notation.

1. 7,100,000

2. 18,900,000,000

3. 0.000 03

4. 0.000 000 068

5. 120 billion

6. 4.5 million

7. 8 ten-thousandths

8. 375 millionths

9. 25×10^5

10. 76×10^{-4}

11. 0.025×10^9

12. 0.98×10^{-3}

Write each number in standard notation.

13. 6×10^3

14. 8×10^{-3}

15. 4.5×10^4

16. 2.9×10^{-6}

17. 8.01×10^{-4}

18. 9.075×10^8

19. 1.0092×10^6

20. 5.045×10^{-7}

21. 17.8×10^4

22. 31.9×10^{-2}

23. 0.002×10^{-3}

24. 0.098×10^7

Example 2

Simplify. Give each answer in scientific notation.

25. $5 \times (3.2 \times 10^6)$

26. $(6.4 \times 10^6) \div 8$

27. $8 \times (4.1 \times 10^{-2})$

28. $(4.5 \times 10^{-5}) \div 9$

29. $3 \times (7.4 \times 10^7)$

30. $(4.2 \times 10^{-3}) \div 6$

31. $(9.3 \times 10^9) \div 3$

32. $2 \times (3.7 \times 10^{-5})$

33. $2.1 \times (6 \times 10^3)$

34. $15 \times (4 \times 10^{-7})$

35. $(1.8 \times 10^{-8}) \div 9$

36. $(2.4 \times 10^5) \div 8$

37. $(3.2 \times 10^{-4}) \div 8$

38. $5 \times (4.1 \times 10^{-3})$

39. $(3.5 \times 10^{10}) \div 5$

Example 3

Simplify. Give each answer in scientific notation rounded to the nearest hundredth.

40. $(3.5 \times 10^8)(7.1 \times 10^2)$

41. $\dfrac{7.52 \times 10^{10}}{3.9 \times 10^4}$

42. $(5.1 \times 10^{10})(6.79 \times 10^{-4})$

43. $(4.16 \times 10^{-3})(7.7 \times 10^{-4})$

44. $\dfrac{8.015 \times 10^6}{1.754 \times 10^{11}}$

45. $\dfrac{3.013 \times 10^{-6}}{7.187 \times 10^{-13}}$

46. $\dfrac{5.72 \times 10^3}{6.11 \times 10^{-4}}$

47. $(9.28 \times 10^{-9})(3.75 \times 10^6)$

48. $\dfrac{9.97 \times 10^{-3}}{8.01 \times 10^5}$

49. $(6.1 \times 10^{15})(5.32 \times 10^{-8})$

50. $\dfrac{5.125 \times 10^6}{1.927 \times 10^{-3}}$

51. $(4.87 \times 10^{-15})(3.9 \times 10^{12})$

52. $\dfrac{3.975 \times 10^9}{2.15 \times 10^7}$

53. $(5.75 \times 10^7)(1.98 \times 10^{-5})$

54. $(7.9 \times 10^{-13})(6.41 \times 10^{10})$

Practice 8-5
· ·
Mixed Exercises

Write each number in standard notation.

1. 7×10^4 **2.** 3×10^{-2} **3.** 2.6×10^5 **4.** 7.1×10^{-4}

5. 5.71×10^{-5} **6.** 4.155×10^7 **7.** 3.0107×10^2 **8.** 9.407×10^{-5}

9. 31.3×10^6 **10.** 83.7×10^{-4} **11.** 0.018×10^{-1} **12.** 0.016×10^5

13. 8.0023×10^{-3} **14.** 6.902×10^8 **15.** 1005×10^2 **16.** 0.095×10^{-1}

Write each number in scientific notation.

17. 51,000,000   **18.** 975,000,000,000   **19.** 0.000 000 12   **20.** 0.000 005 008

21. 1560 billion   **22.** 0.5 million   **23.** 2 thousandths   **24.** 1095 millionths

25. 194×10^3 **26.** 154×10^{-3} **27.** 0.05×10^6 **28.** 0.031×10^{-4}

29. 790 thousand   **30.** 25 hundredths   **31.** 0.000 000 000 159   **32.** 5,000,900,000,000

Simplify. Give each answer in scientific notation rounded to the nearest hundredth when necessary.

33. $(3 \times 10^{-4})(5 \times 10^6)$ **34.** $(8 \times 10^{-4}) \div 2$ **35.** $4 \times (3 \times 10^5)$

36. $5 \times (7 \times 10^{-2})$ **37.** $(2.8 \times 10^{-5})(5 \times 10^7)$ **38.** $(7.5 \times 10^{-4}) \div 5$

39. $(1.6 \times 10^5) \div 4$ **40.** $\dfrac{6.8 \times 10^{10}}{3.7 \times 10^4}$ **41.** $(6.2 \times 10^{-9})(1.91 \times 10^3)$

42. $\dfrac{5.3 \times 10^5}{6.9 \times 10^8}$ **43.** $8 \times (9 \times 10^9)$ **44.** $(6 \times 10^{-6}) \div 8$

45. $7 \times (9 \times 10^6)$ **46.** $\dfrac{7.13 \times 10^3}{1.92 \times 10^{-4}}$ **47.** $\dfrac{8.175 \times 10^{-4}}{3.792 \times 10^{-8}}$

48. $(2.7 \times 10^9) \div 9$ **49.** $(4.12 \times 10^3)(7.38 \times 10^5)$ **50.** $3 \times (1.2 \times 10^{-4})$

51. $\dfrac{5.3 \times 10^5}{6.9 \times 10^8}$ **52.** $(7.13 \times 10^{-3})(1.7 \times 10^{-7})$ **53.** $(3.11 \times 10^{-2})(2.7 \times 10^{-4})$

54. $2 \times (6.1 \times 10^{-8})$ **55.** $(3.9 \times 10^{-1})(8.2 \times 10^4)$ **56.** $(8.4 \times 10^{-9}) \div 4$

57. $(3.7 \times 10^{-4})(7.25 \times 10^{10})$ **58.** $\dfrac{4.785 \times 10^{-9}}{8.131 \times 10^{-6}}$ **59.** $\dfrac{2.9 \times 10^{-10}}{7.85 \times 10^{-15}}$

60. $(6.3 \times 10^8) \div 7$ **61.** $\dfrac{3.918 \times 10^8}{4.382 \times 10^{-2}}$ **62.** $3 \times (3.2 \times 10^{-2})$

63. $(9.2 \times 10^8)(2.7 \times 10^{10})$ **64.** $(8.7 \times 10^{-2})(7.7 \times 10^{-5})$ **65.** $\dfrac{9.72 \times 10^{-8}}{3.89 \times 10^{-6}}$

Practice 8-6

· ·

Example Exercises

Example 1

Simplify each expression.

1. $a^2 \cdot a^3$ 2. $b^4 \cdot b^6$ 3. $x^5 \cdot x$ 4. $5^2 \cdot 5^4$

5. $m^3 \cdot n^4 \cdot m^5$ 6. $x^2 \cdot y^3 \cdot y^2 \cdot x$ 7. $p^3 \cdot q^5 \cdot p^7$ 8. $s^4 \cdot t^5 \cdot t^3$

9. $(3m^3)(2m^5)$ 10. $(-5m^2)(-2m^4)$ 11. $4^3 \cdot 4^4$ 12. $(6p^5)(8p^4)$

13. $(2x^2y)(3xy^4)$ 14. $(-2a^2b^3)(3a^4)$ 15. $(5x^2y^3)(-2x^4y^5)$ 16. $(3m^2n^5)(-8mn^2)$

Example 2

Simplify. Give the answer in scientific notation.

17. $(2 \times 10^3)(4 \times 10^5)$ 18. $(3.5 \times 10^5)(2 \times 10^9)$ 19. $(8 \times 10^{11})(2.5 \times 10^3)$

20. $3(4 \times 10^5)(5 \times 10^3)$ 21. $200(5 \times 10^3)(1 \times 10^7)$ 22. $(9 \times 10^8)(0.2 \times 10^4)$

23. The speed of light is approximately 1.86×10^5 mi/s. If it takes light from the sun 5.1×10^2 s to reach the earth, how far away is the sun?

24. One liter equals 1×10^6 mm^3. There are 5×10^6 red blood cells in 1 mm^3 of human blood. How many red blood cells are there in 1 L of human blood?

25. Suppose you are an astronaut on a mission to Mars. Your spacecraft is traveling at a speed of 2.5×10^4 mi/h. It takes you 5.5×10^3 h to reach Mars. How many miles do you travel?

Example 3

Simplify each expression. Use only positive exponents.

26. $m^8 \cdot m^{-5}$ 27. $r^3 \cdot r^{-2}$ 28. $a^{-5} \cdot a^3$ 29. $x^{-4} \cdot x^{-7} \cdot x^5$

30. $n^{-3} \cdot n^{-4}$ 31. $(2a^{-3})(5a^4)$ 32. $(-3p^{-5})(2p^8)$ 33. $s^3 \cdot s^{-5} \cdot s^7$

34. $\dfrac{1}{b^{-8} \cdot b^{-1}}$ 35. $\dfrac{1}{x^3 \cdot x^{-7}}$ 36. $\dfrac{1}{y^{-5} \cdot y^8}$ 37. $\dfrac{1}{m \cdot m^{-3}}$

Simplify. Give the answer in scientific notation.

38. $(2 \times 10^{-4})(5 \times 10^2)$ 39. $(3 \times 10^{-2})(4 \times 10^{-3})$ 40. $(8 \times 10^5)(7 \times 10^{-2})$

41. $(6 \times 10^8)(7 \times 10^{-12})$ 42. $(7.5 \times 10^{-1})(2 \times 10^3)$ 43. $(2 \times 10^{13})(3.6 \times 10^{-9})$

44. $(4 \times 10^6)(2.5 \times 10^{-3})$ 45. $(4.6 \times 10^{-3})(3 \times 10^{-1})$ 46. $(3.4 \times 10^{-11})(4 \times 10^{-8})$

Practice 8-6
. . . .
Mixed Exercises

Simplify each expression. Use only positive exponents.

1. $(3d^{-4})(5d^8)$ **2.** $(-8m^4)(4m^8)$ **3.** $n^{-6} \cdot n^{-9}$

4. $a^3 \cdot a$ **5.** $k^8 \cdot k^5$ **6.** $(3p^{-15})(6p^{11})$

7. $p^7 \cdot q^5 \cdot p^6$ **8.** $(-1.5a^5b^2)(6a)$ **9.** $(-2d^3e^3)(6d^4e^6)$

10. $\dfrac{1}{b^{-7} \cdot b^5}$ **11.** $p^5 \cdot q^2 \cdot p^4$ **12.** $\dfrac{1}{n^6 \cdot n^{-5}}$

13. $(8d^4)(4d^7)$ **14.** $x^{-9} \cdot x^3 \cdot x^2$ **15.** $2^3 \cdot 2^2$

16. $r^7 \cdot s^4 \cdot s \cdot r^3$ **17.** $b^7 \cdot b^{13}$ **18.** $(7p^4)(5p^9)$

19. $s^8 \cdot s^{-9} \cdot s^3$ **20.** $(6r^4s^3)(9rs^2)$ **21.** $4^3 \cdot 4^2$

22. $m^{12} \cdot m^{-14}$ **23.** $s^7 \cdot t^4 \cdot t^8$ **24.** $(-3xy^6)(3.2x^5y)$

25. $a^{-7} \cdot a^9$ **26.** $\dfrac{1}{h^7 \cdot h^3}$ **27.** $\dfrac{1}{t^{-5} \cdot t^{-3}}$

28. $f^5 \cdot f^2 \cdot f^0$ **29.** $r^6 \cdot r^{-13}$ **30.** $5^{-6} \cdot 5^4$

Simplify. Give the answer in scientific notation.

31. $(7 \times 10^7)(5 \times 10^{-5})$ **32.** $5(3 \times 10^8)(3 \times 10^4)$ **33.** $(9.5 \times 10^{-4})(2 \times 10^{-5})$

34. $(4 \times 10^9)(4.1 \times 10^8)$ **35.** $(7.2 \times 10^{-7})(2 \times 10^{-5})$ **36.** $13(5 \times 10^7)(4 \times 10^3)$

37. $(6 \times 10^{-6})(5.2 \times 10^4)$ **38.** $(4 \times 10^6)(9 \times 10^8)$ **39.** $(6.1 \times 10^9)(8 \times 10^{14})$

40. $(2.1 \times 10^{-4})(4 \times 10^{-7})$ **41.** $(1.6 \times 10^5)(3 \times 10^{11})$ **42.** $(9 \times 10^{12})(0.3 \times 10^{-18})$

43. $2(4 \times 10^9)(11 \times 10^3)$ **44.** $(5 \times 10^{13})(9 \times 10^{-9})$ **45.** $10(7 \times 10^6)(4 \times 10^9)$

46. $(6 \times 10^{-8})(12 \times 10^{-7})$ **47.** $(6 \times 10^{15})(3.2 \times 10^2)$ **48.** $(5 \times 10^8)(2.6 \times 10^{-16})$

49. In 1990, the St. Louis metropolitan area had an average of $82 \times 10^{-6} \, \text{g/m}^3$ of pollutants in the air. How many grams of pollutants were there in $2 \times 10^3 \, \text{m}^3$ of air?

50. Light will travel approximately 5.88×10^{12} mi in one year. This is called a light-year. Suppose a star is 2×10^4 light-years away. How many miles is it to that star?

51. The weight of $1 \, \text{m}^3$ of air is approximately 1.3×10^3 g. Suppose that the volume of air inside of a building is $3 \times 10^6 \, \text{m}^3$. How much does the air inside the building weigh?

52. Light will travel 1.18×10^{10} in. in 1 s. How far will light travel in 1 nanosecond, 1×10^{-9} s?

Practice 8-7
• •
Example Exercises

Example 1

Simplify each expression. Use positive exponents.

1. $(x^2)^3$ **2.** $(a^4)^2$ **3.** $(2^3)^2$ **4.** $(d^3)^{-2}$

5. $(b^{-7})^2$ **6.** $(m^{-2})^{-4}$ **7.** $(3^{-2})^2$ **8.** $x^2 \cdot (x^2)^5$

9. $(y^3)^4$ **10.** $d^2 \cdot (d^3)^4$ **11.** $n^8 \cdot (n^{-2})^2$ **12.** $(a^3)^{-3} \cdot a^5$

13. $3^2 \cdot (3^2)^2$ **14.** $x \cdot (x^4)^6$ **15.** $b^{-3} \cdot (b^2)^3$ **16.** $(y^3)^{-5} \cdot y^{20}$

Example 2

Simplify each expression. Use positive exponents.

17. $(xy)^3$ **18.** $(x^2y)^4$ **19.** $(m^{-2}n^3)^{-2}$

20. $(5a^3)^2$ **21.** $(7b^{-1})^2$ **22.** $(2a^2b^3)^2$

23. $a^3 \cdot (a^2b)^4$ **24.** $(x^{-2})^3(x^2y^3)^4$ **25.** $(6x^2)^2(3x^2y)^3$

26. $(m^2)^{-4}(m^2n^3)^2$ **27.** $(x^3y^2)^2(xy^3)^4$ **28.** $(a^2b^3)^{-1}(a^{-2}b)^{-5}$

Example 3

Multiply. Give your answers in scientific notation.

29. $(3 \times 10^4)^3$ **30.** $(3 \times 10^{-5})^2$ **31.** $(8 \times 10^{10})^2$

32. $(4 \times 10^{-7})^2$ **33.** $(6 \times 10^7)^3$ **34.** $(2 \times 10^3)^5$

35. $(2 \times 10^6)^{-2}$ **36.** $10^3 \cdot (5 \times 10^8)^2$ **37.** $10^2 \cdot (6 \times 10^9)^2$

38. $10^{-4} \cdot (3 \times 10^4)^2$ **39.** $10^{-7} \cdot (5 \times 10^3)^3$ **40.** $(10^5)^2(8 \times 10^{-4})^2$

41. The Earth is shaped somewhat like a sphere. The volume of a sphere can be calculated by using the formula $V = \frac{4}{3}\pi r^3$. The radius of the Earth is 2.1×10^7 ft. What is the volume of the Earth?

42. The volume of a cylindrical water storage tank can be calculated by using the formula $V = 3.14r^2h$. The radius of the tank is 1×10^2 ft. The height of the tank is 5×10^1 ft. What is the volume of the tank?

43. The kinetic energy, in joules, of a moving object can be found by using the formula $E = \frac{1}{2}mv^2$, where m is the mass and v is the speed of the object. The mass of a proton is 1.67×10^{-27} kg. Find the kinetic energy of a proton traveling 2.5×10^8 m/s.

Practice 8-7
· ·
Mixed Exercises

Simplify each expression. Use positive exponents.

1. $(4a^5)^3$　　　　　　　　**2.** $(2^{-3})^4$　　　　　　　　**3.** $(m^{-3}n^4)^{-4}$

4. $(x^5)^2$　　　　　　　　**5.** $2^5 \cdot (2^4)^2$　　　　　　**6.** $(4x^4)^3(2xy^3)^2$

7. $x^4 \cdot (x^4)^3$　　　　　**8.** $(x^5y^3)^3(xy^5)^2$　　　　**9.** $(5^2)^2$

10. $(a^4)^{-5} \cdot a^{13}$　　　**11.** $(3f^4g^{-3})^3(f^2g^{-2})^{-1}$　**12.** $x^3 \cdot (x^3)^5$

13. $(d^2)^{-4}$　　　　　　　**14.** $(a^3b^4)^{-2}(a^{-3}b^{-5})^{-4}$　**15.** $(x^2y)^4$

16. $(12b^{-2})^2$　　　　　　**17.** $(m^{-5})^{-3}$　　　　　　**18.** $(x^{-4})^5(x^3y^2)^5$

19. $(y^6)^{-3} \cdot y^{21}$　　　**20.** $n^6 \cdot (n^{-2})^5$　　　　**21.** $(m^5)^{-3}(m^4n^5)^4$

22. $(a^3)^6$　　　　　　　　**23.** $b^{-9} \cdot (b^2)^4$　　　　　**24.** $(4^{-1}s^3)^{-2}$

25. $(5a^3b^5)^4$　　　　　　**26.** $(b^{-3})^6$　　　　　　　**27.** $(y^6)^3$

28. $a^{-4} \cdot (a^4b^3)^2$　　　**29.** $(x^4y)^3$　　　　　　　**30.** $d^3 \cdot (d^2)^5$

Multiply. Give your answers in scientific notation.

31. $10^{-9} \cdot (2 \times 10^2)^2$　　**32.** $(3 \times 10^{-6})^3$　　　**33.** $10^4 \cdot (4 \times 10^6)^3$

34. $(9 \times 10^7)^2$　　　　**35.** $10^{-3} \cdot (2 \times 10^3)^5$　**36.** $(7 \times 10^5)^3$

37. $(5 \times 10^5)^4$　　　　**38.** $(2 \times 10^{-3})^3$　　　**39.** $(5 \times 10^2)^{-3}$

40. $(3 \times 10^5)^4$　　　　**41.** $(4 \times 10^8)^{-3}$　　　**42.** $(1 \times 10^{-5})^{-5}$

43. $10^5 \cdot (8 \times 10^7)^3$　　**44.** $(10^2)^3(6 \times 10^{-3})^3$　**45.** $10^7 \cdot (2 \times 10^2)^4$

46. The kinetic energy, in joules, of a moving object is found by using the
formula $E = \frac{1}{2}mv^2$, where m is the mass and v is the speed of the
object. The mass of a car is 1.59×10^3 kg. The car is traveling at
2.7×10^1 m/s. What is the kinetic energy of the car?

47. The moon is shaped somewhat like a sphere. The surface area of the
moon is found by using the formula $S = 12.56r^2$. What is the surface
area of the moon if the radius is 1.08×10^3 mi?

48. Because of a record corn harvest, excess corn is stored on the ground in
a pile. The pile is shaped liked a cone. The height of the pile is 25 ft and
the radius of the pile is 1.2×10^2 ft. Use the formula $V = \frac{1}{3}\pi r^2 h$ to
find the volume.

49. The distance in feet that an object travels in t seconds is given by the
formula $d = 64t^2$. How far has the object traveled after 1.5×10^3 s?

© Prentice-Hall, Inc.

Practice 8-8

Example Exercises

Example 1

Simplify each expression. Use only positive exponents.

1. $\dfrac{2^5}{2^3}$

2. $\dfrac{5^4}{5^7}$

3. $\dfrac{a^{10}}{a^7}$

4. $\dfrac{x^{12}}{x^8}$

5. $\dfrac{m^5 n^2}{m^8 n^7}$

6. $\dfrac{x y^6}{x^4 y^3}$

7. $\dfrac{a^3 b^4}{a b^2}$

8. $\dfrac{3^{-2}}{3^2}$

9. $\dfrac{6^{-3}}{6^{-5}}$

10. $\dfrac{d^{-3}}{d^{-9}}$

11. $\dfrac{a^{-6}}{a^4}$

12. $\dfrac{x^{10}}{x^{-7}}$

13. $\dfrac{a^4 b^{-7} c}{a^8 b^3 c^{-6}}$

14. $\dfrac{s^{-14}}{s^{-10}}$

15. $\dfrac{a^2 b^{-3}}{a^{-4} b^3}$

16. $\dfrac{p^{-4} q^{-6}}{p q^{-1}}$

Example 2

Simplify each expression. Give your answer in scientific notation.

17. $\dfrac{5 \times 10^6}{2.5 \times 10^4}$

18. $\dfrac{8.4 \times 10^8}{4 \times 10^3}$

19. $\dfrac{7.2 \times 10^3}{8 \times 10^{-5}}$

20. $\dfrac{2.8 \times 10^{-3}}{7 \times 10^{-9}}$

21. $\dfrac{4.7 \times 10^{10}}{3.2 \times 10^6}$

22. $\dfrac{3.9 \times 10^6}{5.7 \times 10^{10}}$

23. $\dfrac{4.71 \times 10^3}{6.13 \times 10^{-3}}$

24. $\dfrac{7.91 \times 10^{-6}}{4.43 \times 10^{-4}}$

25. $\dfrac{525 \text{ billion}}{355 \text{ million}}$

26. $\dfrac{25 \text{ million}}{65 \text{ million}}$

27. $\dfrac{21.6 \text{ million}}{537.1 \text{ million}}$

28. $\dfrac{905 \text{ million}}{6.1 \text{ million}}$

Example 3

Simplify each expression. Use only positive exponents.

29. $\left(\dfrac{3}{4}\right)^2$

30. $\left(\dfrac{4}{a^2}\right)^4$

31. $\left(\dfrac{3}{x^3}\right)^4$

32. $\left(\dfrac{3}{5}\right)^{-3}$

33. $\left(-\dfrac{4}{3^2}\right)^{-2}$

34. $\left(\dfrac{a^4}{b}\right)^3$

35. $\left(\dfrac{x^{-3}}{y^{-2}}\right)^{-1}$

36. $\left(\dfrac{a^2 b}{c^3}\right)^4$

37. $\left(\dfrac{2 x^3 y^2}{z}\right)^2$

38. $\left(\dfrac{3 a^{-2} b^3}{c^{-4}}\right)^3$

39. $\left(\dfrac{x^4 y^0}{z^{-3}}\right)^{-2}$

40. $\left(\dfrac{8 a^2 b^{-1}}{c^4}\right)^0$

41. $\left(\dfrac{2^3 m^2 n^{-2}}{p^{-4}}\right)^2$

42. $\left(\dfrac{a^3 b^4}{a^5}\right)^3$

43. $\left(\dfrac{2 x^4 y^{-3}}{x^2 y^4}\right)^0$

44. $\left(\dfrac{p^3 q^{-2}}{q^2 r^{-4}}\right)^1$

Practice 8-8
· ·
Mixed Exercises

Simplify each expression. Use only positive exponents.

1. $\dfrac{c^{15}}{c^9}$

2. $\left(\dfrac{x^3 y^{-2}}{z^{-5}}\right)^{-4}$

3. $\dfrac{x^7 y^9 z^3}{x^4 y^7 z^8}$

4. $\left(\dfrac{a^2}{b^3}\right)^5$

5. $\dfrac{3^7}{3^4}$

6. $\left(\dfrac{a^3}{b^2}\right)^4$

7. $\left(\dfrac{2}{3}\right)^{-2}$

8. $\left(\dfrac{p^{-3} q^{-2}}{q^{-3} r^5}\right)^4$

9. $\dfrac{a^6 b^{-5}}{a^{-2} b^7}$

10. $\dfrac{7^{-4}}{7^{-7}}$

11. $\dfrac{a^7 b^6}{a^5 b}$

12. $\left(\dfrac{a^2 b^{-4}}{b^2}\right)^5$

13. $\left(-\dfrac{3}{2^3}\right)^{-2}$

14. $\dfrac{z^7}{z^{-3}}$

15. $\left(\dfrac{5 a^0 b^4}{c^{-3}}\right)^2$

16. $\dfrac{x^4 y^{-8} z^{-2}}{x^{-1} y^6 z^{-10}}$

17. $\dfrac{m^6}{m^{10}}$

18. $\left(\dfrac{2^3 m^4 n^{-1}}{p^2}\right)^0$

19. $\left(\dfrac{s^{-4}}{t^{-1}}\right)^{-2}$

20. $\left(\dfrac{2 a^3 b^{-2}}{c^3}\right)^5$

21. $\left(\dfrac{x^{-3} y}{x z^{-4}}\right)^{-2}$

22. $\dfrac{h^{-13}}{h^{-8}}$

23. $\dfrac{4^6}{4^8}$

24. $\left(\dfrac{1}{3}\right)^3$

25. $\dfrac{x^5 y^3}{x^2 y^9}$

26. $\left(\dfrac{m^{-3} n^4}{n^{-2}}\right)^4$

27. $\dfrac{4^{-1}}{4^2}$

28. $\left(\dfrac{a^8 b^6}{a^{11}}\right)^5$

29. $\dfrac{n^9}{n^{15}}$

30. $\left(\dfrac{r^3 s^{-1}}{r^2 s^6}\right)^{-1}$

31. $\dfrac{n^{-8}}{n^4}$

32. $\dfrac{m^8 n^3}{m^{10} n^5}$

Simplify each expression. Give your answer in scientific notation.

33. $\dfrac{3.54 \times 10^{-9}}{6.15 \times 10^{-5}}$

34. $\dfrac{9.35 \times 10^{-3}}{3.71 \times 10^{-5}}$

35. $\dfrac{495 \text{ billion}}{23.9 \text{ million}}$

36. $\dfrac{8 \times 10^9}{4 \times 10^5}$

37. $\dfrac{9.5 \times 10^9}{5 \times 10^{12}}$

38. $\dfrac{6.4 \times 10^9}{8 \times 10^7}$

39. $\dfrac{298 \text{ billion}}{49 \text{ million}}$

40. $\dfrac{1.8 \times 10^{-8}}{0.9 \times 10^3}$

41. $\dfrac{3.6 \times 10^6}{9 \times 10^{-3}}$

42. $\dfrac{8.19 \times 10^7}{4.76 \times 10^{-2}}$

43. $\dfrac{65 \text{ million}}{19.5 \text{ billion}}$

44. $\dfrac{4.9 \times 10^{12}}{7 \times 10^3}$

45. $\dfrac{36.2 \text{ trillion}}{98.5 \text{ billion}}$

46. $\dfrac{3.9 \times 10^3}{1.3 \times 10^8}$

47. $\dfrac{5.6 \times 10^{-5}}{8 \times 10^{-7}}$

48. $\dfrac{40 \text{ million}}{985 \text{ million}}$

Practice 9-1

Example Exercises

Example 1

Given the lengths of the two legs of a right triangle, find the length of the hypotenuse to the nearest tenth.

1. 12 and 16   **2.** 10 and 24   **3.** 20 and 15   **4.** 36 and 15

5. 3 and 5   **6.** 7 and 4   **7.** 8 and 12   **8.** 6 and 6

9. 9 and 13   **10.** 14 and 27   **11.** 19 and 15   **12.** 32 and 18

13. 40 and 45   **14.** 30 and 40   **15.** 27 and 42   **16.** 25 and 25

Example 2

Use the triangle at the right. Find the length of the missing side to the nearest tenth.

17. $a = \blacksquare, b = 18, c = 30$ **18.** $a = 24, b = \blacksquare, c = 25$

19. $a = \blacksquare, b = 10, c = 20$ **20.** $a = 13, b = \blacksquare, c = 19$

21. $a = 11, b = \blacksquare, c = 15$ **22.** $a = \blacksquare, b = 9, c = 22$

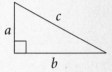

23. A flower garden is in the shape of a right triangle. One leg of the triangle is 6 ft long and the hypotenuse is 12 ft long. What is the length of the other leg?

24. A 20-ft-long wire is used to support a television antenna. The wire is connected to the antenna 15 ft above the ground. How far away from the base of the tower will the other end of the wire be located?

25. Suppose you are making a banner in the shape of a right triangle. The hypotenuse is 36 in. long. One of the legs is 15 in. long. What is the length of the other leg?

Example 3

Can each set of three numbers represent the lengths of the sides of a right triangle? Explain your answer.

26. 16, 63, 65   **27.** 15, 35, 40   **28.** 7, 9, 12   **29.** 15, 18, 12

30. 17, 31, 18   **31.** 2.9, 2.0, 2.1   **32.** $\frac{5}{7}, \frac{12}{7}, \frac{13}{7}$ **33.** $\frac{4}{3}, \frac{5}{3}, \frac{4}{3}$

34. 9, 41, 40   **35.** 2.8, 5.3, 4.5   **36.** 12.5, 30, 32.5   **37.** 30, 50, 35

38. 48, 14, 50   **39.** 10, 12, 5   **40.** 2.6, 8.1, 8.4   **41.** 29, 21, 20

© Prentice-Hall, Inc.

Practice 9-1
• •
Mixed Exercises

**Use the triangle at the right.
Find the length of the missing
side to the nearest tenth.**

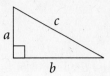

1. $a = 12, b = 35, c = \blacksquare$ **2.** $a = 10, b = \blacksquare, c = 26$ **3.** $a = 11, b = \blacksquare, c = 61$

4. $a = 36, b = 15, c = \blacksquare$ **5.** $a = 8, b = 15, c = \blacksquare$ **6.** $a = \blacksquare, b = 24, c = 40$

7. $a = 18, b = \blacksquare, c = 35$ **8.** $a = 17, b = \blacksquare, c = 49$ **9.** $a = 42, b = 37, c = \blacksquare$

10. $a = \blacksquare, b = 80, c = 90$ **11.** $a = 8, b = 8, c = \blacksquare$ **12.** $a = 19, b = \blacksquare, c = 26$

13. $a = \blacksquare, b = 27, c = 33$ **14.** $a = \blacksquare, b = 13, c = 24$ **15.** $a = 9, b = \blacksquare, c = 13$

16. $a = 19, b = 45, c = \blacksquare$ **17.** $a = \blacksquare, b = 24, c = 39$ **18.** $a = 14, b = 14, c = \blacksquare$

**Can each set of three numbers represent the lengths of the sides of a right
triangle? Explain your answer.**

19. 20, 21, 29   **20.** 16, 30, 34   **21.** 24, 60, 66   **22.** 23, 18, 14

23. 10, 24, 28   **24.** 45, 28, 53   **25.** $\frac{4}{5}, \frac{3}{5}, 1$ **26.** $\frac{2}{3}, \frac{4}{3}, \frac{1}{3}$

27. 3.5, 4.4, 5.5   **28.** 10.5, 11.3, 13.8   **29.** 3.3, 6.5, 5.6   **30.** 24, 70, 74

31. 4.2, 7.0, 5.6   **32.** 5.2, 6.5, 3.9   **33.** 2.1, 3.5, 2.8   **34.** 4.8, 7.5, 5.4

35. 7.5, 4.3, 6.7   **36.** $\frac{1}{9}, \frac{1}{15}, \frac{1}{18}$ **37.** $\frac{1}{2}, \frac{6}{5}, \frac{13}{10}$ **38.** $\frac{1}{5}, \frac{1}{4}, \frac{1}{3}$

Find the missing length to the nearest tenth.

39. A ladder is 25 ft long. The ladder needs to reach to a window that is 24 ft
above the ground. How far away from the building should the bottom of
the ladder be placed?

40. Suppose you are making a sail in the shape of a right triangle for a
sailboat. The length of the longest side of the sail is 65 ft. The sail is to be
63 ft high. What is the length of the third side of the sail?

41. Suppose you leave your house and travel 13 mi due west. Then you
travel 3 mi due south. How far are you from your house?

42. A wire is run between the tops of two poles. One pole is 23 ft taller than
the other pole. The poles are 37 ft apart. How long does the wire need to
be to reach between the two poles?

Practice 9-2

• •

Example Exercises

Example 1

1. You live three blocks west and four blocks north of the library. Your friend lives two blocks east and eight blocks north of the library. How many blocks apart do you and your friend live?

2. You work for a delivery service. Your first delivery is 4 mi west and 6 mi north of the office. Your second delivery is 3 mi east and 7 mi south of the office. How far apart are the two deliveries?

3. Two small planes take off from the same airport. Each plane flies to a different airport. The first plane flies to an airport that is 50 mi east and 75 mi north of the original airport. The second plane flies to an airport that is 60 mi west and 40 mi south of the original airport. How far apart are the two planes when they land at the airports?

4. Forest rangers use lookout towers to locate forest fires. One tower is 5 km west and 3 km north of a fire. A second tower is 3 km west and 4 km south of the fire. How far apart are the two towers?

Example 2

Find the distance between each pair of points. Round your answer to the nearest tenth.

5. $(0, 6), (8, 0)$ 6. $(1, 2), (4, 6)$ 7. $(-3, 1), (2, 13)$ 8. $(3, -2), (5, -4)$

9. $(8, 7), (3, 10)$ 10. $(-2, -1), (4, -3)$ 11. $(2, -7), (-3, -1)$ 12. $(5, 1), (2, 9)$

13. $(3, -4), (8, 6)$ 14. $(6, -2), (-8, 12)$ 15. $(7, 5), (3, -1)$ 16. $(9, 15), (-6, -2)$

17. $(-6, 12), (13, 21)$ 18. $(8, -10), (14, -22)$ 19. $(4, -9), (10, -15)$ 20. $(23, 8), (3, -19)$

Example 3

Find the midpoint of $\overline{XY}$.

21. $X(2, 4)$ and $Y(6, 10)$ 22. $X(3, 5)$ and $Y(9, 17)$ 23. $X(-3, 2)$ and $Y(5, -4)$

24. $X(-1, -8)$ and $Y(6, -4)$ 25. $X(-1, -5)$ and $Y(-3, 9)$ 26. $X(1, 7)$ and $Y(6, 9)$

27. $X(-4, 1)$ and $Y(6, 4)$ 28. $X(9, -2)$ and $Y(8, 3)$ 29. $X(6, -11)$ and $Y(0, -7)$

30. $X(6\frac{1}{2}, 8)$ and $Y(3\frac{1}{2}, 2)$ 31. $X(7, -7)$ and $Y(4, -11)$ 32. $X(3, -2)$ and $Y(7, -15)$

33. $X(-3, -2)$ and $Y(-6, -17)$ 34. $X(-1, -11)$ and $Y(8, 16)$ 35. $X(8, 13)$ and $Y(2, -5)$

© Prentice-Hall, Inc.

Practice 9-2

· ·
Mixed Exercises

Find the midpoint of $\overline{XY}$.

1. $X(8, 14)$ and $Y(2, 6)$ **2.** $X(11, 7)$ and $Y(3, 19)$ **3.** $X(-7, 6)$ and $Y(11, -2)$

4. $X(-3, -2)$ and $Y(7, 8)$ **5.** $X(-4, -1)$ and $Y(-8, 5)$ **6.** $X(6, 15)$ and $Y(4, 8)$

7. $X(-3, 5)$ and $Y(8, 9)$ **8.** $X(16, -8)$ and $Y(5, 9)$ **9.** $X(0, -15)$ and $Y(9, -15)$

10. $X(9\frac{1}{2}, 7)$ and $Y(7\frac{1}{2}, 5)$ **11.** $X(6, -2)$ and $Y(9, -1)$ **12.** $X(8, -13)$ and $Y(1, -7)$

13. $X(-7, -5)$ and $Y(-3, 16)$ **14.** $X(-7, -17)$ and $Y(11, 4)$ **15.** $X(11, 19)$ and $Y(6, -4)$

16. $X(3, -8)$ and $Y(-5, -13)$ **17.** $X(-2, 2)$ and $Y(6, -13)$ **18.** $X(-9, -4)$ and $Y(16, 12)$

Find the distance between each pair of points. Round your answer to the nearest tenth.

19. $(3, 0), (0, 4)$ **20.** $(3, 5), (12, 17)$ **21.** $(-4, 2), (2, -6)$ **22.** $(5, -7), (9, -2)$

23. $(4, 9), (15, 4)$ **24.** $(-7, 4), (2, -9)$ **25.** $(6, -1), (-5, 5)$ **26.** $(9, 8), (1, 12)$

27. $(13, -8), (2, 15)$ **28.** $(16, -7), (-2, -3)$ **29.** $(9, 15), (5, 12)$ **30.** $(7, 5), (-9, -6)$

31. $(-7, 15), (19, 2)$ **32.** $(9, -1), (11, -28)$ **33.** $(14, -29), (10, -25)$ **34.** $(2, -8), (8, -1)$

35. $(-11, 1), (7, 13)$ **36.** $(-1, 9), (19, 23)$ **37.** $(-9, 33), (13, 31)$ **38.** $(7, 2), (1, -2)$

39. You live 4 mi west and 7 mi south of a park. Your friend lives 9 mi east and 3 mi north of the park. How far apart do you and your friend live?

40. You are on a camping trip. One day you walk 2 mi east and 4 mi north of your campsite to a lake. Another day you walk 1 mi west and 2 mi north of your campsite to a waterfall. How far apart are the lake and the waterfall?

41. There is a large building on fire. Fire trucks from two different stations respond to the fire. One station is 1 mi east and 2 mi north of the fire. The other station is 2 mi west and 1 mi south of the fire. How far apart are the two fire stations?

42. The Anderson and McCready families decide to go to a concert together. The Andersons live 4 km west and 6 km north of the concert hall. The McCreadys live 5 km east and 2 km south of the concert hall. How far apart do the two families live?

43. According to the map, a ball field is 4 km west and 2 km north of where you live. A theater is 1 km east and 4 km south of where you live. How far apart are the ball field and the theater?

© Prentice-Hall, Inc.

Practice 9-3

Example Exercises

Example 1

Use △XYZ to evaluate each expression.

1. sin X   **2.** cos X   **3.** tan X

4. sin Z   **5.** cos Z   **6.** tan Z

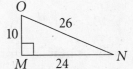

Use △MNO to evaluate each expression.

7. sin N   **8.** cos N   **9.** tan N

10. sin O   **11.** cos O   **12.** tan O

Example 2

Find the values of *x* and *y* to the nearest tenth.

13.

14.

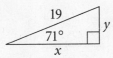

15.

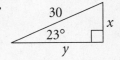

Example 3

Find the value of *x* to the nearest tenth.

16.

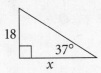

17.

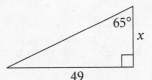

18.

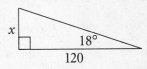

19. Suppose the angle of elevation to the top of a tree is 50°. If you are standing 35 ft from the tree, how tall is the tree?

20. Suppose the angle of elevation to the top of a light pole is 20°. The light pole is 50 ft tall. How far are you standing from the pole?

Practice 9-3
· ·
Mixed Exercises

Use △*ABC* to evaluate each expression.

1. sin *A*   **2.** cos *A*   **3.** tan *A*

4. sin *B*   **5.** cos *B*   **6.** tan *B*

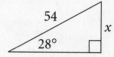

Evaluate each expression. Round to four decimal places.

7. tan 59°   **8.** sin 75°   **9.** sin 8°   **10.** cos 13°   **11.** sin 32°

12. tan 67°   **13.** cos 17°   **14.** cos 36°   **15.** tan 19°   **16.** cos 58°

Find the value of *x* to the nearest tenth.

17. 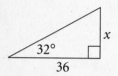   **18.** 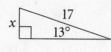   **19.**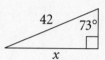

20. 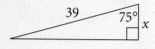   **21.** 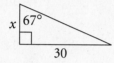   **22.**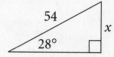

Use △*PQR* to evaluate each expression.

23. sin *P*   **24.** cos *P*   **25.** tan *P*

26. sin *R*   **27.** cos *R*   **28.** tan *R*

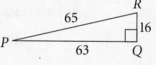

29. A tree casts a shadow that is 20 ft long. The angle of elevation of the sun is 29°. How tall is the tree?

30. Suppose your angle of elevation to the top of a water tower is 78°. If the water tower is 145 ft tall, how far are you standing from the water tower?

31. The angle of elevation from the control tower to an airplane is 49°. The airplane is flying at 5000 ft. How far away from the control tower is the plane?

© Prentice-Hall, Inc.

Practice 9-4

••

Example Exercises

Example 1

Simplify each radical expression. Assume that all variables under radicals represent positive numbers.

1. $\sqrt{50}$ **2.** $\sqrt{48}$ **3.** $\sqrt{20}$ **4.** $\sqrt{8}$ **5.** $\sqrt{25x^5}$ **6.** $\sqrt{75}$

7. $\sqrt{300}$ **8.** $\sqrt{49a^3}$ **9.** $\sqrt{125}$ **10.** $\sqrt{28}$ **11.** $\sqrt{63}$ **12.** $\sqrt{72}$

Example 2

Simplify each radical expression. Assume that all variables under radicals represent positive numbers.

13. $6\sqrt{20}$ **14.** $\sqrt{8} \cdot \sqrt{2}$ **15.** $\sqrt{ab^3}$ **16.** $\sqrt{30} \cdot \sqrt{6}$ **17.** $12\sqrt{60x^2}$

18. $\left(2\sqrt{3}\right)^2$ **19.** $\sqrt{12} \cdot \sqrt{27}$ **20.** $\left(7\sqrt{5}\right)^2$ **21.** $\sqrt{a^5b^6}$ **22.** $\sqrt{14} \cdot \sqrt{8}$

Example 3

Find *g*. Evaluate any radicals and round to the nearest tenth.

23.
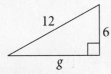

24.
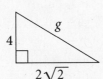

25.
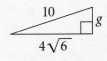

Examples 4-6

Simplify each radical expression. Assume that all variables under radicals represent positive numbers.

26. $\sqrt{\dfrac{7}{9}}$ **27.** $\sqrt{\dfrac{17}{64}}$ **28.** $\dfrac{\sqrt{48}}{\sqrt{8}}$ **29.** $\dfrac{\sqrt{120}}{\sqrt{10}}$ **30.** $\dfrac{5}{\sqrt{2}}$

31. $\dfrac{7}{\sqrt{3}}$ **32.** $\sqrt{\dfrac{15}{49}}$ **33.** $\dfrac{\sqrt{60}}{\sqrt{12}}$ **34.** $\dfrac{3}{\sqrt{3}}$ **35.** $\dfrac{4}{\sqrt{8}}$

Practice 9-4
Mixed Exercises

Simplify each radical expression. Assume that all variables under radicals represent positive numbers.

1. $\sqrt{32}$ **2.** $\sqrt{22} \cdot \sqrt{8}$ **3.** $\sqrt{147}$ **4.** $\sqrt{\frac{17}{144}}$ **5.** $\sqrt{a^2 b^5}$

6. $\frac{2}{\sqrt{6}}$ **7.** $\sqrt{80}$ **8.** $\sqrt{27}$ **9.** $\frac{\sqrt{256}}{\sqrt{32}}$ **10.** $\frac{8}{\sqrt{7}}$

11. $\sqrt{12x^4}$ **12.** $\frac{\sqrt{96}}{\sqrt{12}}$ **13.** $\sqrt{200}$ **14.** $\sqrt{\frac{12}{225}}$ **15.** $\sqrt{15} \cdot \sqrt{6}$

16. $\sqrt{120}$ **17.** $\frac{4}{\sqrt{2a}}$ **18.** $\left(3\sqrt{2}\right)^3$ **19.** $\sqrt{250}$ **20.** $\frac{\sqrt{65}}{\sqrt{13}}$

21. $\sqrt{84}$ **22.** $\sqrt{\frac{18}{121}}$ **23.** $\sqrt{48s^3}$ **24.** $3\sqrt{24}$ **25.** $\sqrt{15} \cdot \sqrt{35}$

26. $\sqrt{160}$ **27.** $\frac{6}{\sqrt{3}}$ **28.** $\frac{\sqrt{48n^6}}{\sqrt{6n^3}}$ **29.** $\sqrt{136}$ **30.** $\sqrt{\frac{27x^2}{256}}$

31. $\sqrt{m^3 n^2}$ **32.** $\frac{\sqrt{180}}{\sqrt{9}}$ **33.** $\sqrt{18} \cdot \sqrt{8}$ **34.** $\left(10\sqrt{3}\right)^2$ **35.** $\sqrt{\frac{17}{64}}$

Use the Pythagorean theorem to find *n*. Express *n* as a radical in simplest form.

36.

37.

38.

39.
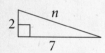

40.

41.
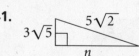

42.

43.
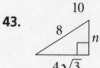

44.
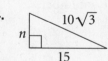

Practice 9-5

Example Exercises

Example 1

Simplify each expression.

1. $5\sqrt{2} + 3\sqrt{2}$ **2.** $8\sqrt{5} + 6\sqrt{5}$ **3.** $\sqrt{6} + 2\sqrt{6}$

4. $4\sqrt{7} + 3\sqrt{7}$ **5.** $8\sqrt{10} + \sqrt{10}$ **6.** $7\sqrt{3} - 2\sqrt{3}$

7. $10\sqrt{6} - 8\sqrt{6}$ **8.** $2\sqrt{11} - 6\sqrt{11}$ **9.** $-8\sqrt{15} + 10\sqrt{15}$

Example 2

Simplify each expression.

10. $3\sqrt{2} + \sqrt{8}$ **11.** $\sqrt{27} + 4\sqrt{3}$ **12.** $\sqrt{12} + 3\sqrt{3}$

13. $\sqrt{28} + 6\sqrt{7}$ **14.** $5\sqrt{3} - \sqrt{12}$ **15.** $\sqrt{18} - 2\sqrt{2}$

16. $6\sqrt{2} - \sqrt{32}$ **17.** $9\sqrt{5} - \sqrt{20}$ **18.** $\sqrt{12} + \sqrt{27}$

19. $\sqrt{32} - \sqrt{8}$ **20.** $4\sqrt{3} - \sqrt{12}$ **21.** $\sqrt{18} + \sqrt{27}$

Example 3

Solve each exercise by using the golden ratio $\left(1 + \sqrt{5}\right) : 2$.

22. The ratio of the width : height of a door is equal to the golden ratio. The height of the door is 60 in. Find the width of the door in inches.

23. The ratio of the length : width of a pool is equal to the golden ratio. The width is 30 ft. Find the length of the pool in feet.

Example 4

Simplify each expression.

24. $3\left(4 + 2\sqrt{5}\right)$ **25.** $-2\left(6\sqrt{2} - 8\right)$ **26.** $5\left(3\sqrt{2} + 4\sqrt{3}\right)$

27. $\sqrt{3}\left(6 + 2\sqrt{2}\right)$ **28.** $\sqrt{5}\left(8 - 3\sqrt{5}\right)$ **29.** $2\sqrt{3}\left(1 + 8\sqrt{2}\right)$

30. $\sqrt{6}\left(\sqrt{2} - 6\right)$ **31.** $\sqrt{3}\left(4\sqrt{5} - 6\sqrt{3}\right)$ **32.** $\sqrt{5}\left(\sqrt{12} - \sqrt{10}\right)$

Practice 9-5

Mixed Exercises

Simplify each expression.

1. $3\sqrt{7} + 5\sqrt{7}$

2. $10\sqrt{4} - \sqrt{4}$

3. $4\sqrt{2}\left(2 + 2\sqrt{3}\right)$

4. $\sqrt{45} + 2\sqrt{5}$

5. $12\sqrt{11} + 7\sqrt{11}$

6. $\sqrt{2}\left(2\sqrt{3} - 4\sqrt{2}\right)$

7. $\sqrt{28} + \sqrt{63}$

8. $3\sqrt{6} - 8\sqrt{6}$

9. $\sqrt{3}\left(\sqrt{6} - \sqrt{12}\right)$

10. $\sqrt{18} - \sqrt{50}$

11. $4\sqrt{2} + 2\sqrt{8}$

12. $13\sqrt{15} - 11\sqrt{15}$

13. $3\left(8\sqrt{3} - 7\right)$

14. $8\left(2\sqrt{5} + 5\sqrt{2}\right)$

15. $17\sqrt{21} - 12\sqrt{21}$

16. $\sqrt{6}\left(7 + 3\sqrt{3}\right)$

17. $8\left(4 - 3\sqrt{2}\right)$

18. $2\sqrt{12} + 6\sqrt{27}$

19. $19\sqrt{3} + \sqrt{12}$

20. $8\sqrt{26} + 10\sqrt{26}$

21. $\sqrt{10}\left(3 - 2\sqrt{6}\right)$

22. $9\sqrt{2} - \sqrt{50}$

23. $10\sqrt{13} - 7\sqrt{13}$

24. $12\sqrt{6} - 4\sqrt{24}$

25. $5\sqrt{7} + \sqrt{28}$

26. $8\sqrt{13} - 12\sqrt{13}$

27. $13\sqrt{40} + 6\sqrt{10}$

28. $-3\sqrt{3}\left(\sqrt{6} + \sqrt{3}\right)$

29. $12\sqrt{29} - 15\sqrt{29}$

30. $10\sqrt{6} - 2\sqrt{6}$

31. $8\sqrt{3} - \sqrt{75}$

32. $3\sqrt{6}\left(2\sqrt{3} + \sqrt{6}\right)$

33. $17\sqrt{35} + 2\sqrt{35}$

34. $\sqrt{19} + 4\sqrt{19}$

35. $12\sqrt{9} - 4\sqrt{9}$

36. $\sqrt{8}\left(\sqrt{2} - 7\right)$

Solve each exercise by using the golden ratio $\left(1 + \sqrt{5}\right) : 2$.

37. The ratio of the height : width of a window is equal to the golden ratio. The width of the door is 36 in. Find the height of the door. Express your answer in simplest radical form and in inches.

38. The ratio of the length : width of a flower garden is equal to the golden ratio. The width of the garden is 14 ft. Find the length of the garden. Express your answer in simplest radical form and in feet.

39. The ratio of the width : height of the front side of a building is equal to the golden ratio. The height of the building is 40 ft. Find the width of the building. Express your answer in simplest radical form and in feet.

© Prentice-Hall, Inc.

Practice for 9-6

Example Exercises

Example 1

Solve each radical equation. Check your solutions.

1. $\sqrt{x} = 8$ **2.** $\sqrt{x} + 2 = 7$ **3.** $\sqrt{x} - 1 = 6x$ **4.** $\sqrt{x + 1} = 4$

5. $\sqrt{x - 1} + 1 = 3$ **6.** $9 = \sqrt{3x}$ **7.** $\sqrt{3x + 6} = 6$ **8.** $4 + \sqrt{x - 8} = 10$

9. $8 = \sqrt{x + 5}$ **10.** $8 - \sqrt{4x} = 4$ **11.** $\sqrt{2x} - 4 = 10$ **12.** $\sqrt{4x} - 6 = 2$

Example 2

13. The equation $V = \sqrt{64d}$ gives the speed V in ft/s of a falling object after it has fallen d ft.

   a. How far has an object fallen when its speed is 8 ft/s?

   b. How far has an object fallen when its speed is 128 ft/s?

14. The equation $P = I^2R$ gives the electrical power P in watts used for current I and resistance R.

   a. Find P when $I = 2$ amps and $R = 100$ ohms.

   b. Find I when $P = 1000$ watts and $R = 25$ ohms.

Example 3

Solve each radical equation. Check your solutions.

15. $\sqrt{2x} = \sqrt{x + 3}$ **16.** $\sqrt{x} = \sqrt{2x - 5}$ **17.** $\sqrt{x + 6} = \sqrt{4x}$

18. $\sqrt{5x - 8} = \sqrt{4x}$ **19.** $\sqrt{x + 1} = \sqrt{2x - 3}$ **20.** $\sqrt{4x + 3} = \sqrt{x + 15}$

21. $\sqrt{2x - 1} = \sqrt{x + 8}$ **22.** $\sqrt{3x - 5} = \sqrt{x + 3}$ **23.** $\sqrt{7x} = \sqrt{2x + 15}$

Example 4

Solve each radical equation. Check your solutions.

24. $x = \sqrt{x + 2}$ **25.** $x = \sqrt{x + 12}$ **26.** $\sqrt{9x - 20} = x$

27. $x = \sqrt{2x + 3}$ **28.** $x = \sqrt{2x + 15}$ **29.** $x = \sqrt{5x - 6}$

30. $x = \sqrt{2x + 8}$ **31.** $x = \sqrt{18 - 3x}$ **32.** $x = \sqrt{4x + 5}$

© Prentice-Hall, Inc.

Practice 9-6

Mixed Exercises

Solve each radical equation. Check your solutions.

1. $\sqrt{x} + 3 = 11$

2. $\sqrt{x + 2} = \sqrt{3x - 6}$

3. $x = \sqrt{24 - 10x}$

4. $\sqrt{4x - 7} = 1$

5. $\sqrt{x} = \sqrt{4x - 12}$

6. $x = \sqrt{11x - 28}$

7. $\sqrt{x} = 12$

8. $x = \sqrt{12x - 32}$

9. $x = \sqrt{13x - 40}$

10. $\sqrt{3x + 5} = \sqrt{x + 1}$

11. $\sqrt{x + 3} = 5$

12. $\sqrt{6x - 4} = \sqrt{4x + 6}$

13. $2 = \sqrt{x + 6}$

14. $x = \sqrt{2 - x}$

15. $\sqrt{4x + 2} = \sqrt{x + 14}$

16. $\sqrt{x + 8} = 9$

17. $x = \sqrt{7x + 8}$

18. $\sqrt{3x + 8} = \sqrt{2x + 12}$

19. $\sqrt{2x + 3} = 5$

20. $\sqrt{3x + 13} = \sqrt{7x - 3}$

21. $x = \sqrt{6 - 5x}$

22. $\sqrt{3x} - 5 = 4$

23. $\sqrt{3x + 4} = \sqrt{5x}$

24. $x = \sqrt{x - 12}$

25. $\sqrt{x - 4} + 3 = 9$

26. $x = \sqrt{8x + 20}$

27. $12 = \sqrt{6x}$

28. $x = \sqrt{60 - 7x}$

29. $\sqrt{x + 14} = \sqrt{6x - 1}$

30. $\sqrt{5x - 7} = \sqrt{6x + 11}$

31. $7 + \sqrt{2x} = 3$

32. $\sqrt{x + 56} = x$

33. $5 + \sqrt{x + 4} = 12$

34. The equation $d = \frac{1}{2}at^2$ gives the distance d in ft that an object travels from rest while accelerating where a is the acceleration and t is the time.

   a. How far has an object traveled in 4 s when the acceleration is 5 ft/s²?

   b. How long did it take an object to travel 100 ft when the acceleration is 8 ft/s²?

35. The equation $v = 20\sqrt{t + 273}$ relates the speed v, in m/s, with the air temperature t in Celsius degrees.

   a. Find the temperature when the speed of sound is 340 m/s.

   b. Find the temperature when the speed of sound is 320 m/s.

36. The equation $V = \sqrt{\frac{Fr}{m}}$ gives the speed V in m/s of an object moving in a horizontal circle where F is centripetal force, r is radius, and m is mass of the object.

   a. Find r when $F = 6$ newtons, $m = 2$ kg, and $V = 3$ m/s.

   b. Find F when $r = 1$ m, $m = 3$ kg, and $V = 2$ m/s.

Practice 9-7

* *

Example Exercises

Example 1

Graph each function. Use a graphing calculator.

1. $y = \sqrt{x + 3}$ **2.** $y = \sqrt{x - 4}$ **3.** $y = \sqrt{x} - 5$

4. $y = \sqrt{x} + 3$ **5.** $y = \sqrt{x + 4} - 2$ **6.** $y = \sqrt{x - 1} + 3$

Using words like "shift up," "shift down," "shift left," and "shift right,"

describe how each of the graphs compare to the graph of $y = \sqrt{x}$ **.**

7. $y = \sqrt{x} - 7$ **8.** $y = \sqrt{x} + 6$ **9.** $y = \sqrt{x + 3}$

10. $y = \sqrt{x} - 1$ **11.** $y = \sqrt{x + 5}$ **12.** $y = \sqrt{x - 12}$

Example 2

Find the domain of each function and graph.

13. $y = \sqrt{x + 4}$ **14.** $y = \sqrt{3x}$ **15.** $f(x) = \sqrt{x - 1}$

16. $y = \sqrt{2x + 6}$ **17.** $y = \sqrt{x - 7}$ **18.** $f(x) = \sqrt{3x + 9}$

Example 3

19. The function $e = 9\sqrt{t} + 10$ models the earnings for a small
company. The earnings e, in millions of dollars, is a function of time t,
the number of years since the company started.

     a. Graph the function.

     b. Evaluate the function to find the earnings at the end of ten years.

     c. Solve an equation to find the year for which the year-end earnings
        were about $28 million.

20. The population of a town is modeled by the function $p = 50\sqrt{2t} + 1500$.
The population p is a function of time t, the number of years since 1985.
Graph the function. Find the population in 1993.

Practice 9-7

Mixed Exercises

Find the domain of each function.

1. $f(x) = \sqrt{x - 7}$

2. $f(x) = \sqrt{3x - 12}$

3. $y = \sqrt{4x + 11}$

4. $y = \sqrt{x - 12}$

5. $f(x) = \sqrt{x + 14}$

6. $y = \sqrt{x + 8}$

7. $y = \sqrt{5x + 13}$

8. $y = \sqrt{2x}$

9. $y = \sqrt{6x}$

Graph each function. Use a graphing calculator.

10. $y = \sqrt{x} - 12$

11. $y = 3\sqrt{x}$

12. $y = \sqrt{x + 8}$

13. $y = \sqrt{x + 7} - 6$

14. $y = \sqrt{x - 6} - 8$

15. $y = \sqrt{x - 10}$

16. $y = 2\sqrt{x - 2}$

17. $y = \sqrt{x - 8} + 6$

18. $y = \sqrt{x} + 7$

Using words like "shift up," "shift down," "shift left," and "shift right," describe how each of the graphs compare to the graph of $y = \sqrt{x}$.

19. $y = \sqrt{x} - 9$

20. $y = \sqrt{x} - 8$

21. $y = \sqrt{x} + 20$

22. $y = \sqrt{x} - 19$

23. $y = \sqrt{x} + 18$

24. $y = \sqrt{x} - 32$

25. $y = \sqrt{x} + 11$

26. $y = \sqrt{x} + 14$

27. $y = \sqrt{x - 4} - 7$

28. The number of people involved in recycling in a community is modeled by the function $n = 90\sqrt{3t} + 400$, where t is the number of months the recycling plant has been open.

a. Graph the function.

b. Find the number of people recycling when the plant has been open for 6 mo.

c. Find the month when about 670 people were recycling.

29. The time t, in seconds, that it takes for an object to drop a distance d, in feet, is modeled by the function $t = \sqrt{\frac{d}{16}}$. Assume no air resistance.

a. Graph the function.

b. Find the time it takes for an object to fall 1000 ft.

c. How far does an object fall in 10 s?

Practice 9-8

Example Exercises

Example 1

Complete each table to find the standard deviation for each data set.

1.

x	x̄	(x − x̄)	(x − x̄)²
94			
90			
88			
87			
81			
		Sum:	
	Standard Deviation:		

2.

x	x̄	(x − x̄)	(x − x̄)²
97			
93			
80			
76			
84			
		Sum:	
	Standard Deviation:		

Make a table like the one above to find the standard deviation for each data set.

3. $\{4, 8, 9, 7, 2\}$

4. $\{7, 9, 8, 4, 7\}$

5. $\{6, 2, 9, 7, 8, 10\}$

6. $\{6, 10, 7, 5, 3, 4, 9, 4\}$

7. $\{40, 30, 25, 18, 36, 28, 33\}$

8. $\{3.5, 2.5, 4.0, 3.5, 2.0, 2.5, 3.0\}$

9. $\{4, 5, 6, 6, 4\}$

10. $\{8, 6, 2, 6, 9, 2\}$

11. $\{11, 13, 19, 15, 14, 16, 13, 15\}$

12. $\{8, 6, 7, 9, 3, 5, 8, 7, 1\}$

13. $\{90, 92, 88, 91, 90, 89\}$

14. $\{9.5, 10.0, 9.0, 8.5, 7.5, 9.5\}$

Example 2

Use a calculator to find the standard deviation for each set of data.

15. $\{37, 38, 27, 21, 25, 39\}$

16. $\{96, 94, 88, 82, 86, 87, 81\}$

17. $\{11, 14, 18, 21, 22, 15, 19, 15\}$

18. $\{5, 8, 11, 14, 18, 6, 19\}$

19. $\{78, 56, 23, 54, 87, 78\}$

20. $\{40, 42, 44, 47, 48, 44, 45, 43, 44\}$

21. $\{5.3, 6.3, 7.1, 8.3, 4.6\}$

22. $\{1.5, 4.8, 4.1, 2.6, 5.3, 4.0\}$

Four people are in a bowling tournament. They bowl five games. Use the data in the table below to find the mean and standard deviation for each of the bowlers.

		Game 1	Game 2	Game 3	Game 4	Game 5
23.	**Bowler 1**	210	200	245	187	236
24.	**Bowler 2**	186	212	221	179	256
25.	**Bowler 3**	197	212	191	246	210
26.	**Bowler 4**	240	182	203	196	264

Practice 9-8
• •
Mixed Exercises

Use a calculator to find the standard deviation for each set of data.

1. {8, 6, 7, 1, 9, 14, 5, 7}   **2.** {11, 13, 12, 9, 6, 19, 17}   **3.** {5, 7, 3, 4, 6, 8, 2, 5, 5}

4. {4.6, 2.7, 1.9, 8.4, 7.2}   **5.** {9.8, 9.5, 9.6, 9.2, 9.6, 9.9}   **6.** {5.7, 3.5, 8.2, 5.7, 7.2, 6.3, 7.3}

7. {120, 250, 512, 245, 158}   **8.** {78, 89, 34, 65, 92, 26, 66}   **9.** {67, 34, 98, 23, 66, 19, 85, 79, 82}

Complete each table to find the standard deviation for each data set.

10.

x	$\bar{x}$	$(x - \bar{x})$	$(x - \bar{x})^2$
125			
140			
145			
155			
160			
		Sum:	
	Standard Deviation:		

11.

x	$\bar{x}$	$(x - \bar{x})$	$(x - \bar{x})^2$
210			
200			
190			
180			
170			
		Sum:	
	Standard Deviation:		

Make a table like the one above to find the standard deviation for each data set.

12. {10, 12, 17, 21, 25}   **13.** {25, 46, 81, 72, 56}   **14.** {100, 130, 107, 118, 115}

15. {3, 4, 2, 7, 5, 9}   **16.** {2.5, 5.5, 6.5, 7.5, 8.0}   **17.** {9, 1, 8, 6, 3, 1, 7}

18. {10, 18, 43, 76, 24, 33}   **19.** {92, 91, 86, 72, 78, 85}   **20.** {3, 4, 5, 1, 8, 9, 2, 8}

Use a graphing calculator to find the standard deviation for each set of data.

21. {23, 67, 87, 45, 92, 55}   **22.** {5, 7, 2, 8, 12, 22, 39, 3, 1}

23. {34, 12, 98, 90, 123, 63, 82, 216}   **24.** {67, 56, 87, 67, 66, 68}

25. {5.7, 2.6, 8.3, 1.7, 5.3, 1.0}   **26.** {12.5, 19.3, 25.4, 61.5, 78.9, 2.6}

27. {3.4, 6.5, 8.3, 8.2, 5.5}   **28.** {234, 654, 789, 123, 563}

An exercise research study has five groups. Each group has at most six members in it. The body weight of each member of the group is in the table below. Find the mean and standard deviation for each group.

29.	**Group A**	125 lb	189 lb	202 lb	149 lb	156 lb	208 lb
30.	**Group B**	187 lb	241 lb	146 lb	174 lb		
31.	**Group C**	210 lb	112 lb	168 lb	187 lb	176 lb	
32.	**Group D**	155 lb	178 lb	213 lb	224 lb	192 lb	164 lb
33.	**Group E**	198 lb	207 lb	167 lb	182 lb		

Name _____ Class _____ Date _____

Practice 10-1
Example Exercises

Example 1

Write each polynomial in standard form. Then name each polynomial by
its degree and the number of its terms.

1. $x + 2x^2$ **2.** $3n^2 + 6 - 5n$ **3.** $8 - 2x^3 + 4x^2$

4. $2 + x^2 + 4x$ **5.** $6 + 7x$ **6.** $7 - 8a^2 + 6a^3$

7. $y^3 - 4y + 6 - y^2$ **8.** $x^2 + 4 - x$ **9.** $x^2 + x^4$

10. $3m - 7m^3 + 3$ **11.** $5a + 7a^4$ **12.** $6x^3 + x + x^2$

13. $6 + x^2 - 4x$ **14.** $x^3 - 8$ **15.** $y^2 - 7y - 3y^3$

16. $x - 6x^2$ **17.** $6x + 8x^3 - 2x^2$ **18.** $12x^2 - 6x^3 + 7 + x$

Example 2

Find each sum. Write your answer in standard form.

19. $(3x^2 - 4) + (5x^2 + 8)$ **20.** $(5x^3 + 6x^2) + (x^3 - 12x^2)$

21. $(4y^2 - 3y + 8) + (6y^2 + 6y - 9)$ **22.** $(a^3 + 8a^2 + 6a) + (8a^3 + 2a^2 - 6a)$

23. $(7x^2 + 8x + 1) + (x^2 - 5x - 3)$ **24.** $(9x^2 + 3x + 4) + (2x^2 + 2x + 1)$

25. $(3a + 4a^3 - 8) + (a^2 + 2a - 7)$ **26.** $(2x^3 + 6x - 7) + (3x^2 - 9x - 5)$

27. $(3x - 7x^2 - 3) + (x^2 + 5x)$ **28.** $(3y^3 + 8y^2 - 3) + (2y - 5y^2)$

29. $(5s^2 + 7s - 11) + (s + 4 - 5s^2)$ **30.** $(6 - 8x) + (7x^3 + 2x + 15)$

31. $(4x^3 + 2x - 3x^2 + 1) + (2x^3 - 5x + 2)$ **32.** $(3n^4 - 2n^2 + 6) + (2n - 3n^4 - 6)$

33. $(3x + 4x^2 - 8) + (x^3 - 6x + 9x^2)$ **34.** $(9 - 5x^3 - 6x^2) + (x + 6x^3 - 4)$

Example 3

Find each difference. Write your answer in standard form.

35. $(5x^2 + 4x + 8) - (3x^2 + x + 3)$ **36.** $(8x^2 - 4x + 1) - (3x^2 + 6x - 4)$

37. $(7y^3 + 2y - 7) - (2y^3 + y + 3)$ **38.** $(n^3 + n^2 + n) - (2n^3 + 3n^2 - 2n)$

39. $(x^3 + 3x^2 - 4x) - (2x^2 + 3x + 1)$ **40.** $(4x^2 - 7x + 8) - (2x^3 + 8x - 5)$

41. $(3c^2 + 4c - 6) - (3c + 8)$ **42.** $(2y^3 - 7y + 10) - (y^3 + 6y - 7)$

43. $(5y^2 - 9y + 11) - (4y + 8 - y^2)$ **44.** $(7c^2 - 10c + 1) - (9 + 2c^2 - 8c)$

45. $(2x - 10x^2 + 7) - (x^2 + 8)$ **46.** $(3x^3 - 10x + 8) - (2x^2 + 7x + 8)$

47. $(x^2 + 7x^3) - (3x^2 + 4x - 12)$ **48.** $(x + 3x^2 - 4x^3 + 6) - (x^3 + 3x^2 + x)$

49. $(x^2 - 3 + 7x) - (2x^3 + 3x^2 - 7x)$ **50.** $(6x^3 - 9 + 8x) - (2x^2 + 6x - 11)$

Algebra Chapter 10   Adding and Subtracting Polynomials   **157**

Practice 10-1

· ·

Mixed Exercises

Write each polynomial in standard form. Then name each polynomial by its degree and the number of its terms.

1. $4y^3 - 4y^2 + 3 - y$ **2.** $x^2 + x^4 - 6$ **3.** $x + 2$

4. $2m^2 - 7m^3 + 3m$ **5.** $4 - x + 2x^2$ **6.** $7x^3 + 2x^2$

7. $n^2 - 5n$ **8.** $6 + 7x^2$ **9.** $3a^2 + a^3 - 4a + 3$

10. $5 + 3x$ **11.** $7 - 8a^2 + 6a$ **12.** $5x + 4 - x^2$

13. $2 + 4x^2 - x^3$ **14.** $4x^3 - 2x^2$ **15.** $y^2 - 7 - 3y$

16. $x - 6x^2 - 3$ **17.** $v^3 - v + 2v^2$ **18.** $8d + 3d^2$

Find each sum or difference. Write your answer in standard form.

19. $(3x^2 - 5x) - (x^2 + 4x + 3)$ **20.** $(2x^3 - 4x^2 + 3) + (x^3 - 3x^2 + 1)$

21. $(3y^3 - 11y + 3) - (5y^3 + y^2 + 2)$ **22.** $(3x^2 + 2x^3) - (3x^2 + 7x - 1)$

23. $(2a^3 + 3a^2 + 7a) + (a^3 + a^2 - 2a)$ **24.** $(8y^3 - y + 7) - (6y^3 + 3y - 3)$

25. $(x^2 - 6) + (5x^2 + x - 3)$ **26.** $(5n^2 - 7) - (2n^2 + n - 3)$

27. $(5n^3 + 2n^2 + 2) - (n^3 + 3n^2 - 2)$ **28.** $(3y^2 - 7y + 3) - (5y + 3 - 4y^2)$

29. $(2x^2 + 9x - 17) + (x^2 - 6x - 3)$ **30.** $(3 - x^3 - 5x^2) + (x + 2x^3 - 3)$

31. $(3x + x^2 - x^3) - (x^3 + 2x^2 + 5x)$ **32.** $(d^2 + 8 - 5d) - (5d^2 + d - 2d^3 + 3)$

33. $(3x^3 + 7x^2) + (x^2 - 2x^3)$ **34.** $(6c^2 + 5c - 3) - (3c^2 + 8c)$

35. $(3y^2 - 5y - 7) + (y^2 - 6y + 7)$ **36.** $(3c^2 - 8c + 4) - (7 + c^2 - 8c)$

37. $(4x^2 + 13x + 9) + (12x^2 + x + 6)$ **38.** $(2x - 13x^2 + 3) - (2x^2 + 8x)$

39. $(7x - 4x^2 + 11) + (7x^2 + 5)$ **40.** $(4x + 7x^3 - 9x^2) + (3 - 2x^2 - 5x)$

41. $(y^3 + y^2 - 2) + (y - 6y^2)$ **42.** $(x^2 - 8x - 3) - (x^3 + 8x^2 - 8)$

43. $(3x^2 - 2x + 9) - (x^2 - x + 7)$ **44.** $(2x^2 - 6x + 3) - (2x + 4x^2 + 2)$

45. $(2x^2 - 2x^3 - 7) + (9x^2 + 2 + x)$ **46.** $(3a^2 + a^3 - 1) + (2a^2 + 3a + 1)$

47. $(2x^2 + 3 - x) - (2 + 2x^2 - 5x)$ **48.** $(n^4 - 2n - 1) + (5n - n^4 + 5)$

49. $(x^3 + 3x) - (x^2 + 6 - 4x)$ **50.** $(7s^2 + 4s + 2) + (3s + 2 - s^2)$

51. $(6x^2 - 3x + 9) - (x^2 + 3x - 5)$ **52.** $(3x^3 - x^2 + 4) + (2x^3 - 3x + 9)$

53. $(y^3 + 3y - 1) - (y^3 + 3y + 5)$ **54.** $(3 + 5x^3 + 2x) - (x + 2x^2 + 4x^3)$

55. $(x^2 + 15x + 13) + (3x^2 - 15x + 7)$ **56.** $(7 - 8x^2) + (x^3 - x + 5)$

57. $(2x + 3) - (x - 4) + (x + 2)$ **58.** $(x^2 + 4) - (x - 4) + (x^2 - 2x)$

Practice 10-2
Example Exercises

Example 1

Find each product.

1. $3(x + 8)$
2. $-3(x + 6)$
3. $2(x^2 + 6x - 2)$
4. $x(x + 4)$
5. $3x(x^2 + 7)$
6. $2x^2(x + 3)$
7. $2x(2x - 7)$
8. $5x(x^2 - 2x + 1)$
9. $-3x(x - 3)$
10. $-2d(d^2 + d - 3)$
11. $y(y + 1) + 3(y + 4)$
12. $6x(x - 1) - 4(x^2 - x)$

Example 2

Use tiles to factor each polynomial.

13. $3x^2 - 6x$
14. $4n^2 + 8n$
15. $5x^2 - 15x$
16. $2h^2 + 4h$
17. $3x^2 - 9x$
18. $4x^2 - 4x$

Example 3

Find the greatest common factor (GCF) for each polynomial.

19. $6x - 15$
20. $7x - 28$
21. $x^2 + 6x$
22. $n^4 + 6n^3$
23. $3z^2 + 6z - 9$
24. $4x^2 + 8x - 2$
25. $4x^3 + 12x^2$
26. $9x^3 - 6x$
27. $2f^3 + 6f^2 + 8f^2$

Example 4

Use the GCF to factor each expression.

28. $3x + 6$
29. $14d - 7$
30. $x^3 - 4x$
31. $3h^2 - 18h$
32. $2x^2 + 4x - 10$
33. $w^3 + 6w^2 - 5w$
34. $3x^3 + 12x^2 + 6x$
35. $4x^4 - 12x^3 + 6x^2$
36. $3x^4 + 27x^2$
37. $5z^4 - 25z^3 - 20z$
38. $4x^3 + 12x^4$
39. $6m^4 - 9m^3 + 18m^2$

Example 5

40. A triangle is placed inside of a circle of radius $3x$. The base of the triangle is $2x$ and the height is x.

   a. Find the area of the circle not covered by the triangle.

   b. Find the area when $x = 4$ in.

Practice 10-2

• •

Mixed Exercises

Find each product.

1. $4(a - 3)$ **2.** $-5(x - 2)$ **3.** $-3x^2(x^2 + 3x)$

4. $4x^3(x - 3)$ **5.** $-5x^2(x^2 + 2x + 1)$ **6.** $3x(x^2 - 5x - 3)$

7. $-x^2(-2x^2 + 3x - 2)$ **8.** $4d^2(d^2 - 3d - 7)$ **9.** $5m^3(m + 6)$

10. $a^2(2a + 4)$ **11.** $4(x^2 - 3) + x(x + 1)$ **12.** $4x(5x - 6)$

Find the greatest common factor (GCF) for each polynomial.

13. $8x - 4$ **14.** $15x + 45x^2$ **15.** $x^2 + 3x$

16. $4c^3 - 8c^2 + 8$ **17.** $12x - 36$ **18.** $12n^3 + 4n^2$

19. $14x^3 + 7x^2$ **20.** $8x^3 - 12x$ **21.** $9 - 27x^3$

22. $25x^3 - 15x^2$ **23.** $11x^2 - 33x$ **24.** $4n^4 + 6n^3 - 8n^2$

25. $8d^3 + 4d^2 + 12d$ **26.** $6x^2 + 12x - 21$ **27.** $8g^2 + 16g - 8$

Factor each expression.

28. $8x + 10$ **29.** $12n^3 - 8n$ **30.** $14d - 2$

31. $6h^2 - 8h$ **32.** $3z^4 - 15z^3 - 9z^2$ **33.** $3y^3 - 8y^2 - 9y$

34. $x^3 - 5x^2$ **35.** $8x^3 - 12x^2 + 4x$ **36.** $7x^3 + 21x^4$

37. $6a^3 - 12a^2 + 14a$ **38.** $6x^4 + 12x^2$ **39.** $3n^4 - 6n^2 + 9n$

40. $2w^3 + 6w^2 - 4w$ **41.** $12c^3 - 30c^2$ **42.** $2x^2 + 8x - 14$

43. $4x^3 + 12x^2 + 16x$ **44.** $16m^3 - 8m^2 + 12m$ **45.** $4a^3 - 20a^2 - 8a$

46. $18c^4 - 9c^2 + 7c$ **47.** $6y^4 + 9y^3 - 27y^2$ **48.** $6c^2 - 3c$

49. A circular pond will be placed on a square piece of land. The length of a side of the square is $2x$. The radius of the pond is x. The part of the square not covered by the pond will be planted with flowers. What is the area of the square that will be planted with flowers?

50. A square poster of length $3x$ is to have a square painting centered on it. The length of the painting is $2x$. The area of the poster not covered by the painting will be painted black.

    a. What is the area of the poster that will be painted black?

    b. Find the area when $x = 12$ in.

51. The formula for the surface area of a sphere is $A = 4\pi r^2$. A square sticker of side x is placed on a ball of radius x.

    a. What is the area of the sphere not covered by the sticker?

    b. Find the area not covered when $x = 5$ in.

Practice 10-3

Example Exercises

Example 1

Use tiles or the distributive property to find each product.

1. $(x + 1)(x + 3)$ **2.** $(a - 2)(a + 6)$ **3.** $(a - 8)(a + 2)$

4. $(d + 3)(d - 2)$ **5.** $(2x - 1)(x - 4)$ **6.** $(3p - 7)(2p + 1)$

7. $(5x + 2)(x + 3)$ **8.** $(3s - 2)(s - 3)$ **9.** $(2x + 6)(x - 8)$

10. $(3x + 4)(2x - 1)$ **11.** $(2x - 3)(5x - 2)$ **12.** $(3w + 7)(2w - 5)$

Example 2

Find each product using FOIL.

13. $(x + 4)(x + 2)$ **14.** $(b + 6)(b - 1)$ **15.** $(x - 3)(x + 2)$

16. $(n - 6)(n + 6)$ **17.** $(2x - 3)(x + 2)$ **18.** $(r + 3)(4r - 1)$

19. $(2x - 3)(2x - 1)$ **20.** $(3k + 3)(2k - 2)$ **21.** $(5x - 4)(2x + 3)$

22. $(3x + 1)(3x + 2)$ **23.** $(8x - 7)(x + 4)$ **24.** $(3y + 8)(5y + 6)$

Example 3

25. The Santori family built a rectangular swimming pool in their backyard. The length of the pool is 4 times the width. A cement deck 6 ft wide is around the pool. Write an expression for the area of the pool and deck.

26. Suppose you deposit $1200 in a savings account that has an annual interest rate r. At the end of 2 yr the amount of money in your account would be $1200(1 + r)(1 + r)$.

  a. Simplify the expression and write your answer in standard form.

  b. Find the amount of money in the account at the end of 2 yr if the interest rate is 5%.

Example 4

Find each product.

27. $(a^2 + 2a + 1)(a + 1)$ **28.** $(x^2 + 3x - 2)(x + 3)$ **29.** $(x - 2)(x^2 - 5x + 4)$

30. $(x - 3)(x^2 + 3x + 9)$ **31.** $(m^2 - 6m + 4)(2m + 1)$ **32.** $(3g - 2)(g^2 + 5g - 6)$

33. $(2n - 7)(n^2 - n + 3)$ **34.** $(3x + 2)(2x^2 - x + 3)$ **35.** $(3x^2 + 6x - 1)(3x - 1)$

36. $(x + 5)(2x^2 - 5x - 4)$ **37.** $(4b - 1)(3b^2 - 2b - 5)$ **38.** $(4x^2 - 7x + 3)(5x - 2)$

© Prentice-Hall, Inc.

Practice 10-3
• •
Mixed Exercises

Find each product.

1. $(x + 3)(2x - 5)$

2. $(x^2 + x - 1)(x + 1)$

3. $(3w + 4)(2w - 1)$

4. $(x + 5)(x + 4)$

5. $(2b - 1)(b^2 - 3b + 4)$

6. $(a - 11)(a + 5)$

7. $(2g - 3)(2g^2 + g - 4)$

8. $(3s - 4)(s - 5)$

9. $(4x + 3)(x - 7)$

10. $(x + 6)(x^2 - 4x + 3)$

11. $(5x - 3)(4x + 2)$

12. $(3y + 7)(4y + 5)$

13. $(3x + 7)(x + 5)$

14. $(5x - 2)(x + 3)$

15. $(3m^2 - 7m + 8)(m - 2)$

16. $(a - 6)(a + 8)$

17. $(x + 2)(2x^2 - 3x + 2)$

18. $(a^2 + a + 1)(a - 1)$

19. $(x - 2)(x^2 + 4x + 4)$

20. $(2r + 1)(3r - 1)$

21. $(k + 4)(3k - 4)$

22. $(2n - 3)(n^2 - 2n + 5)$

23. $(p - 4)(2p + 3)$

24. $(3x + 1)(4x^2 - 2x + 1)$

25. $(2x^2 - 5x + 2)(4x - 3)$

26. $(x + 7)(x + 5)$

27. $(6x - 11)(x + 2)$

28. $(2x + 1)(4x + 3)$

29. $(3x + 4)(3x - 4)$

30. $(6x - 5)(3x + 1)$

31. $(n - 7)(n + 4)$

32. $(3x - 1)(2x + 1)$

33. $(d + 9)(d - 11)$

34. $(2x^2 + 5x - 3)(2x + 1)$

35. $(b + 8)(2b - 5)$

36. $(2x - 5)(x + 4)$

37. $(3x + 5)(5x - 7)$

38. $(x - 5)(2x^2 - 7x - 2)$

39. $(2x^2 - 9x + 11)(2x + 1)$

40. $(2x^2 + 5x - 4)(2x + 7)$

41. $(x^2 + 6x + 11)(3x + 5)$

42. $(5x + 7)(7x + 3)$

43. $(4x - 7)(2x - 5)$

44. $(x - 9)(3x + 5)$

45. $(2x - 1)(x^2 - 7x + 1)$

46. The width of a rectangular painting is 3 in. more than twice the height. A frame that is 2.5 in. wide goes around the painting.
   a. Write an expression for the area of the painting and frame.
   b. Find the area when the height of the painting is 12 in.
   c. Find the area when the height of the painting is 15 in.

47. The Robertsons put a rectangular pool in their backyard with a stone walkway around it. The total length of the pool and walkway is 3 times the total width. The walkway is 2 ft wide.
   a. Write an expression for the area of the pool.
   b. Find the area of the pool when the total width is 10 ft.
   c. Find the area of the pool when the total width is 9 ft.

48. Suppose you deposit $1500 in a savings account that has an annual interest rate r. At the end of 3 yr the amount of money in your account would be $1500(1 + 2r + r^2)(1 + r)$.
   a. Simplify the expression and write your answer in standard form.
   b. Find the amount of money in the account at the end of three years if the interest rate is 4%.
   c. Find the amount of money in the account at the end of 3 yr if the interest rate is 6%.

Practice 10-4

Example Exercises

Example 1

Use tiles to factor each expression.

1. $x^2 + 3x + 2$ **2.** $x^2 + 6x + 8$ **3.** $x^2 + 4x - 5$

4. $x^2 + 5x - 6$ **5.** $x^2 - 5x + 6$ **6.** $x^2 - 7x - 8$

Example 2

Use FOIL and *Guess and Test* to factor each expression.

7. $n^2 + 8n + 16$ **8.** $x^2 + 9x + 20$ **9.** $x^2 - 9x + 14$

10. $x^2 + 12x + 32$ **11.** $n^2 - 10n + 9$ **12.** $x^2 + 8x + 15$

13. $x^2 - 9x + 20$ **14.** $x^2 - 8x + 16$ **15.** $x^2 - 10x + 24$

16. $x^2 - 5x + 6$ **17.** $x^2 + 7x + 12$ **18.** $n^2 - 10n + 21$

19. $x^2 + 14x + 45$ **20.** $x^2 - 18x + 17$ **21.** $x^2 - 11x + 28$

22. $x^2 + 13x + 22$ **23.** $x^2 + 16x + 28$ **24.** $n^2 - 16n + 48$

Example 3

Use FOIL and *Guess and Test* to factor each expression.

25. $x^2 + 3x - 4$ **26.** $n^2 + n - 20$ **27.** $x^2 + 2x - 15$

28. $x^2 - 6x - 27$ **29.** $x^2 + x - 6$ **30.** $n^2 - n - 42$

31. $x^2 - 16x - 36$ **32.** $x^2 + 4x - 21$ **33.** $x^2 + 6x - 27$

34. $x^2 - 3x - 28$ **35.** $x^2 + 2x - 63$ **36.** $x^2 - 4x - 21$

37. $x^2 + 3x - 10$ **38.** $x^2 - 2x - 8$ **39.** $n^2 - n - 56$

40. $x^2 - 3x - 18$ **41.** $x^2 - 11x - 60$ **42.** $x^2 + 3x - 40$

Example 4

Factor each expression.

43. $3x^2 + 8x + 5$ **44.** $2x^2 + 5x - 3$ **45.** $3x^2 + 8x + 4$

46. $3x^2 - 10x + 8$ **47.** $2x^2 - 5x + 3$ **48.** $3x^2 - x - 4$

49. $3x^2 + 10x + 3$ **50.** $2x^2 - x - 21$ **51.** $5x^2 - 11x + 2$

52. $4x^2 + 4x - 15$ **53.** $6x^2 - 19x + 15$ **54.** $3x^2 + 7x + 2$

55. $2x^2 - x - 15$ **56.** $3x^2 - 7x - 6$ **57.** $2x^2 + x - 6$

58. $2x^2 - 5x - 12$ **59.** $6x^2 - 7x - 5$ **60.** $4x^2 + 7x + 3$

Practice 10-4

Mixed Exercises

Use tiles to factor each expression.

1. $2x^2 + 3x + 1$
2. $d^2 + 8d + 7$
3. $y^2 + 6y + 8$
4. $b^2 - 2b - 3$
5. $s^2 - 4s - 5$
6. $2a^2 + 5a + 3$
7. $2n^2 + n - 6$
8. $3x^2 - x - 4$
9. $a^2 + 3a + 2$
10. $p^2 - 8p + 7$
11. $d^2 + 6d + 5$
12. $n^2 + n - 6$

Factor each expression.

13. $x^2 + 5x - 14$
14. $b^2 + 9b + 14$
15. $2y^2 - 9y - 5$
16. $a^2 + 7a + 12$
17. $5x^2 - 2x - 7$
18. $7n^2 + 9n + 2$
19. $x^2 - 8x + 12$
20. $x^2 + 7x - 18$
21. $n^2 - 7n + 10$
22. $s^2 - 5s - 14$
23. $x^2 - 9x + 8$
24. $x^2 - 2x - 24$
25. $3c^2 - 17c - 6$
26. $3x^2 + 8x + 4$
27. $x^2 + 7x + 10$
28. $6x^2 - 7x - 10$
29. $m^2 - 4m - 21$
30. $3x^2 - 10x + 8$
31. $x^2 - 5x - 24$
32. $b^2 - 4b - 60$
33. $3a^2 - 16a - 12$
34. $m^2 + 7m + 10$
35. $n^2 - n - 72$
36. $k^2 - 6k + 5$
37. $5x^2 + 2x - 3$
38. $3a^2 + 7a + 2$
39. $3b^2 + 7b + 2$
40. $d^2 - 4d + 3$
41. $b^2 - 26b + 48$
42. $n^2 - 15n + 26$
43. $n^2 - n - 6$
44. $z^2 - 14z + 49$
45. $7r^2 - 10r + 3$
46. $3x^2 + 8x + 5$
47. $2b^2 + 9b + 4$
48. $t^2 - 6t - 27$
49. $b^2 + 4b - 12$
50. $d^2 + 11d + 18$
51. $5x^2 - 7x + 2$
52. $x^2 - 13x + 42$
53. $5x^2 - 22x + 8$
54. $4n^2 + 17n - 15$
55. $3a^2 - 5a - 2$
56. $h^2 + 7h - 18$
57. $x^2 + 3x - 10$
58. $p^2 - 12p - 28$
59. $y^2 + 6y - 55$
60. $b^2 + 3b - 4$
61. $5a^2 - 33a - 14$
62. $3b^2 - 2b - 8$
63. $3x^2 + 7x - 6$
64. $r^2 + 2r - 35$
65. $c^2 - 3c - 10$
66. $x^2 + 8x + 15$
67. $2x^2 + 13x - 24$
68. $n^2 - 23n + 60$
69. $c^2 + 3c - 10$
70. $4r^2 - 11r - 3$
71. $2m^2 + 9m + 7$
72. $5x^2 - 3x - 2$
73. $y^2 - 16y + 64$
74. $n^2 + 10n + 25$
75. $r^2 - 14r - 51$
76. $7a^2 + 19a + 10$
77. $x^2 - x - 42$
78. $n^2 - 2n - 63$
79. $a^2 + 7a + 6$
80. $7a^2 - 30a + 8$
81. $3m^2 + 17m + 10$
82. $n^2 + 16n - 36$
83. $n^2 - 4n - 21$
84. $y^2 + 16y - 17$

Practice 10-5

•••

Example Exercises

Example 1

Factor each expression.

1. $x^2 - 4$

2. $a^2 - 16$

3. $x^2 - 49$

4. $f^2 - 81$

5. $x^2 - 25$

6. $h^2 - 1$

7. $w^2 - 144$

8. $x^2 - 225$

9. $x^2 - 196$

10. $y^2 - 625$

11. $x^2 - 400$

12. $b^2 - 100$

Example 2

Factor each expression.

13. $4x^2 - 9$

14. $9x^2 - 25$

15. $16n^2 - 1$

16. $25m^2 - 4$

17. $49x^2 - 144$

18. $25a^2 - 64$

19. $16x^2 - 81$

20. $64n^2 - 169$

21. $100x^2 - 49$

Example 3

Factor each expression.

22. $x^2 + 8x + 16$

23. $a^2 - 10a + 25$

24. $x^2 + 14x + 49$

25. $f^2 + 16f + 64$

26. $x^2 + 12x + 36$

27. $x^2 - 18x + 81$

28. $x^2 - 22x + 121$

29. $x^2 + 24x + 144$

30. $y^2 - 20y + 100$

Example 4

Factor each expression.

31. $4x^2 + 4x + 1$

32. $9x^2 - 6x + 1$

33. $4x^2 - 12x + 9$

34. $9x^2 + 24x + 16$

35. $4x^2 + 20x + 25$

36. $25c^2 - 40c + 16$

37. $49x^2 - 28x + 4$

38. $16x^2 - 24x + 9$

39. $64x^2 + 112x + 49$

Example 5

Factor each expression.

40. $2d^2 - 18$

41. $3x^2 - 12$

42. $12w^2 - 27$

43. $2x^2 + 20x + 50$

44. $3x^2 - 12x + 12$

45. $4h^3 - 36h$

46. $2x^2 + 4x + 2$

47. $4x^2 + 24x + 36$

48. $n^3 - 8n^2 + 16n$

•••

Practice 10-5

· ·

Mixed Exercises

Factor each expression.

1. $x^2 - 9$
2. $4m^2 - 1$
3. $a^2 + 2a + 1$

4. $4x^2 + 12x + 9$
5. $x^2 - 22x + 121$
6. $n^2 - 4$

7. $9x^2 - 4$
8. $16c^2 - 49$
9. $9x^2 - 30x + 25$

10. $4x^2 - 20x + 25$
11. $2a^2 - 18$
12. $x^2 - 24x + 144$

13. $3n^2 - 3$
14. $9h^2 + 60h + 100$
15. $9d^2 - 49$

16. $81a^2 - 400$
17. $r^2 - 36$
18. $3a^2 - 48$

19. $b^2 + 4b + 4$
20. $10x^2 - 90$
21. $25x^2 - 64$

22. $12w^2 - 27$
23. $g^3 - 25g$
24. $x^2 + 6x + 9$

25. $a^2 - 25$
26. $36s^2 - 225$
27. $4b^2 + 44b + 121$

28. $x^2 - 16x + 64$
29. $x^2 - 2x + 1$
30. $d^2 - 49$

31. $x^3 - 36x$
32. $9y^2 - 289$
33. $x^2 - 30x + 225$

34. $100a^2 - 9$
35. $2x^2 + 4x + 2$
36. $5n^3 - 20n$

37. $9n^2 + 12n + 4$
38. $d^2 - 169$
39. $4a^2 - 81$

40. $x^2 - 121$
41. $5x^2 + 40x + 80$
42. $16n^2 + 56n + 49$

43. $3n^2 - 30n + 75$
44. $a^2 + 26a + 169$
45. $25x^2 - 144$

46. $9d^2 - 64$
47. $n^2 - 28n + 196$
48. $49a^2 - 14a + 1$

49. $y^2 + 8y + 16$
50. $y^2 - 400$
51. $x^2 - 10x + 25$

52. $4x^2 - 60x + 225$
53. $3x^2 - 363$
54. $y^2 - 81$

55. $a^2 - 100$
56. $256a^2 - 1$
57. $n^2 + 34n + 289$

58. $2d^3 - 50d$
59. $y^2 + 22y + 121$
60. $144x^2 - 25$

61. $4x^2 - 169$
62. $x^2 - 12x + 36$
63. $64r^2 + 80r + 25$

64. $50m^3 - 32m$
65. $b^2 - 225$
66. $x^2 - 18x + 81$

67. $b^2 - 64$
68. $16x^2 - 72x + 81$
69. $b^2 - 256$

70. $x^2 + 24x + 144$
71. $225x^2 - 16$
72. $2x^3 + 40x^2 + 200x$

73. $4r^2 - 25$
74. $16x^2 + 8x + 1$
75. $b^2 - 14b + 49$

76. $x^2 + 30x + 225$
77. $m^2 - 28m + 196$
78. $9r^2 - 256$

79. $b^2 + 20b + 100$
80. $m^2 - 16$
81. $4x^2 - 32x + 64$

82. $x^2 - 196$
83. $8x^3 - 32x$
84. $25x^2 - 30x + 9$

85. $8m^2 - 16m + 8$
86. $9x^2 - 400$
87. $m^2 - 144$

Class

Date

Name

Practice 10-6

Example Exercises

Example 1

Solve each equation.

1. $(x + 1)(x + 3) = 0$
2. $(a + 4)(a + 8) = 0$
3. $(x + 6)(x + 2) = 0$
4. $(x - 4)(x + 4) = 0$
5. $(x - 7)(x - 1) = 0$
6. $(x - 3)(x - 10) = 0$
7. $(x + 5)(x - 3) = 0$
8. $(x - 2)(x + 9) = 0$
9. $(b - 12)(b + 12) = 0$
10. $(2n + 3)(n - 4) = 0$
11. $(x + 7)(4x - 5) = 0$
12. $(2x + 7)(2x - 7) = 0$
13. $(3x - 7)(2x + 1) = 0$
14. $(8y - 3)(4y + 1) = 0$
15. $(5x + 6)(4x + 5) = 0$
16. $(x + 8)(6x - 7) = 0$
17. $(5x - 9)(x + 7) = 0$
18. $(6m - 11)(3m + 7) = 0$

Example 2

Solve each equation by factoring.

19. $x^2 + 5x + 6 = 0$
20. $b^2 - 7b - 18 = 0$
21. $r^2 - 4 = 0$
22. $x^2 + 8x - 20 = 0$
23. $y^2 + 14y + 13 = 0$
24. $s^2 - 3s - 10 = 0$
25. $x^2 + 7x = 8$
26. $x^2 = 25$
27. $h^2 + 10h = -21$
28. $2t^2 + 8t - 64 = 0$
29. $3a^2 - 36a + 81 = 0$
30. $5x^2 - 45 = 0$
31. $2a^2 - a - 21 = 0$
32. $3n^2 - 11n + 10 = 0$
33. $2x^2 - 7x - 9 = 0$
34. $2n^2 - 5n = 12$
35. $3m^2 - 5m = -2$
36. $5s^2 - 17s = -6$
37. $6m^2 = 13m + 28$
38. $4a^2 - 4a = 15$
39. $4r^2 = r + 3$

Example 3

40. A rectangular sheet of paper has area 55 in.^{2}. Its dimensions are $(x + 2)$ in. by $(x + 8)$ in. What are the dimensions of the sheet of paper?

41. Suppose you are building an aquarium of volume 2880 in.^{3}. The aquarium will be 12 in. high. The base will be a rectangle with the length 4 in. more than twice the width. Find the dimensions of the base.

42. Suppose you launch a model rocket with an upward starting velocity of v ft/s. You can use the equation $h = -16t^2 + vt$ to find the rocket's altitude h feet t seconds after launch. Suppose the upward starting velocity is 160 ft/s. When will the rocket hit the ground?

© Prentice-Hall, Inc.

Algebra Chapter 10

Solving Equations by Factoring

Practice 10-6
• ●
Mixed Exercises

Solve each equation.

1. $(x - 9)(x + 8) = 0$ **2.** $x^2 - 9x - 10 = 0$ **3.** $(c - 21)(c + 21) = 0$

4. $(x - 12)(5x - 13) = 0$ **5.** $2a^2 - 21a - 65 = 0$ **6.** $(x - 7)(x + 13) = 0$

7. $a^2 + 6a - 72 = 0$ **8.** $(2x - 3)(2x + 7) = 0$ **9.** $(4d - 10)(5d - 8) = 0$

10. $(n + 12)(n - 8) = 0$ **11.** $2s^2 - 13s - 24 = 0$ **12.** $x^2 + 5x - 150$

13. $3c^2 + 8c = 3$ **14.** $(6a - 1)(5a + 21) = 0$ **15.** $(c + 9)(c - 9) = 0$

16. $(x + 18)(x + 17) = 0$ **17.** $x^2 = 121$ **18.** $x^2 - 21x + 108 = 0$

19. $2d^2 + 3d = 54$ **20.** $(5n - 16)(n + 11) = 0$ **21.** $(n - 13)(n - 27) = 0$

22. $(x - 8)(x + 15) = 0$ **23.** $x^2 - 35x + 300 = 0$ **24.** $9x^2 - 4 = 0$

25. Suppose you are building a storage box of volume 4368 in.^{3}. The box will be 24 in. long. The height of the box will be 1 in. more than its width. Find the height and width of the box.

26. A banner is in the shape of a right triangle of area 63 in.^{2}. The height of the banner is 4 in. less than twice the width of the banner. Find the height and width of the banner.

27. A rectangular poster has an area of 190 in.^{2}. The height of the poster is 1 in. less than twice its width. Find the dimensions of the poster.

28. A diver is standing on a platform 24 ft above the pool. He jumps from the platform with an initial upward velocity of 8 ft/s. Use the formula $h = -16t^2 + vt + s$, where h is his height above the water, t is time, v is his starting upward velocity, and s is his starting height. How long will it take for him to hit the water?

Simplify each equation and write in standard form. Then solve the equation.

29. $(x + 11)(x - 10) = 0$ **30.** $m^2 - 169 = 0$ **31.** $2m^2 + 5m = 42$

32. $m^2 = 8m + 9$ **33.** $(2t - 5)(2t - 1) = 0$ **34.** $(b - 17)(b - 21) = 0$

35. $(3y - 1)(y + 6) = 0$ **36.** $2x^2 + 50 = 25x$ **37.** $(x + 6)(x + 7) = 0$

38. $x^2 - 26x + 168 = 0$ **39.** $m^2 + 13m = 30$ **40.** $(x + 14)(x - 3) = 0$

41. $4x^2 + 2x = 2$ **42.** $x^2 = 13x - 42$ **43.** $3t^2 = 75$

44. $(2b - 7)(2b + 13) = 0$ **45.** $(4t - 5)(t + 8) = 0$ **46.** $3x^2 - 5x + 2 = 0$

47. $t^2 + 23t = -132$ **48.** $5b^2 + 37b - 130 = 0$ **49.** $2b^2 + b = 28$

50. $(x - 8)(5x - 3) = 0$ **51.** $3x^2 - 21x = 54$ **52.** $2x^2 = 512$

53. $y^2 - 8y = 65$ **54.** $(y - 2)(5y - 9) = 0$ **55.** $(y - 4)(5y + 8) = 0$

© Prentice-Hall, Inc.

Name _____ Class _____ Date _____

Practice 10-7
Example Exercises

Example 1

Use the quadratic formula to solve each equation. Round to the nearest tenth.

1. $x^2 - 6x + 3 = 0$
2. $g^2 - 2g - 6 = 0$
3. $2x^2 + 4x - 1 = 0$
4. $4a^2 + 8a - 13 = 0$
5. $3a^2 + 10a + 4 = 0$
6. $5g^2 - g - 1 = 0$
7. $3y^2 - 6y + 12 = 20$
8. $6x^2 + 17x - 51 = 0$
9. $12x^2 - 3x = 31$
10. $6n^2 - 17n + 8 = 40$
11. $10n^2 - 32n - 7 = 20$
12. $15n^2 - 36n = 103$

13. A rectangular courtyard covers 20 ft². The courtyard is 3 ft longer than it is wide. Find the dimensions of the courtyard.

Example 2

Solve each equation by using square roots or factoring.

14. $9a^2 - 49 = 0$
15. $36h^2 = 1$
16. $5x^2 - 500 = 0$
17. $4x^2 = 36$
18. $100x^2 - 81 = 0$
19. $6g^2 - 96 = 0$
20. $12n^2 - 243 = 0$
21. $15k^2 - 60 = 0$
22. $20x^2 = 125$
23. $18m^2 = 200$
24. $9c^2 - 144 = 0$
25. $16t^2 - 100 = 0$

Example 3

Solve each equation by graphing. If there are no real solutions, write *no real solutions*.

26. $x^2 + x - 6 = 0$
27. $x^2 - x - 12 = 0$
28. $2d^2 - 3d + 2 = 0$
29. $4b^2 + 5b + 1 = 0$
30. $3s^2 + 7s + 3 = 0$
31. $6a^2 - 2a - 15 = 0$
32. $3x^2 + 5x - 12 = 0$
33. $m^2 + 10m + 12 = 0$
34. $3x^2 - 5x - 10 = 0$
35. $2f^2 - 7f + 11 = 0$
36. $x^2 + 9x - 8 = 0$
37. $y^2 - 3y + 4 = 0$

Example 4

Solve each equation by factoring.

38. $y^2 - 6y - 16 = 0$
39. $x^2 + 9x - 52 = 0$
40. $n^2 - 10n + 21 = 0$
41. $x^2 + 12x + 32 = 0$
42. $2p^2 + 11p - 21 = 0$
43. $2x^2 - 19x + 42 = 0$
44. $2d^2 - 11d - 90 = 0$
45. $3g^2 - 19g - 72 = 0$
46. $3m^2 - 42m + 120 = 0$
47. $5n^2 + 39n - 8 = 0$
48. $4x^2 + 54x + 110 = 0$
49. $6x^2 + 11x - 35 = 0$

Practice 10-7
• •
Mixed Exercises

Solve each quadratic equation by any method. If the equation has no real solutions write *no real solutions*. Round your answers to the nearest hundredth.

1. $x^2 + 8x + 5 = 0$ 2. $x^2 - 36 = 0$ 3. $d^2 - 4d - 96 = 0$

4. $a^2 - 3a - 154 = 0$ 5. $4p^2 - 12p - 91 = 0$ 6. $5m^2 + 9m = 126$

7. $r^2 - 35r + 70 = 0$ 8. $y^2 + 6y - 247 = 0$ 9. $x^2 + 12x - 40 = 0$

10. $4n^2 - 81 = 0$ 11. $x^2 + 13x + 30 = 0$ 12. $a^2 - a = 132$

13. $6w^2 - 23w + 7 = 0$ 14. $4x^2 + 33x = 27$ 15. $7s^2 - 7 = 0$

16. $x^2 + 5x - 90 = 0$ 17. $5b^2 - 20 = 0$ 18. $4x^2 - 3x + 6 = 0$

19. $6h^2 + 77h - 13 = 0$ 20. $5y^2 = 17y + 12$ 21. $g^2 - 15g = 54$

22. $27f^2 = 12$ 23. $4x^2 - 52x + 133 = 0$ 24. $x^2 + 36x + 60 = 0$

25. $a^2 - 2a - 360 = 0$ 26. $x^2 + 10x + 40 = 0$ 27. $t^2 - 10t = 39$

28. $4x^2 + 7x - 9 = 0$ 29. $2c^2 - 39c + 135 = 0$ 30. $4x^2 + 33x + 340 = 0$

31. $m^2 - 40m + 100 = 0$ 32. $8x^2 + 25x + 19 = 0$ 33. $36w^2 - 289 = 0$

34. $4d^2 + 29d - 60 = 0$ 35. $4z^2 + 43z + 108 = 0$ 36. $3x^2 - 19x + 40 = 0$

37. $14x^2 = 56$ 38. $32x^2 - 18 = 0$ 39. $r^2 + r - 650 = 0$

40. $2y^2 = 39y - 17$ 41. $5a^2 - 9a + 5 = 0$ 42. $x^2 = 9x + 120$

43. $8h^2 - 38h + 9 = 0$ 44. $20x^2 = 245$ 45. $9h^2 - 72h = -119$

46. $x^2 + 3x + 8 = 0$ 47. $6m^2 - 13m = 19$ 48. $9x^2 - 81 = 0$

49. $4s^2 + 8s = 221$ 50. $6p^2 + 25p - 119 = 0$ 51. $2s^2 - 59s + 17 = 0$

52. A rectangular painting has dimensions x and $x + 10$. The picture is in a frame 2 in. wide. The total area of the picture and frame is 900 in.^{2}. What are the dimensions of the painting?

53. A ball is thrown upward from a height of 15 ft with an initial upward velocity of 5 ft/s. Use the formula $h = -16t^2 + vt + s$ to find how long it will take for the ball to hit the ground.

54. Your community wants to put a square fountain in a park. Around the fountain will be a sidewalk that is 3.5 ft wide. The total area that the fountain and sidewalk can be is 700 ft^2. What are the dimensions of the fountain?

55. The Garys have a triangular pennant of area 420 in.^{2} flying from the flag pole in their yard. The height of the triangle is 10 in. less than 5 times the base of the triangle. What are the dimensions of the pennant?

© Prentice-Hall, Inc.

Practice 11-1
· ·
Example Exercises

Example 1

Each pair of points is from an inverse variation. Find the missing value.

1. $(4, 2)$ and $(1, a)$ **2.** $(12, 2)$ and $(8, b)$ **3.** $(6, 6)$ and $(c, 18)$

4. $(5, 15)$ and $(d, 25)$ **5.** $\left(\frac{3}{4}, 8\right)$ and $\left(\frac{1}{2}, w\right)$ **6.** $\left(\frac{2}{3}, \frac{1}{2}\right)$ and $\left(x, \frac{1}{3}\right)$

7. $(x, 10)$ and $(3, 5)$ **8.** $\left(\frac{3}{7}, z\right)$ and $\left(\frac{2}{3}, \frac{3}{2}\right)$ **9.** $(2.4, 0.6)$ and $(x, 1.6)$

10. $(8.6, 1.2)$ and $(n, 17.2)$ **11.** $(m, 6)$ and $(50, 60)$ **12.** $(4.8, p)$ and $(3.6, 6.4)$

13. $(12, 27)$ and $(18, b)$ **14.** $(2.7, 11.8)$ and $(x, 1.8)$ **15.** $\left(\frac{3}{5}, y\right)$ and $\left(\frac{2}{25}, 5\right)$

16. In an electric circuit, the current I varies inversely with the resistance R.

    a. If $I = 10$ amps when $R = 12$ ohms, find R when $I = 2$ amps.

    b. If $I = 3$ amps when $R = 100$ ohms, find I when $R = 20$ ohms.

    c. If $I = 0.5$ amps when $R = 510$ ohms, find R when $I = 1.5$ amps.

Example 2

Find the constant of variation k for each inverse variation.

17. $y = 11$ when $x = 3$ **18.** $g = 5$ when $h = 18$ **19.** $j = 12$ when $k = 6.5$

20. $n = \frac{3}{5}$ when $m = \frac{1}{3}$ **21.** $p = \frac{1}{2}$ when $d = \frac{3}{4}$ **22.** $y = 15$ when $x = \frac{3}{2}$

Tell whether the data in each table is a *direct variation*, or an *inverse variation*. Write an equation to model the data.

23.

x	2	4	5
y	14	28	35

24.

x	2	4	16
y	16	8	2

25.

x	2	3	5
y	15	10	6

26.

x	1	2	4
y	10	5	2.5

27.

x	4	8	10
y	10	20	25

28.

x	7	10	15
y	3.5	5	7.5

29.

x	4	8	16
y	1	0.5	0.25

30.

x	2	7	11
y	4.6	16.1	25.3

31.

x	30	20	10
y	0.5	0.75	1.5

Practice 11-1

•••

Mixed Exercises

Find the constant of variation k for each inverse variation.

1. $m = 9$ when $n = 6$ **2.** $w = 3.6$ when $x = 5$ **3.** $r = \frac{3}{4}$ when $t = \frac{2}{9}$

4. $x = 7$ when $y = 13$ **5.** $f = 8$ when $g = 9$ **6.** $m = 4.9$ when $n = 0.8$

7. $x = 11$ when $y = 44$ **8.** $y = 8$ when $x = 9.5$ **9.** $w = 12$ when $x = \frac{5}{6}$

Each pair of points is from an inverse variation. Find the missing value.

10. $(5, 8)$ and $(4, m)$ **11.** $(16, 5)$ and $(10, h)$ **12.** $(14, 8)$ and $(c, 7)$

13. $(3, 18)$ and $(a, 27)$ **14.** $(4, 28)$ and $(3, p)$ **15.** $(100, 25)$ and $(4, a)$

16. $(x, 7)$ and $(2, 14)$ **17.** $\left(\frac{2}{5}, \frac{3}{2}\right)$ and $\left(k, \frac{5}{2}\right)$ **18.** $(16, 3)$ and $(g, 24)$

19. $(2.4, 19.8)$ and $(h, 13.2)$ **20.** $(12.4, 6.6)$ and $(f, 8.8)$ **21.** $(3.2, k)$ and $(9.2, 0.8)$

22. $(18, 24)$ and $(72, v)$ **23.** $(17, 0.9)$ and $(5.1, x)$ **24.** $\left(\frac{3}{4}, y\right)$ and $\left(\frac{2}{3}, 18\right)$

Tell whether the data in each table is a *direct variation,* or an *inverse variation.* Write an equation to model the data.

25.
x	2	7	10
y	35	10	7

26.
x	3	6	24
y	16	8	2

27.
x	5	6	8
y	55	66	88

28.
x	2	8	16
y	9	36	72

29.
x	2	3	9
y	18	12	4

30.
x	2	6	10
y	4.2	12.6	21

31.
x	2	5	12
y	12.8	32	76.8

32.
x	1.2	1.5	2.4
y	5	4	2.5

33.
x	6	9	36
y	3	2	0.5

37. The volume V of a gas in a closed container varies inversely with pressure p, in atmospheres, that is applied to that gas.

   a. If $V = 20$ m³ when $p = 1$ atm, find V when $p = 4$ atm.

   b. If $V = 24$ m³ when $p = 3$ atm, find p when $V = 36$ m³.

   c. If $V = 48$ m³ when $p = 2$ atm, find V when $p = 5$ atm.

38. The time t to travel a fixed distance varies inversely with the rate r of travel.

   a. If $t = 3$ h and $r = 25$ mi/h, find t when $r = 50$ mi/h.

   b. If $t = 120$ s and $r = 40$ ft/s, find r when $t = 25$ s.

© Prentice-Hall, Inc.

Practice 11-2

• •

Example Exercises

Example 1

Evaluate each function for $x = -3$, $x = 1$, and $x = 3$.

1. $y = \frac{3}{x}$ 　　　　**2.** $y = \frac{6}{x + 1}$ 　　　　**3.** $y = \frac{x + 3}{x}$ 　　　　**4.** $y = \frac{2x}{3x + 3}$

5. $y = \frac{27}{x^2}$ 　　　　**6.** $y = \frac{3x}{x + 2}$ 　　　　**7.** $y = \frac{2x - 1}{x}$ 　　　　**8.** $y = \frac{36}{x^2}$

What value of x makes the denominator of each function equal to zero?

9. $y = \frac{4}{x}$ 　　　　**10.** $y = \frac{3}{x + 2}$ 　　　　**11.** $y = \frac{8}{x - 1}$ 　　　　**12.** $y = \frac{10x}{x + 6}$

13. $y = \frac{5}{2x + 4}$ 　　　**14.** $y = \frac{-7x}{3x - 9}$ 　　　**15.** $y = \frac{5}{2x + 1}$ 　　　**16.** $y = \frac{6x}{3x - 2}$

Graph each function. Include a dashed line for each asymptote.

17. $y = \frac{5}{x}$ 　　　　**18.** $y = \frac{3}{x + 2}$ 　　　　**19.** $y = \frac{2}{x - 3}$ 　　　　**20.** $y = \frac{3}{x} - 2$

21. $y = \frac{-5}{x - 1}$ 　　　**22.** $y = \frac{x}{x + 3}$ 　　　　**23.** $y = \frac{x - 1}{x + 1}$ 　　　**24.** $y = \frac{1}{x - 3} + 4$

Example 2

25. As you move farther away from a sound source the sound level

decreases. The function $I = \frac{120}{d^2}$ relates the sound level I to the

distance d in feet from the sound source.

   a. What is the sound level 2 ft from the sound source?

   b. What is the sound level 4 ft from the sound source?

   c. What is the sound level 10 ft from the sound source?

   d. What is the sound level 12 ft from the sound source?

26. Light intensity decreases as you move farther away from the source of

light. The function $I = \frac{800}{d^2}$ relates the light intensity I, in lumens, to

the distance d, in feet, from the light source.

   a. What is the light intensity 4 ft away from the light source?

   b. What is the light intensity 5 ft away from the light source?

   c. What is the light intensity 10 ft away from the light source?

   d. What is the light intensity 15 ft away from the light source?

Name _____ Class _____ Date _____

Practice 11-2
• •
Mixed Exercises

Evaluate each function for $x = -2$, $x = 2$, and $x = 4$.

1. $y = \dfrac{24}{x + 4}$ **2.** $y = \dfrac{8}{x}$ **3.** $y = \dfrac{4x}{2x + 2}$ **4.** $y = \dfrac{6x}{x + 1}$

5. $y = \dfrac{5x - 2}{x}$ **6.** $y = \dfrac{x + 4}{2x}$ **7.** $y = \dfrac{32}{x^2}$ **8.** $y = \dfrac{144}{x^2}$

9. In an electric circuit the resistance R, in ohms, increases when the current I, in amps, in the circuit increases. The function $R = \dfrac{1000}{I^2}$ relates the resistance to the current.
  a. What is the resistance when the current is 4 amps?
  b. What is the resistance when the current is 20 amps?
  c. What is the resistance when the current is 10 amps?

10. Light intensity decreases as you move farther away from the source of light. The function $I = \dfrac{12{,}000}{d^2}$ relates the light intensity I, in lumens, to the distance d, in feet, from the light source.
  a. What is the light intensity 2 ft away from the light source?
  b. What is the light intensity 8 ft away from the light source?
  c. What is the light intensity 25 ft away from the light source?

11. In a cylinder of constant volume, the height increases as the radius decreases. The function $h = \dfrac{360}{r^2}$ relates height of the cylinder to the radius of the cylinder.
  a. What is the height of the cylinder when the radius is 5 m?
  b. What is the height of the cylinder when the radius is 12 m?

What value of x makes the denominator of each function equal to zero?

12. $y = \dfrac{5}{2x - 8}$ **13.** $y = \dfrac{12}{x}$ **14.** $y = \dfrac{5}{x + 7}$ **15.** $y = \dfrac{5x}{4x - 10}$

16. $y = \dfrac{7x}{x + 3}$ **17.** $y = \dfrac{3}{x - 8}$ **18.** $y = \dfrac{6}{5x - 6}$ **19.** $y = \dfrac{9x}{3x + 5}$

Graph each function. Include a dashed line for each asymptote.

20. $y = \dfrac{2}{x}$ **21.** $y = \dfrac{2}{x - 1}$ **22.** $y = \dfrac{1}{x + 4}$ **23.** $y = \dfrac{2}{x} + 3$

24. $y = \dfrac{-2}{x + 6}$ **25.** $y = \dfrac{2x}{x - 6}$ **26.** $y = \dfrac{x + 3}{x - 2}$ **27.** $y = \dfrac{3}{x - 1} - 3$

© Prentice-Hall, Inc.

Practice 11-3
....
Example Exercises

Example 1

Simplify each expression and state any values restricted from the domain.

1. $\dfrac{8a^3}{36a^4}$

2. $\dfrac{12d^3}{20d}$

3. $\dfrac{16x^2}{24x^4}$

4. $\dfrac{18h^5}{27h^2}$

5. $\dfrac{4x + 6}{2}$

6. $\dfrac{3x - 9}{3x}$

7. $\dfrac{3n^2 + 6n}{n + 2}$

8. $\dfrac{6c - 9}{4c - 6}$

Example 2

9. Write and simplify the ratio $\dfrac{\text{surface area of cube}}{\text{volume of cube}}$. The formula for volume of a cube is s^3 and the formula for surface area of a cube is $6s^2$.

10. The ratio $\dfrac{\text{volume of rectangular solid}}{\text{area of rectangular base}}$ determines the height of a

rectangular solid. Find the height when the volume is $4a^3 + 4a^2$ and the area is $4a^2$.

Example 3

Find each product.

11. $\dfrac{9}{11} \cdot \dfrac{2}{3}$

12. $\dfrac{3x}{14x^2} \cdot \dfrac{7x^2}{15x}$

13. $\dfrac{8a^2}{3} \cdot \dfrac{9}{16a}$

14. $\dfrac{x + 2}{12} \cdot \dfrac{8}{x + 2}$

15. $\dfrac{x^3}{8} \cdot \dfrac{2}{x^2}$

16. $\dfrac{12n^2}{8n} \cdot \dfrac{12n}{6n^2}$

17. $\dfrac{3a^7}{5a^4} \cdot \dfrac{10a^5}{6a^5}$

18. $\dfrac{m - 2}{3(m + 1)} \cdot \dfrac{9(m + 1)}{m + 2}$

19. $\dfrac{x + 1}{6} \cdot \dfrac{3}{2x + 2}$

Example 4

Find each quotient.

20. $\dfrac{7}{8} \div \dfrac{3}{4}$

21. $\dfrac{5}{4} \div \left(-\dfrac{7}{9}\right)$

22. $\dfrac{9a}{14} \div \dfrac{3a^2}{7}$

23. $\dfrac{m^3}{8} \div \dfrac{m^2}{6}$

24. $\dfrac{x + 3}{3} \div \dfrac{x + 3}{6}$

25. $\dfrac{4b^3}{3} \div \dfrac{16b}{6}$

26. $\dfrac{10y^3}{9y} \div \dfrac{8y}{5y^2}$

27. $\dfrac{4s - 5}{6} \div \dfrac{8s - 10}{12}$

28. $\dfrac{3x}{x^2 - 4} \div \dfrac{x}{x + 2}$

....

Practice 11-3

Mixed Exercises

Simplify each expression and state any values restricted from the domain.

1. $\dfrac{6x^4}{18x^2}$ **2.** $\dfrac{15a^2}{25a^4}$ **3.** $\dfrac{32h^3}{48h^2}$ **4.** $\dfrac{12n^4}{21n^6}$

5. $\dfrac{3x-6}{6}$ **6.** $\dfrac{x^2-2x}{x}$ **7.** $\dfrac{4t^2-2t}{2t}$ **8.** $\dfrac{a^3-2a^2}{2a^2-4a}$

Find each product or quotient.

9. $\dfrac{5}{9} \cdot \dfrac{6}{15}$ **10.** $\dfrac{8}{3} \div \dfrac{16}{27}$ **11.** $\left(-\dfrac{3}{4}\right) \div \dfrac{16}{21}$

12. $\dfrac{2}{9} \div \left(-\dfrac{10}{3}\right)$ **13.** $\dfrac{18m}{4m^2} \div \dfrac{9m}{8}$ **14.** $\dfrac{8x}{12} \cdot \dfrac{4x}{6}$

15. $\dfrac{9}{15x} \cdot \dfrac{25x}{27}$ **16.** $\dfrac{12x^3}{25} \div \dfrac{16x}{5}$ **17.** $\dfrac{6x^3}{18x} \div \dfrac{9x^2}{10x^4}$

18. $\dfrac{4r^3}{10} \cdot \dfrac{25}{16r^2}$ **19.** $\dfrac{8n^2}{3} \div \dfrac{20n}{9}$ **20.** $\dfrac{14x^2}{5} \div 7x^4$

21. $\dfrac{4n^3}{11} \cdot \dfrac{33n}{36n^2}$ **22.** $\dfrac{24r^3}{35r^2} \div \dfrac{12r}{14r^3}$ **23.** $\dfrac{a^2-4}{3} \cdot \dfrac{9}{a+2}$

24. $\dfrac{4b-12}{5b^2} \cdot \dfrac{6b}{b-3}$ **25.** $\dfrac{2b}{5} \cdot \dfrac{10}{b^2}$ **26.** $\dfrac{2b}{b+3} \div \dfrac{b}{b+3}$

27. $\dfrac{5y^3}{7} \cdot \dfrac{14y}{30y^2}$ **28.** $\dfrac{4p+16}{5p} \div \dfrac{p+4}{15p^3}$ **29.** $\dfrac{3(h+2)}{h+3} \div \dfrac{h+2}{h+3}$

30. $\dfrac{a^3-a^2}{a^3} \cdot \dfrac{a^2}{a-1}$ **31.** $\dfrac{h^2+6h}{h+3} \cdot \dfrac{4h+12}{h+6}$ **32.** $\dfrac{n^2-1}{n+2} \cdot \dfrac{n^2-4}{n+1}$

33. Write and simplify the ratio $\dfrac{\text{perimeter of rectangle}}{\text{area of rectangle}}$. The perimeter of the rectangle is $10w$ and the area of the rectangle is $4w^2$.

34. The ratio $\dfrac{3 \cdot \text{volume of cone}}{\text{area of base}}$ determines the height of a cone. Find the height when the volume is $4r^3 + 2r^2$ and the area of the base is $6r^2$.

35. The ratio $\dfrac{2 \cdot \text{area of triangle}}{\text{height of triangle}}$ determines the length of the base of a triangle. Find the length of the base when the area is $3n^2 + 6n$ and the height is $2n + 4$.

36. The ratio $\dfrac{\text{volume of rectangular solid}}{\text{area of rectangular base}}$ determines the height of a rectangular solid. Find the height when the volume is $5s^3 + 10s^2$ and the area is $5s^2$.

Practice 11-4

Example Exercises

Example 1

Simplify.

1. $\dfrac{3}{x} + \dfrac{5}{x}$

2. $\dfrac{8}{x-5} + \dfrac{6}{x-5}$

3. $\dfrac{7}{h} - \dfrac{3}{h}$

4. $\dfrac{10}{2x-3} - \dfrac{8}{2x-3}$

5. $\dfrac{3a}{2a+5} + \dfrac{5a}{2a+5}$

6. $\dfrac{2b}{b+6} - \dfrac{4b}{b+6}$

7. $\dfrac{8n}{3n-7} - \dfrac{2n}{3n-7}$

8. $\dfrac{5y}{y+9} + \dfrac{8y}{y+9}$

Example 2

Find the LCD.

9. $\dfrac{1}{x}, \dfrac{1}{x^3}$

10. $\dfrac{1}{2}, \dfrac{5}{6x^4}$

11. $\dfrac{3}{4a^3}, \dfrac{1}{6a^6}$

12. $\dfrac{6}{5n^2}, \dfrac{9}{10n^3}$

13. $\dfrac{5}{8s^6}, \dfrac{4}{6s^8}$

Simplify.

14. $\dfrac{3}{2} + \dfrac{5}{4a}$

15. $\dfrac{8}{3x} - \dfrac{5}{6x}$

16. $\dfrac{5}{2b^4} - \dfrac{1}{3b^3}$

17. $\dfrac{8}{5n^2} + \dfrac{3}{5n}$

18. $\dfrac{7}{6x^3} + \dfrac{5}{8x^2}$

19. $\dfrac{5}{12g^2} - \dfrac{3}{10g}$

20. $\dfrac{1}{6a^3} + \dfrac{5}{9a^5}$

21. $\dfrac{3c}{4} - \dfrac{5c}{6}$

Example 3

Simplify.

22. $\dfrac{4}{x-2} + \dfrac{3}{x+1}$

23. $\dfrac{5}{n-1} + \dfrac{3}{n+5}$

24. $\dfrac{4a}{a+1} - \dfrac{2a}{a^2-1}$

25. $\dfrac{4}{b+1} + \dfrac{b}{b^2-1}$

26. $\dfrac{2}{x-4} - \dfrac{6}{x^3-16x}$

27. $\dfrac{i}{7i+14} + \dfrac{6}{3i+6}$

Example 4

28. For her daily exercise, Andrea jogs 1 mi and then walks 1 mi. Her walking rate is 60% of her jogging rate.

   a. Write and simplify an expression for the amount of time Andrea spends exercising daily.

   b. If Andrea's jogging rate is 5 mi/h, how much time daily does she spend exercising?

Practice 11-4

Mixed Exercises

Simplify.

1. $\frac{3x}{4} - \frac{x}{4}$

2. $\frac{3}{x} + \frac{5}{x}$

3. $\frac{5x}{6} - \frac{2x}{3}$

4. $\frac{x}{3} + \frac{x}{5}$

5. $\frac{3m}{4} + \frac{5m}{12}$

6. $\frac{4x}{7} - \frac{3x}{14}$

7. $\frac{6}{7t} - \frac{3}{7t}$

8. $\frac{d}{3} + \frac{4d}{3}$

9. $\frac{7}{2d} - \frac{3}{2d}$

10. $\frac{3}{2d^2} + \frac{4}{3d}$

11. $\frac{9}{m+1} - \frac{6}{m-1}$

12. $\frac{3}{x} - \frac{7}{x}$

13. $\frac{7a}{6} + \frac{a}{6}$

14. $\frac{4}{k+3} - \frac{8}{k+3}$

15. $\frac{3}{4z^2} + \frac{7}{4z^2}$

16. $\frac{6}{x^2-1} + \frac{7}{x-1}$

17. $\frac{2x}{x^2-1} - \frac{3}{x+1}$

18. $\frac{3t}{8} + \frac{3t}{8}$

19. $\frac{4}{3a^2} - \frac{1}{2a^3}$

20. $\frac{4}{a+4} + \frac{6}{a+4}$

21. $\frac{4}{x+3} + \frac{6}{x-2}$

22. $\frac{6}{7t^3} - \frac{8}{3t}$

23. $\frac{3}{2x+6} + \frac{4}{6x+18}$

24. $\frac{5}{8a} - \frac{3}{8a}$

25. $\frac{5}{r^2-4} + \frac{7}{r+2}$

26. $\frac{6}{a^2-2} + \frac{9}{a^2-2}$

27. $\frac{5x}{4} - \frac{x}{4}$

28. $\frac{4}{3x+6} - \frac{3}{2x+4}$

29. $\frac{4}{c^2+4c+3} + \frac{1}{c+3}$

30. $\frac{6}{x^2-3x+2} - \frac{4}{x-2}$

31. Brian rode his bike 2 mi to his friend's house. His bike had a flat tire so he had to walk home. His walking rate is 25% of his biking rate.

   a. Write an expression for the amount of time Brian spent walking and riding his bike.

   b. If Brian's bike riding rate is 12 mi/h, how much time did he spend walking and riding his bike?

32. Trudi and Sean are on a river canoeing. Because of the current of the river, their downstream rate is 250% of their upstream rate. They canoe 3 mi upstream and then return to their starting point.

   a. Write an expression for the amount of time Trudi and Sean spend canoeing.

   b. If their upstream rate is 2 mi/h, how much time do Trudi and Sean spend canoeing?

   c. If their upstream rate is 3 mi/h, how much time do Trudi and Sean spend canoeing?

Practice 11-5

• •

Example Exercises

Example 1

Solve each equation. Be sure to check your answers!

1. $\frac{1}{x} - \frac{1}{3x} = \frac{1}{3}$ **2.** $\frac{1}{n} + \frac{1}{12} = \frac{1}{6}$ **3.** $\frac{3}{c} - \frac{1}{12} = \frac{5}{2c}$ **4.** $\frac{1}{t} + \frac{2}{3t} = \frac{5}{6}$

5. $\frac{4}{a} - \frac{7}{a} = -\frac{1}{2}$ **6.** $\frac{4}{b^2} + \frac{3}{b} = 1$ **7.** $1 + \frac{6}{x} = \frac{16}{x^2}$ **8.** $\frac{1}{2} - \frac{3}{x} = -\frac{4}{x^2}$

9. $\frac{5}{3x} - \frac{1}{9} = \frac{1}{x}$ **10.** $\frac{11}{b} - \frac{3}{b} = 2$ **11.** $\frac{a}{3} - \frac{2}{3} = \frac{1}{a}$ **12.** $1 + \frac{3}{m} = -\frac{2}{m^2}$

Example 2

13. Abby and Wade have a lawn care service. With a riding mower, Wade can mow the hospital's lawn in 2 h. Abby with a push mower can mow the lawn in 6 h. How long would it take both of them working together to mow the hospital's lawn?

14. The Moe Woodworking Company has two planers. The newer planer works twice as fast as the older planer. When both planers are working they can fill an order in 30 min. How long would it take each planer working alone to fill the order?

15. Dawn and Michael are long distance runners. During practice Michael runs 3 mi/h faster than Dawn. In the same amount of time, Dawn runs 8 mi and Michael runs 12 mi. What is the rate of each runner?

16. Paula can do a plumbing job in 3 h. If Maria and Paula work together they can complete the job in 2 h. How long would it take Maria, working alone, to complete the job?

Example 3

Solve each equation. Be sure to check your answers!

17. $\frac{3}{a+1} = \frac{2}{a-3}$ **18.** $\frac{1}{3(g+2)} + 2 = \frac{3}{g+2}$ **19.** $\frac{n-1}{n-3} = \frac{2}{n-3}$

20. $\frac{7}{x+3} = \frac{7}{x^2-9}$ **21.** $\frac{2}{x(x-1)} + 1 = \frac{2}{x-1}$ **22.** $\frac{4}{b+3} = \frac{1}{b+3} + 3$

23. $\frac{6}{v} - \frac{5}{v-2} = \frac{v-7}{v-2}$ **24.** $\frac{2}{h(h-1)} = \frac{2}{h-1} - 1$ **25.** $\frac{d+1}{d-2} = \frac{3}{d-2}$

Practice 11-5

•••

Mixed Exercises

Solve each equation.

1. $\frac{1}{x} + \frac{1}{2x} = \frac{1}{6}$

2. $\frac{x}{x+2} + \frac{4}{x-2} = 1$

3. $\frac{1}{3s} = \frac{s}{2} - \frac{1}{6s}$

4. $\frac{1}{b-3} = \frac{b}{4}$

5. $1 - \frac{3}{x} = \frac{4}{x^2}$

6. $\frac{7}{3(a-2)} - \frac{1}{a-2} = \frac{2}{3}$

7. $\frac{n}{n-4} = \frac{2n}{n+4}$

8. $x + \frac{6}{x} = -7$

9. $\frac{2}{r^2-r} - 1 = \frac{2}{r-1}$

10. $\frac{y}{y+3} = \frac{6}{y+9}$

11. $\frac{d}{3} + \frac{1}{2} = \frac{1}{3d}$

12. $\frac{2}{3n} + \frac{3}{4} = \frac{2}{3}$

13. $\frac{1}{m-4} + \frac{1}{m+4} = \frac{8}{m^2-16}$

14. $\frac{1}{t^2} - \frac{2}{t} = \frac{3}{t^2}$

15. $\frac{k^2}{k+3} = \frac{9}{k+3}$

16. $\frac{h-3}{h+6} = \frac{2h+3}{h+6}$

17. $\frac{h}{6} - \frac{3}{2h} = \frac{8}{3h}$

18. $4 - \frac{3}{y} = \frac{5}{y}$

19. David and Fiona have a house painting business. It takes Fiona 3 da to paint a certain house. David could paint the same house in 4 da. How long would it take them to paint the house if David and Fiona work together?

20. Suppose the Williams Spring Water Company has two machines that bottle the spring water. Machine X fills the bottles twice as fast as Machine Y. Working together is takes them 20 min to fill 450 bottles. How long would it take each machine working alone to fill the 450 bottles?

21. Chao, who is an experienced architect, can draw a certain set of plans in 6 h. It takes Carl, who is a new architect, 10 h to draw the same set of plans. How long would it take them working together to draw the set of plans?

22. For exercise, Joseph likes to walk and Vincent likes to ride his bike. Vincent rides his bike 12 km/h faster than Joseph walks. Joseph walks 20 km in the same amount of time that Vincent rides 44 km. Find the rate that each of them travels.

23. The Ryan Publishing Company has two printing presses. It takes the new printing press 45 min to print 10,000 fliers. Together the two presses can print the 10,000 fliers in 30 min. How long does it take the older printing press by itself to print the 10,000 fliers?

Practice 11-6

. . . .

Example Exercises

Example 1

1. Suppose you have two shirts, three pairs of pants, and two pairs of shoes. How many different outfits do you have?

2. Suppose a restaurant has nine different main courses and six kinds of dessert. How many ways can you order a meal?

Example 2

3. In how many ways can five students stand in a line?

4. In how many ways can ten different books be arranged on a bookshelf?

5. In how many ways can six students be arranged in a row in a classroom?

6. In how many ways can a car dealer arrange his nine new cars in the show room?

Example 3

Use a calculator to evaluate.

7. $_8P_4$ 8. $_{10}P_6$ 9. $_{11}P_2$ 10. $_5P_3$ 11. $_8P_7$

12. $_9P_3$ 13. $_{26}P_6$ 14. $_8P_3$ 15. $_6P_2$ 16. $_4P_2$

17. Suppose the basketball team consists of 15 players. Each player can play any position. In how many ways can the five starters be introduced?

18. How many four-digit code numbers are possible using different digits?

19. Suppose a license plate consists of five different digits using the digits 1, 2, 3, 4, 5, 6, 7. How many five-digit license plates are possible?

20. The order of the finalists in a spelling competition are determined by a draw. If there are eight finalists, how many orders are possible for the final competition?

21. You have a collection of trophies that you would like to arrange on a shelf. If there are 15 trophies in all, how many ways can they be arranged in groups of three?

Practice 11-6
· ·
Mixed Exercises

Use a calculator to evaluate.

1. $_7P_2$ **2.** $_{12}P_6$ **3.** $_{11}P_3$ **4.** $_{10}P_3$ **5.** $_9P_8$ **6.** $_{12}P_7$

7. $_{20}P_7$ **8.** $_{15}P_3$ **9.** $_{16}P_4$ **10.** $_{25}P_3$ **11.** $_{17}P_2$ **12.** $_{15}P_2$

13. Suppose a license plate consists of five different letters.

     a. How many five-letter license plates are possible?

     b. How many ways can a five-letter license plate be made with the letters from APRIL if none of the letters are repeated?

     c. Suppose a license plate is assigned randomly. What is the probability that it will contain the letters from APRIL?

14. In how many ways can nine mopeds be parked in a row?

15. Suppose there are three different ways that you could go from your house to a friend's house. From you friend's house there are four different ways that you could go to the library. How many different ways can you go from your house to the library after meeting your friend?

16. A sports card collection contains 20 baseball players, 15 basketball players, and 25 football players. In how many ways can you select one of each?

17. Suppose you are electing student council officers. The student council contains 24 students. In how many ways can a president, vice-president, and a secretary be elected?

18. Suppose the code to a lock consists of three different numbers from the numbers 1 to 20, inclusive.

     a. How many three-number codes are possible?

     b. How many of the codes contain the numbers 6, 13, and 17?

     c. What is the probability that the code will contain the numbers 6, 13, and 17?

19. A car dealer sells four different models of cars. Each of the cars can come in six different colors. For each of the cars there are two different option packages available. How many different ways can you select a car?

20. Teams in a math competition consist of six students. In how many ways can the six students be selected to work a problem on the board?

Practice 11-7

• •

Example Exercises

Example 1

Use a calculator to evaluate.

1. $_8C_4$ **2.** $_{10}C_6$ **3.** $_{10}C_2$ **4.** $_5C_3$ **5.** $_8C_7$ **6.** $_9C_4$

7. $_{12}C_5$ **8.** $_{12}C_2$ **9.** $_{10}C_7$ **10.** $_9C_5$ **11.** $_{15}C_4$ **12.** $_{15}C_7$

13. The math club consists of 28 members. In how many ways can a committee of three students be selected?

14. There are 15 people out for softball. How many teams of nine players can be formed if a player can play any position?

15. How many conbinations of three items can be selected from a choice of ten items at a salad bar?

16. From a track team of twelve students, a coach selects four students for a relay race. How many different groups of four can the coach select?

Example 2

17. Suppose your school is forming a vocal music group of three students. The students are chosen from a group of four girls and three boys.

   a. How many different groups of three students are possible?

   b. How many groups could have all girls?

   c. What is the probability that the group will have all girls?

18. A box of books contains five fiction and six biographies. Two books are selected at random.

   a. How many different groups of two books are possible?

   b. How many groups of books will contain only biographies?

   c. What is the probability that the books will be only biographies?

19. Suppose a shipment of 24 video cameras contains two that were damaged in shipment. Four video cameras are tested at random.

   a. How many different groups of four video cameras are possible?

   b. How many groups of four video cameras contain both of the defective ones?

   c. What is the probability of finding both defective cameras?

Name _____ Class _____ Date _____

Practice 11-7
* *
Mixed Exercises

Use a calculator to evaluate.

1. $_9C_4$ **2.** $_{12}C_8$ **3.** $_9C_6$ **4.** $_{15}C_9$ **5.** $_{10}C_8$ **6.** $_{13}C_6$

7. $_{18}C_5$ **8.** $_{16}C_3$ **9.** $_{17}C_7$ **10.** $_9C_5$ **11.** $_{17}C_{13}$ **12.** $_{14}C_7$

13. A group of six tourists arrive at the airport 15 min before flight time. At the gate they learn there are only three seats left on the airplane. How many different groups of three could get on the airplane?

14. How many ways can you select 5 cards from a choice of 12 cards at a store?

15. A committee of four students is to be formed from members of the student council. The student council contains 13 girls and 12 boys.

  a. How many different committees of four students are possible?

  b. How many committees will only contain boys?

  c. What is the probability that the committee will only contain boys?

16. Suppose your math class consists of 24 students. In how many ways can a group of five students be selected to form a math team?

17. A jar of marbles contains six yellow and eight red marbles. Three marbles are selected at random.

  a. How many different groups of three marbles are possible?

  b. How many groups of three marbles will contain only red ones?

  c. What is the probability that the group of marbles will contain only red ones?

18. Suppose two members of your class need to be selected as members of the student council. Your class has 26 students in it. How many groups of two students can be selected?

19. The letters of the alphabet are written on slips of paper and placed in a hat. Three letters are selected at random.

  a. How many different combinations of three letters are possible?

  b. How many combinations consist only of the letters A, C, H, I, K, or Y?

  c. What is the probability that the letters selected consist only of the letters A, C, H, I, K, or Y?